Spy Trade

Books by Grant F. Smith

NEOCON MIDDLE EAST POLICY
The "Clean Break" Plan Damage Assessment

DEADLY DOGMA
How Neoconservatives Broke the Law to Deceive America

VISA DENIED
How Anti-Arab Visa Policies Destroy U.S. Exports,
Jobs and Higher Education

FOREIGN AGENTS
The American Israel Public Affairs Committee from the 1963 Fulbright
Hearings to the 2005 Espionage Scandal

AMERICA'S DEFENSE LINE
The Justice Department's Battle to Register the Israel Lobby as Agents of a
Foreign Government

Spy
Trade

❧❧

*How Israel's Lobby Undermines
America's Economy*

Published by the Institute for Research: Middle Eastern Policy, Inc.
Calvert Station
PO Box 32041
Washington, DC 20007

First published in 2008 by the Institute for Research: Middle Eastern Policy

7 9 10 8 6
Copyright Institute for Research: Middle Eastern Policy, Inc.
All Rights Reserved

Paperback ISBN-13 978-0-9764437-1-1

Library of Congress Cataloging-in-Publication Data

Smith, Grant F.
Spy trade : how Israel's lobby undermines America's economy / by Grant F. Smith.
p. cm.
Includes index.
ISBN 978-0-9764437-1-1 (alk. paper)
1. Zionists--United States--Political activity. 2. Lobbying--Moral and ethical aspects--United States. 3. Espionage, Israeli. 4. Illegal arms transfers--Israel. 5. United States--Foreign economic relations--Israel. 6. Israel--Foreign economic relations--United States. I. Title.
E184.36.P64S655 2009
337.7305694--dc22

2009036408

"The fact that Israel had the report caused no economic damage to any U.S. business or interest...the entire issue seems to have received more attention than it deserved."
– Dan Halpern, Economics Minister, Israeli Embassy in Washington, DC

Table of Contents

Table of Exhibits

About the Author

Grant F. Smith is director at the Washington, DC-based Institute for Research: Middle Eastern Policy (IRmep). IRmep is an independent nonprofit that studies U.S. policy formulation toward the Middle East. Smith's research and analysis about trade, law enforcement, and opportunity costs have appeared in *Antiwar.com*, the *Financial Times of London, Inc. Magazine, Arab News, Kiplinger, Gannet, The Wall Street Journal, The Washington Post, Al-Eqtisadiah, Khaleej Times, The New York Times, The Minneapolis Star Tribune, The Daily Star*, the Associated Press, Reuters, *The Washington Report on Middle East Affairs*, and specialty publications such as the U.S. State Department's *Washington File*. Smith is a frequent guest analyst on Voice of America (VOA) television and Radio France Internationale. He has also appeared on the BBC, C-SPAN, Al Jazeera, CNN, PressTV, and numerous public radio programs. In 2003, Smith launched IRmep at a policy symposium in the Rayburn House Office Building on Capitol Hill warning about the grave dangers of adopting a 1996 neoconservative plan for involving the U.S. military more deeply across the Middle East.

Smith's research assignments have taken him to more than 40 countries. Before joining IRmep, he was a senior analyst and later research program manager at the Boston-based Yankee Group Research, Inc. Smith taught undergraduate, graduate, and executive education courses in finance, research, and marketing for five years at CESA in Bogotá, one of Colombia's top-ranked business schools. Before that, Smith was a marketing manager at the Minneapolis-based Investors Diversified Services (IDS), now Ameriprise Financial Advisors. Smith completed a BA in International Relations from the University of Minnesota and a master's in International Management from the University of St. Thomas in St. Paul, Minnesota. His career in research includes the authorship of over 200 research papers, articles, surveys, and editorials.

Michael F. Scheuer is a former CIA analyst and author of the books Marching Toward Hell: America and Islam After Iraq *(2008) and* Imperial Hubris: Why the West is Losing the War on Terror *(2004). During his 22-year career, he served as chief of the CIA's Bin Laden station.*

Foreword

Grant F. Smith's excellent, deeply disturbing book *Spy Trade: How Israel's Lobby Undermines America's Economy* is a welcome addition to a growing scholarly literature documenting beyond reasonable doubt that the Israel lobby's elite are above U.S. law. The lobby's illegal and sometimes treasonous behavior is empowered by critical support from the rank and file. Further, Smith's work shows that America's problem is not only Israel and its lobby, but perhaps more dangerously, blanket immunity from prosecution. The harmful activities in which Israel lobby leaders engage are only possible because of their ability to corrupt U.S. politics at every level of government.

From the perspective of a former senior U.S. intelligence officer, Smith's well-researched book is a marvel. Israel's intelligence services have created, as this and other recently published works authoritatively demonstrate, a domestic espionage network in the United States whose operatives do the following:

(a) Steal secret business data that benefits Israel's economy and costs America intellectual property, business revenue, and domestic jobs.

(b) Shield the American Israel Public Affairs Committee (AIPAC) from having to register as an agent of a foreign power. AIPAC's mission is to coordinate with the Israeli government in order to push U.S. policies that economically benefit Israel at high costs to U.S. business and workers. This agency relationship has corrupted the U.S. legislative, electoral, and judicial processes, and guarantees that American—not Israeli—kids die fighting wars pushed by Israel and its lobby's leaders.

(c) Purloin highly classified military technology that Israel then sells to the highest bidders, who use it to negate the technical superiority of U.S. weaponry, or even resell it to enemies intent on killing U.S. soldiers and Marines in the field.

(d) Run covert operations against a host of government agencies—from the Pentagon to the U.S. Trade Representative's office—stealing and passing information to Israel that compromises U.S. foreign, economic, and defense policies.

(e) Gain preferential and corrupting access—via illegally coordinated campaign contributions, influence, and intimidation—to leading politicians in the Democratic and Republican parties, as well as serving presidents, congressmen, senior law enforcement officials, journalists, judges, bureaucrats, and even intelligence officers.

(f) Buy pardons from presidents to expunge the criminal records of the handful of operatives who have been convicted of theft and/or espionage-related activity.

By any measure, Israel's espionage program in America is an unqualified success, and would be the envy of any intelligence service in the world. But Israel is not solely or even primarily responsible for this success. Espionage and covert action are only possible if human beings are willing to commit treason against their governments and countrymen. Intelligence services can design goals, plans, rewards, and protections for spies, but without individuals willing to commit treason, espionage is all but impossible.

The hugely unsettling truth detailed by Grant Smith's *Spy Trade* is that Israel's intelligence services have found a seemingly unending number of recruits who are not only willing to betray America, but do so without remuneration because they have decided Israel's—not America's—advancement is paramount and justifies criminal and/or treasonous behavior. And in addition to finding Americans eager to be disloyal, Smith shows that Israel—through the potent influence of allies in the U.S. governing, business, and media elites—is able to effectively put those of its spies who are caught beyond appropriate legal punishment via mysteriously negotiated and dismissed court cases; implausible plea deals; well-staged and slanderous demonstrations of Jewish-American "communal anger" over "persecution," thereby winning absurd judicial rulings; reduced jail sentences; and presidential pardons. In short, Israel's tremendously damaging espionage and covert action campaign works and yields huge dividends not because Israel runs the operations, but because substantial numbers of Jewish-Americans are eager to participate and defend them publicly by leveling toxic charges of "anti-Semitism" and using money and media influence to protect or bury them.

Overall, Grant F. Smith's *Spy Trade: How Israel's Lobby Undermines America's Economy* puts on display a vigorous, widespread, established, and effective fifth column pursuing Israel's interests at the expense of America's. Smith also shows that it has been able to operate for so long because the U.S. governing elite knowingly permits it to do so. Eager for reliable campaign contributions directed by AIPAC and other Israel lobby organizations, and terrified of being smeared as anti-Semites, post-1948 U.S. politicians have governed in a manner that protects Israel's intelligence apparatus and domestic operatives by putting both above the law.

Abraham Lincoln presciently warned us that only actions by Americans can destroy the United States. "If destruction be our lot," Lincoln said in 1838, "we must ourselves be its author and finisher. As a nation of freemen, we must live through all time, or die by suicide." At this point, Israel and its lobby's "authors and finishers" are involving America in the affairs, criminality, and wars of a nation of no strategic value to the United States. The willingness of U.S. political leaders to both ignore and monetarily benefit from that fifth column's activities strongly suggests that suicide is becoming the order of the day.

Introduction

Unpunished crimes have long undermined the prosperity, legal protections, and international standing of Americans, but receive little attention from scholars or the press. Violations of U.S. laws were a major factor in establishing the state of Israel in 1948. Massive illicit arms flows coursed through networks of false-front American nonprofit groups smuggling weapons to Jewish fighters in Palestine in contravention of the 1939 Neutrality and Arms Export Acts. Throughout the 1960s and 1970s, figures operating out of the shadows of parastatal institutions such as the Jewish Agency, the Zionist Organization of America, the American Zionist Council, and Israeli intelligence supplied and provided cover for Israel's fledgling Dimona nuclear weapons program against the explicit foreign policies of President John F. Kennedy. The Kennedy administration attempted to register the American Zionist Council (umbrella of the Zionist Organization of America and Hadassah, among others) as a foreign agent of the quasi-governmental Jewish Agency when the Senate uncovered international money laundering into the U.S. That enforcement effort lost inertia after the assassination of President John F. Kennedy and the dissolution of key DOJ leadership.[1]

AZC activity regrouped within the American Israel Public Affairs Committee (AIPAC), which emerged as the new center of gravity of the Israel lobby by the mid-1970s. Illicit financial flows from the Jewish Agency were replaced by U.S. Political Action Committee donations coordinated by AIPAC. One of AIPAC's greatest accomplishments came quietly in 1985. In tight coordination with the Israeli government, AIPAC won coveted tariff-free export access to the U.S. market through America's very first "free trade" area. The lion's share of trade benefits steadily accrued to Israel, even as AIPAC cut U.S. export access to any market considered potentially hostile to Israel.

As America's first bilateral free trade agreement approached its twenty-fifth anniversary, a little known espionage incident remained cloaked in secrecy. The Reagan administration and Israel were neck deep in intrigues during the tumultuous period when the U.S.-Israel Free Trade Agreement (USIFTA) was negotiated. Both became embroiled in the Iran-Contra affair, in an attempt to restart Israel's lucrative arms sales to Iran that had begun under the Shah. The Iran-Contra affair and the 1986 Jonathan Pollard espionage scandal overshadowed a vastly consequential and related "third scandal."

During the 1984 USIFTA trade negotiations, American industry and interest groups lobbied against it and provided valuable intellectual property and trade secrets compiled by the International Trade Commission. The FBI discovered that this report was surreptitiously obtained by both AIPAC and the Israeli government. This major breach threatened the sanctity of the negotiations, but was quickly buried so as not to slow the "fast track" process. All files on the lengthy FBI investigation into the affair were swept up and classified—until July 31, 2009.

Since 1990 USIFTA has generated a cumulative U.S. trade deficit of $71 billion, the equivalent of 100,000 American jobs for each of the last 10 years. It is the only bilateral trade deal consistently generating deficits, major market access complaints from U.S. industries, and ongoing disputes over misappropriated U.S. intellectual property. Did economic espionage and classified information stolen in 1984 give Israel and its lobby an unfair advantage?

The newly declassified FBI documents clarify a much wider pattern of how the Israel lobby[i] extracts staggering wealth during moments of crisis—at enormous but generally hidden cost to the American people. History reveals systematic tactics for achieving those objectives: false fronts, threatening to bring down related legitimate Israel lobby organizations or U.S. government officials, illegally coordinated campaign contributions, and secret deals with the Justice Department under threats of "systemic risk." These activities have had a corrosive effect on the rule of law in the United States. The highest-level perpetrators of Israel lobby crime are almost never held accountable, since important details are covered up and kept from the public for longer periods of time than other categories of classified U.S. government information.

The Obama administration is now confronting vast, embedded parastatal Israeli interests demanding taxpayer-funded aid, diplomatic cover for apartheid-like policies toward Palestinians, and the preservation of Israeli regional nuclear hegemony. It is critical that Americans understand and confront the Israel lobby's challenge to American prosperity and the rule of law before irreversible damage is done to U.S. governance.

---

[i] The lobby is a coalition of individuals and organizations with leaders that actively work to move U.S. foreign policy in Israel's favor, at times against broader U.S. interests.

"Some prominent people and some important organizations could be hurt..." **Robert R. Nathan, former War Production Board chairman during Jewish Agency delegation talks with the FBI director over arms smuggling.** [2]

Arms Smuggling

Arms smuggling is the root of U.S.-Israel commerce. Massive quantities of surplus American weapons crossed the Atlantic in violation of U.S. laws before the state of Israel was formally declared. Smuggling began under David Ben-Gurion, the chairman of both the World Zionist Organization and the quasi-governmental Jewish Agency, which oversaw Jewish immigration into Palestine. Ben-Gurion traveled to the United States in 1945 in a desperate bid for the funding, arms, capital goods, and skilled people necessary to win and hold a new state in Palestine. The precedents established by Israel's first prime minister strongly influenced the formalized U.S.-Israeli diplomatic and commercial relationships that followed.

Ben-Gurion's colleague Dr. Rudolph Sonneborn convened an elite group of 19 wealthy Zionist activists on July 1, 1945 to hear his grand plan for transferring victims of the Holocaust to Palestine from displaced persons camps across Europe. Henry Montor, the national director of the United Jewish Appeal[3] (UJA), and other prominent Jewish-American fundraisers active in finance, law, and retail businesses began operating under the cover of a charitable front organization—ostensibly dedicated to the relief of European Jews—called the Sonneborn Institute.[4] The subsequent creation of separate but legally chartered corporate entities engaged in illicit activities gave the Jewish Agency and budding Israeli defense forces (the Haganah) operational "plausible deniability" if any of the autonomous cells engaged in "black operations" across the U.S. were uncovered.

Rabbi Irving Miller was instrumental in coordinating higher-level arms smuggling and finance even as he openly served as the chairman of the Jewish Agency's American Section, according to Teddy Kollek, a Haganah and Jewish Agency operative based in New York who later became mayor of Jerusalem.[5] In the years following its first meeting, the Sonneborn Institute spawned a half-dozen organizations conducting both aboveboard and highly illegal activities that gave rise to Israel's military, air transport, and shipping industries.

Vast quantities of war materiel were unleashed onto the American market when the U.S. demobilized after WWII. The War Assets Administration (WAA) administered sales of enormous stocks of highly specialized machinery and military equipment. WAA mandated this had to be either converted to civilian use or decommissioned and sold as scrap. The Sonneborn Institute's drive to build a self-reliant military-industrial capacity began when Ben-Gurion sent engineer Haim Slavin to New York to research modern ammunition and arms production. Slavin operated under the truism that it is faster and cheaper to acquire the technology of others than to develop the same capability oneself. He began researching modern production while commissioning the design of an entirely new weapon (code named "the gun") for the Haganah and searching for highly specialized WWII surplus production machinery across the United States.

The Sonneborn network front companies bore innocuous names such as "Machinery Processing and Converting Company" and acquired, stored, packaged, disguised, and exported capital goods. The first purchases included six tons of machinery from the Remington Arms plant in Bridgeport, CT for manufacturing .303 caliber ammunition for "the gun." The network could acquire state-of-the-art ammunition-making equipment worth hundreds of thousands of dollars at the price of $70 per ton only by promising complete decommissioning. Another WAA deal routed through a friendly entrepreneur's corporation secured 200 tons of M-3 demolition explosive at the price of 10 cents per 2.25-pound block, just as the U.S. Department of State declared an embargo on arms shipments to the Middle East.

The network's core competencies involved high secrecy. Sophisticated military-industrial gear was disassembled, catalogued, and disguised as civilian machinery so it could be divided up into innocent-looking components that would make it past U.S. customs inspectors for shipment to Palestine. Ammunition and firearms were welded into the centers of giant boilers or generators, while TNT crates were stenciled with innocuous labels. The Sonneborn Institute was also active in manpower exports. Friends inside and outside the U.S. government provided timely intelligence for key military personnel recruitment operations. One front, Materials and Manpower for Palestine, surreptitiously obtained the entire data set used by U.S. armed service chaplains, which allowed the Haganah to direct targeted appeals to Jewish veterans in the United States during its drive to recruit military volunteers to fight in Palestine.

The network also thought big. Even after the U.S. State Department declared its embargo on arms shipments to the Middle East, it purchased a baby flat-top aircraft carrier from the WAA for $125,000. The plan was for the *U.S.S. Attu* to ferry arms and DPs to Palestine and be fully restored for air attacks.[6]

Nathan Liff, who had acquired a WAA contract for scrapping surplus arms, owned a Honolulu scrap yard that was the site of a major arms theft operation. Liff notified Sonneborn during a visit to New York about his access to surplus war planes. Al Schwimmer, a wartime TWA flight engineer who worked in an aircraft reconditioning and air freight business in Burbank, sent Haganah West Coast coordinator Hank Greenspun to Hawaii to look over Liff's inventory and procure functioning surplus aircraft engines.[7]

Greenspun noticed brand-new crated .30 and .50 caliber machine guns in a military section of the yard full of stock that had not been rendered inoperable.

The crates were not only still owned by the military, but actively patrolled by U.S. Marines. Greenspun observed the sentries' timetable and used a forklift to steal 58 crates containing 500 machine guns. He carefully replaced the new stock with crates of guns already rendered inoperable from Liff's side of the yard.[8] Greenspun moved the guns to Los Angeles for transshipment to Palestine via Mexico. He almost lost the 35 tons of machine guns out of San Pedro harbor while employing a civilian yacht for the Los Angeles-to-Acapulco leg of the smuggling operation. The machine guns arrived in Israel by October of 1948.[9]

Kolleck also established front operations with Latin American dictators, including Anastasio Somoza in Nicaragua. Somoza bought operable WAA stock from the U.S. as a sovereign state, which he reshipped to Palestine in exchange for a 3.5 percent kickback. Haganah operatives also coordinated with gangster boss Sam Kay to traffic arms through Cuba and Panama. [10]

Israel's proto–air transportation service began when Al Schwimmer purchased three surplus military Lockheed Constellations from the WAA for $45,000. The sticker price for the new commercial service version, depending on the equipment configuration, was $685,000 to $720,000. The airplanes were capable of flying 300 miles per hour, had a service ceiling of 16,000 feet, and could carry 100 passengers or 10 tons of cargo. Schwimmer used another $20,000 of the network's funds to rent space at the Lockheed Air Terminal, where he added 10 smaller surplus C-46 Commando cargo planes under the name of Schwimmer Aviation.

Schwimmer also made a proposal to an out-of-luck Florida cargo entrepreneur, Charles Winters, who had purchased two B-17 bombers and converted them for civilian use. Each was capable of carrying seven tons of bombs and cost $204,370 to manufacture. When Winters' Caribbean fruit cargo business failed to prosper, Schwimmer asked if he was interested in flying the bombers to "somewhere in Europe." Winters navigated the bombers across the Atlantic to Czechoslovakia, where they were refitted for war and used to attack Egypt.

Schwimmer's air fleet left the United States for Panama, registered under a shell corporation as a Panamanian airline to evade export controls. It soon departed Panama and went into service in Europe, ferrying military supplies between Czechoslovakia and Tel Aviv. The U.S. Central Intelligence Agency detected the activity and filed a report titled "Clandestine Air Transport Operations" on May 28, 1948. The report cover letter advised that "U.S. National Security is unfavorably affected by these developments and that it could be seriously jeopardized by continued illicit traffic in the 'implements of war.'" The CIA noted that Schwimmer's crews operating in Europe "dressed in U.S. Army uniforms without insignia," which deceived airport authorities in sovereign nations such as Switzerland into believing Schwimmer's air transport smuggling ring was really a "U.S. Air Force Operation."[11]

Arab nations attacked the newly founded Israel in 1948 after a United Nations decision to partition the British-controlled territory of Palestine into

Jewish and Arab states. Jewish forces armed by the Sonneborn network prevailed, seizing territories far beyond those won in the United Nations. Egypt and Jordan absorbed much of what was left of the territories intended for a Palestinian state. The smugglers were largely immunized by Israel's victory. Sonneborn smuggling organizations handling "black" goods gradually became legitimate after Israel won independence. The Supply Mission of the State of Israel in New York absorbed Machinery and Metals Company to manage military acquisitions. Materials for Palestine became Materials for Israel and stopped handling military equipment in favor of basic civilian goods for immigrants, including medical supplies, clothing, footwear, and vehicles. Land and Labor for Israel quietly shut down for less formal recruiting efforts.

The FBI, like the CIA in Europe, was alerted early on to the massive smuggling activities taking place across the United States, but took little effective action. In 1949, Charles Winters pled guilty to illegally exporting airplanes and was sentenced to 18 months in prison. Schwimmer was charged with conspiracy to violate the Neutrality Act, and along with Leo Gardner, Rey Selk, and Service Airways, was found guilty. All were ordered to pay fines of $10,000.

But none of the truly "big fish" of the Sonneborn arms smuggling network were ever indicted. Henry Montor, leader of the United Jewish Appeal, who organized the first Sonneborn meeting, became founder of the Israel Bond Organization, which successfully floated its first issue of $52 million in 1951. His smuggling network fundraising efforts that operated in tandem with the UJA were never prosecuted. Montor left the U.S. to live in Rome and Jerusalem in 1957.[12] Rudolf G. Sonneborn retired quietly as director of Witco Chemical Company and died in 1986. William Levitt is celebrated as the entrepreneur famous for postwar American mass production housing such as his "Levittown" development. Levitt provided a $1 million loan at no interest for the purchase of 15 Messerschmitt ME-109 fighter aircraft from Czechoslovakia for the Haganah, but never faced legal consequences for violating the Neutrality Act.[13]

Al Schwimmer prospered, as he went on to become managing director of Israel Aircraft Industries (later Israel Aerospace Industries) after Israel's war of independence.[b] With the backing of Ben-Gurion and Shimon Peres (Director General of the Ministry of Defense), Schwimmer worked to make IAI an indispensable vendor to the Israeli Air Force in the 1950s. The ambitious IAI attempted to manufacture complete modern fighter jets suitable for domestic military use and export. Later, recognizing necessary economies of scale and industrial capacity shortcomings, it settled into a more specialized role as an advanced modification, upgrade, and improvement vendor for existing fighters, commercial aircraft, and helicopter airframes, as well as manufacturing engines and electronics systems.

---

[b] Known by Arab Palestinians as "al Nakba" or "the disaster."

The organizations and individuals in the Sonneborn Institute's network all engaged in legitimate charitable activities as well as theft and smuggling. This cover and connection to elites involved across U.S. politics, business, and government made it a difficult target for law enforcement. After network members were arrested in Canada for smuggling prototype assault rifle components across the border in 1947, an unusual meeting was held. Leaders of the network traveled with a high-level Jewish Agency representative to Washington, DC and met with Robert R. Nathan, who had led the U.S. industrial mobilization in WWII, becoming the War Production Board's chairman in 1942.[14]

Nathan brokered a summit with FBI Director J. Edgar Hoover. The Royal Canadian Mounted Police had already "asked the FBI to cooperate in tracking down the sources and personnel involved and maybe prosecuting." This law enforcement initiative presented a major threat to the Sonneborn network and the Jewish Agency. Nathan flatly told the FBI director that the network's activities were not "anything damaging to the United States. But it is not straight up and aboveboard. Some prominent people and some important organizations could be hurt." Nathan assured Hoover that none of the weapons involved in the smuggling ring would ever be used in or against the United States, and left the meeting feeling that the FBI director was "sympathetic," but with no indication that he would "cooperate."[15]

Over time, the criminal records of Sonneborn smugglers have been expunged, and even the reputations of the "little fish" convicted in court have been carefully rehabilitated to hero status. In 1950, Nathan Liff offered compelling testimony in a Los Angeles courtroom during the trial over Greenspun and Schwimmer's violations of the Neutrality and Export Control Acts. Liff explained to jurors that he gave guns to "young Jewish boys who went to the door of Hitler's ovens" to bring Holocaust survivors to Palestine.[16] John F. Kennedy pardoned Hank Greenspun in 1961 after winning Israel lobby support in his presidential election campaign. Bill Clinton pardoned Al Schwimmer in the year 2000, even though Schwimmer never personally applied for a pardon or expressed any contrition for his actions. U.S. supporters, led by Hank Greenspun's son, filed on his behalf. Schwimmer felt pardon requests demanded he "fill out all sorts of papers asking for forgiveness, telling the Justice Department you're sorry, you did wrong, and you regret it, and you won't do it again. I didn't feel that way, and I still don't. I didn't feel I had done anything wrong, so I never applied."[17]

Charles Winters, the only network member to actually serve a meaningful prison sentence, was posthumously pardoned in December of 2008 by President George W. Bush after intense lobbying by Steven Spielberg and other prominent American Jews eager to repair the historical record.

The massive theft and smuggling campaign in the U.S. that was absolutely vital in the creation of Israel preceded more legitimate trade—but the general disregard for inconvenient U.S. laws exhibited by the people who became Israel's new leaders and their U.S. supporters continues to this day. The U.S.'s inexhaustible economic benevolence is increasingly attributed to the growth in power of Israel's lobby. The values system of Israel's lobby—that almost any crime committed in the name of Israel is acceptable and must be defended—challenges American principles of blind justice.

American support for Israel was sorely tested by illicit nuclear weapons technology, despite Israel's diplomatic immunity. The tendrils of criminality and scandal later enveloped the Reagan administration as Al Schwimmer again surfaced in the midst of the Iran-Contra scandal. Espionage and covert action were also an integral but secret factor during negotiations for preferential access to the U.S. market for Israeli exporters. The plea for crimes committed in the name of Israel to be immune from U.S. law enforcement continued, as the ethos of the righteous smuggler spread into all areas of the U.S.-Israel relationship.

Conclusion

Israel was not the first or last destination for smuggled U.S. arms. U.S. gunrunning over the border into Mexico at the turn of the century fueled rebel and bandit activity, and continues to generate clashes between drug cartels and state authorities today. But the massive quantities of modern military weapons brought to Israel, the lobby's coordinated fundraising, and the ability of elite American members of the network to preempt law enforcement are unprecedented in American history.

The network's financial and intellectual leadership directed an independent and successful foreign policy undeterred by laws such as the Logan Act and arms export controls. The network short-circuited advice and consent governance by creating "facts on the ground" that became politically convenient for U.S. politicians to applaud and reward, rather than questioning how they were accomplished. The implicit threat made to the director of the FBI that "prominent people and some important organizations could be hurt" if it investigated would today be known as a "systemic risk"[c] threat. Robert Nathan was able to convince the FBI director that the Sonneborn network was too "interconnected" for the criminal justice system to successfully prosecute any high-ranking individual or major component. The threat was credible and would later be deployed when the Israel lobby successfully quashed regulation efforts under the Foreign Agents Registration Act, campaign finance laws, and even the Espionage Act.

The "ends justify the means" operations of the Sonneborn network and its willingness to break the law transferred the costs of dangerous foreign policies to unsuspecting taxpayers as the Israel lobby magnified its influence and power in America.

---

[c] Systemic risks threaten the collapse of an entire system, as opposed to solitary risks associated with a particular individual, organization, or system component.

"Sometime in the late 1950s, that world-class gossip and occasional historian, John F. Kennedy, told me how, in 1948, Harry S. Truman had been pretty much abandoned by everyone when he came to run for president. Then an American Zionist brought him two million dollars in cash, in a suitcase, aboard his whistle-stop campaign train. 'That's why our recognition of Israel was rushed through so fast.' As neither Jack nor I was an antisemite (unlike his father and my grandfather) we took this to be just another funny story about Truman and the serene corruption of American politics." **Gore Vidal, author and intellectual**[18]

The Israel Lobby

The Israel lobby's rise to power involves enormously important but generally unknown encounters with U.S. law enforcement. Israel's economic and military needs have long been acutely felt in Washington, DC thanks to a lobby that coordinates with (and preceded) the Israeli government. The current tip of Israel's lobbying spear, the American Israel Public Affairs Committee (AIPAC), traces its ancestry to groups instrumental in Israel's creation. AIPAC's founder left the Israeli Ministry of Foreign Affairs payroll to launch the organization.

Before WWII and the horrors of the Holocaust, the strength of the Zionist lobby in America peaked and waned. On August 30, 1914, 150 leaders committed to realizing the vision of the new country codified in Theodor Herzl's[iv] book *The Jewish State* met in New York City. Louis D. Brandeis became president of the Provisional Executive Committee for General Zionist Affairs and drove group membership from 12,000 to 176,000 by 1919. But the lack of any binding urgency led to the movement's stagnation.

The Jewish Agency, a corporation envisaged by Theodor Herzl to be charged with land acquisition and transfer of Jews to Palestine, came into existence in Switzerland in 1929. As Arab-Jewish armed conflict over land and control of Palestine accelerated in the 1930s, the Jewish Agency established an American section in New York. The American Zionist Emergency Council coordinated closely with the Jewish Agency's American Section between 1943 and 1949 as a "fire brigade" pressure group bent on securing U.S. government support for the creation of a Jewish state in Palestine. The group claimed a collective membership of 171,000 by 1940.

Fundraising organizations such as the United Jewish Appeal financed aid and fraternal activities through tax-exempt U.S. donations. Harry S Truman—

[iv] The father of modern political Zionism.

intensively lobbied as a senator, vice president, and later president after the death of Roosevelt—recognized the State of Israel within minutes after it declared independence in 1948. He was duly repaid with huge cash donations during his "whistle-stop" cross-country election campaign. This financing, organized by the legendary Abraham Feinberg, saved his presidential election bid from certain ruin.

Isaiah L. Kenen, a public relations operator for the Jewish Agency at the United Nations until statehood who was later employed by the Israeli Ministry of Foreign Affairs until 1951, worked tirelessly to institutionalize U.S. arms sales and aid to Israel on Capitol Hill. The AZEC morphed into the American Zionist Council (AZC)—a lobbying umbrella group composed of powerful Zionist organizations such as Hadassah, the Zionist Organization of America, and others.

The AZC, despite claiming high numeric support based on the membership rolls of its constituent American nonprofit corporations, encountered chronic financial problems. The Eisenhower administration investigated the AZC, which was established as a charity, for prohibited use of tax-exempt funds to lobby Congress. Kenen noted the AZC's narrow escape and favorable ruling: "A government agency had ruled that only an insubstantial portion of AZC funds had been used for lobbying."[19] By the early 1960s, in coordination with the Israeli government, the AZC overcame its funding crisis by secretly tapping the Jewish Agency's own funding—raised tax-exempt in the U.S. and internationally by Jewish charities—and laundering it back into the U.S. for seed money, lobbying, public relations, and community organizing.

The Senate Foreign Relations Committee investigated the activities of a wide range of U.S. agents of foreign principals in 1962-1963. It found that the equivalent of $35 million had been surreptitiously laundered from the Jewish Agency through U.S. "conduits," including $38,000 sent to Kenen via orders from the Jewish Agency in Jerusalem.[20] After thousands of pages of damning testimony and evidence was entered into the Senate record documenting the funding flows, the Jewish Agency's legal counsel boldly told Senator J.W. Fulbright that the 1938 Foreign Agents Registration Act, which required timely public disclosure of foreign lobbying activity, simply didn't apply to Israel.

> Senator Fulbright: Mr. Boukstein, you haven't enlightened me as to how we may deal with this matter because you only confirmed my view that under the existing law and practices, at least, as they are illustrated here, it completely thwarts the purpose of the Foreign Agents Registration Act, because we are not given any information—neither the public or government—as to the nature of these activities and the nature of these projects for which this registrant here is supplied the money.

> Mr. Boukstein: Mr. Chairman, if you would go back to the time when the Foreign Agents Act was made law, in 1938, I think the purpose was altogether different. The language, of course, comprehends everybody; but the purpose at the time

was to bring out, into the open, subversive, at that time particularly Nazi activities, and I hope that the law in this respect served its purpose.

But to the extent that it is still law and to the extent that it is to be applied to other purpose, I certainly agree with you that it needs considerable modification and change.[21]

In 1962, the U.S. Department of Justice, under the leadership of Attorney General Robert F. Kennedy, ordered the AZC, as a recipient of Jewish Agency funds and direction, to openly register as Israel's foreign agent. The 1938 Foreign Agents Registration Act had been enacted to protect Congress from foreign lobbying by requiring all lobbyists for foreign principals to declare their activities to a special DOJ office open to review by the news media and concerned parties. In August of 1963, FBI Director J. Edgar Hoover offered the Justice Department his assistance: "In view of recent public hearings, it is requested that you advise whether any investigation is desired..."[22] The DOJ considered having the FBI raid the American Zionist Council headquarters as a series of meetings between FARA section leadership and the AZC escalated.[23]

The AZC contracted Simon Rifkind, a close confidant of JFK over labor disputes, as its head legal counsel. According to internal DOJ meeting notes from October 17, 1963, Rifkind made a "plea for no registration, stating that it was the opinion of most of the persons affiliated with the [American Zionist] Council that such registration would be so publicized...that it would eventually destroy the Zionist movement."[24] At the time of the secret battle to register the AZC, the Kennedy administration was also battling to reverse Israel's Dimona nuclear weapons development program through U.S. inspections.

After John F. Kennedy was assassinated in November of 1963, the DOJ lost the political cover necessary to proceed. Before he assumed new responsibilities as attorney general in the Johnson administration, Nicholas Katzenbach brokered a preferential deal. The AZC was permitted to file a nonstandard FARA declaration for a "representative" time period of its own choosing. The U.S. Department of Justice also accepted the AZC's request that the most important portion of its FARA declaration (individuals receiving Jewish Agency funding, amounts, and purpose) be secretly filed apart from the public registration. Acquiescing to the AZC was necessary, in the frank assessment of the Justice Department's FARA chief Nathan Lenvin, since the only alternative to backing down was "to institute prosecutive proceedings, which would be impractical..."[25]

The FARA section lost more momentum shortly after Robert F. Kennedy was assassinated on June 6, 1968. Lenvin, who had pursued Isaiah Kenen to register as a foreign agent since 1951,[26] died in his hotel room at the age of 58 while on a DOJ recruiting drive in Chicago a few months later.[27] The AZC passed the mantle of Israel lobbying leadership to the American Israel Public Affairs Committee, or AIPAC, which also refused to register as a foreign agent.[28] The DOJ kept the AZC's FARA filing—which revealed payments to scholars, media outlets such as the *New York Times,* and other recipients and administrative records—secret until 2008.

After the AZC battle, FARA enforcement slowly waned at the Justice Department. Lobbying firms with foreign clients challenged FARA oversight, claiming "attorney-client privilege" covered documents pertaining to lobbying activities conducted on behalf of foreign clients.[29]

The Jewish Agency's American Section also underwent a shell corporation reorganization. On June 9, 1970, the anti-Zionist American Council for Judaism leader Rabbi Elmer Berger and George Washington University legal scholar William T. Mallison forced the DOJ FARA section to request and file the Jewish Agency's covenant agreement with the Israeli government. This 1953 agreement revealed the Jewish Agency as a quasi-arm of the Israeli government, able to review legislation before it went to the Knesset in addition to receiving government funding. The Jewish Agency's American Section abruptly shut down and reemerged on paper as the American Section of the World Zionist Organization, operating in the same building with the same staff and activities.[30] It would later join the executive committee of AIPAC.[31]

Under the leadership of Isaiah L. Kenen, AIPAC grew in power and influence. Fundraising in the aftermath of the 1967 Six-Day War ballooned as Kenen's public relations campaigns spread the theme of "Israel in danger" across constituent groups and yielded unprecedented amounts of direct non-tax-deductible donations from American Jews concerned about the fate of Israel. By the early 1980s, in tight coordination with the Israeli government, larger numbers of U.S. donors, and regional political bosses, Congress passed laws that positioned AIPAC to push through not just foreign aid and military sales, but an unprecedented trade deal. Changes in U.S. campaign finance laws touched off a surge in activity among Israel lobby Political Action Committees (PACs) that ruthlessly, and sometimes lawlessly, bullied Congress with fervor and intense dedication.

U.S. efforts to regulate the financing of political campaigns in the 1970s delivered a powerful tool into the hands of the Israel lobby. In 1972, the Federal Election Campaign Act (FECA) required candidates to disclose sources of campaign contributions and campaign expenditures for the first time. Large unreported cash contributions, which were the specialty of Abraham Feinberg and other lobby organization donors, had long undermined public confidence in the legitimacy of U.S. elections. But rather than quell the quiet role of campaign cash channeled by the Israel lobby, FECA accelerated it.

FECA, as amended in 1974, attempted to limit the influence of wealthy individuals by capping their donations to candidates at $1,000 and the donations of Political Action Committees (PACs) at $5,000. Individuals were prohibited from spending more than $25,000 on all candidates in each election cycle. The Federal Election Commission (FEC) was founded in 1975 to regulate campaign finance and enforce limits. In 1976, only a single PAC was openly chartered to support candidates favorable to Israel; it gathered $99,150 in contributions. By

1980, there were 10 single-issue PACs specifically designed to give contributions to candidates who supported Israel. They gathered $657,668 and dispersed $414,000 to 107 congressional candidates.[32]

Across the United States, Israel PACs soon became absolute enforcers of Israeli government prerogatives by monitoring AIPAC-published scorecards on candidate votes. After executive director Morris Amitay resigned from AIPAC in 1980, he formed one of the largest Israel PACs in existence. By 1982, 40 Israel PACs had gathered $3,900,818 and contributed $2,027,200 to candidates who supported foreign aid grants and arms to Israel. The stealth PAC's capacity to secretly pool resources and tip critical elections became an object of fear as brute financial force and AIPAC support in ground campaigns unseated legislators who did not toe the AIPAC line.[v]

Stealth Israel Political Action Committees 1976-1988[33]

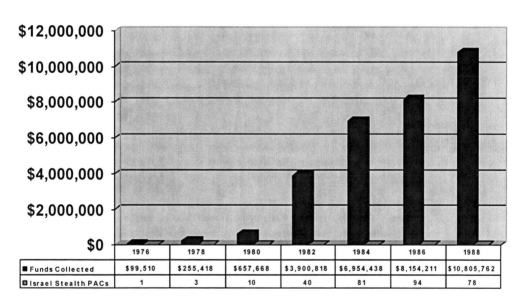

	1976	1978	1980	1982	1984	1986	1988
■ Funds Collected	$99,510	$255,418	$657,668	$3,900,818	$6,954,438	$8,154,211	$10,805,762
▣ Israel Stealth PACs	1	3	10	40	81	94	78

Israel PACs gained their dominance not through sheer financial muscle, but through illicit stealth coordination. Though most American PACs were openly associated with a particular company, industry, union, or trade association, the Israel stealth PACs strove for public anonymity. Those with names that were too easily identified as single-issue Israel PACs changed them in the early 1980s. "Texans for a Sound Middle East Policy" changed its name to "TxPAC." By 1984,

---

[v] Adlai Stevenson, 1981; Paul Findley, 1983; Paul McCloskey, 1982; Charles Percy, 1984; James Abdnor, 1987

81 stealth Israel PACs were active, gathering $6,954,438 and spending $3,772,994 to support AIPAC initiatives. An outside audit of this constellation of ostensibly independent PACs found that it was suspiciously well coordinated: in aggregate, it spent up to $300,000 per candidate in tight races. The results and reputation of the PACs gave AIPAC unprecedented lobbying power.

In 1986, AIPAC passed the U.S.-Israel Free Trade Area and was also able to boost U.S. aid to Israel to $3 billion annually while simultaneously heading off the Reagan administration's planned weapons sales to Jordan and Saudi Arabia. But AIPAC left an inconvenient paper trail that scandalously exploded into the press in 1988 and verified long held suspicions of illegality. AIPAC was not only establishing, but actually coordinating stealth PACS, in violation of U.S. campaign finance laws.

The *New York Times* explored AIPAC's many connections to Israel stealth PACs and the ties between its senior and former senior officials and political candidate election "hit lists" quietly circulated to voters.[34] AIPAC's public assertions that it was not coordinating strategy or funds to political candidates were again demolished in 1988, when the *Washington Post* published internal AIPAC memos revealing that it was highly active in identifying which candidates to support, drafting appeal letters, and directly coordinating PAC disbursements to favored candidates. Internal AIPAC documents made available to the *Washington Post* revealed that the group's top political operative Elizabeth Schrayer was directing stealth PAC candidate contributions in the 1986 Senate races.

> A memo from Elizabeth A. Schrayer, then AIPAC's deputy political director, five weeks before that election urged an assistant to call several pro-Israel PACs and "try" to get $500 to $1,000 donations for five specific Senate candidates.
>
> In the Sept. 30, 1986 memo, Schrayer listed nine pro-Israel PACs and noted that some had not contributed to certain candidates. For example, the memo said that one of the PACs, called ICEPAC, had given nothing to three candidates in whom she was interested. "Try for 1,000 to Bond, Moore, Evans, Daschle, & Reid. Call ASAP," Schrayer wrote, referring to Senate candidates Christopher S. (Kit) Bond (R) in Missouri, W. Henson Moore (R) in Louisiana, John V. Evans (D) in Idaho, Thomas A. Daschle (D) in South Dakota and Harry Reid (D) in Nevada. [35]

AIPAC documents also revealed that it was deeply involved in the mechanics of establishing more PACs in the mid-1980s.

> Four other documents are 1985 letters from Schrayer to individuals in Massachusetts, California and Hawaii. In them, she offers to provide fund-raising ideas and arrange speakers for a new pro-Israel PAC, sends a sample solicitation letter and list of pro-Israel

PACs to a fund-raiser for Evans, and volunteers to answer questions about starting a PAC.

...In addition to the Schrayer memo and letters, a "how to" booklet on setting up a pro-Israel PAC, dated February 1985, was available in Schrayer's office, according to a former AIPAC employee.[36]

The lengthy bombshell *Washington Post* story was unequivocal. Based upon its examination of the AIPAC documents and applicable statutes, the *Post* bluntly declared that U.S. election laws appeared to have been broken.

Federal law permits membership organizations such as AIPAC to communicate on a partisan basis with its members. The law also stipulates that political committees that establish, maintain, finance or control other committees are "affiliated" and thus subject to the contribution limits for one committee.

Over the past few years the number of pro-Israel PACs has grown dramatically. During the 1986 election cycle, for example, *The Wall Street Journal* compiled figures that 80 of these PACs donated nearly $7 million to candidates, sometimes more than $200,000 to a single candidate. This made them the most generous single-issue givers. A single PAC would be limited to giving $10,000 to a candidate in an election cycle.[37]

The *Washington Post* made these assessments based on meticulous examination of how the handwritten notes on the AIPAC memos matched PAC donations reported to the FEC. The publicity generated by a televised *60 Minutes* investigative report and letters to newspaper editors turned public attention toward the regulatory role of the Federal Election Commission and what efforts it would take. Despite the exposés and public protests, the FEC bluntly stated to the press that it would not be taking any action, since no complaints had been filed.[38]

On January 12, 1989, a group of prominent former U.S. government officials filed a complaint charging that the Federal Election Commission failed to require AIPAC to publish details of its income and expenditures, a legal requirement for all political action committees and affiliates. Richard Curtiss alleged "conspiracy and collusion," as reported by the Associated Press:

"AIPAC's formidable ability to mobilize congressional support...is based not upon an appeal to the American national interest but upon threats by a special interest that has resorted to conspiracy and collusion," said a statement by Richard Curtiss, formerly the chief inspector of the U.S. Information Agency and one of the plaintiffs...[39]

The FEC began to reluctantly investigate the charges, but found AIPAC unwilling to cooperate or release documents.[40] Amid minimal press coverage, the FEC delivered a "final" investigatory report on Friday, December 22, 1990. It indicated that the PACs named in the complaint were no longer under investigation, but that some of the allegations against AIPAC itself were still being studied.[41]

The complainants were not satisfied with the FEC response. There was no investigatory documentation in the FEC's initial release or any findings or proposed enforcement actions against AIPAC. There was also no indication of whether or not the investigation had been stymied by AIPAC's outright refusal to comply with the FEC's requests for internal financial records.[42] Time passed, and subsequent findings by the FEC proved less than adequate to the complainants. The FEC then issued a written finding that AIPAC had made "in-kind donations" that "likely crossed the $1,000 threshold"—the highest amount an individual or organization could then donate to a candidate seeking office in a single election. AIPAC therefore functioned as a "political committee" from the FEC perspective. In spite of the violation, the FEC ruled that it would not require AIPAC to register as a political action committee or disclose its donors and recipients, because organizing these types of campaign contributions was not "the major purpose of AIPAC."[43]

Unsatisfied and angered, the original seven complainants filed a lawsuit in the Washington, DC Federal District Court against the FEC. They then went on to file a third appeal alleging that the FEC acted in bad faith by dismissing the January 1989 complaint against AIPAC, and that this faulty interpretation of the rules was not cause for exempting AIPAC from disclosing all details of its donors, donations, and expenditures.

The battle raged into 1995. In March, the DC Circuit Court of Appeals found two to one against the complainants. They then sought a hearing before the entire appeals court, and on May 8, 1996 eight justices ruled for the complainants and against the FEC with two dissenting. The ruling identified a dangerous "slippery slope." Exempting a large and powerful organization like AIPAC from rules governing political activities on the grounds that they weren't the organization's "major purpose" would facilitate abuse, as other corporations began to conduct large-scale political activities and candidate efforts with none of the required FEC oversight and compliance measures.

In 1998, AIPAC appealed the Court of Appeals decision to the Supreme Court. On June 1, 1998, the Supreme Court decided that, in spite of AIPAC challenges, the complainants did have "standing" to demand a resolution in court. However, the Supreme Court refused to rule on the substance of the issue.[44]

The U.S. Supreme Court sent the case back down to the original U.S. District Court. The surviving complainants (one has since passed away) continue to insist that whether or not AIPAC is a membership organization, as it claims, or has other functions (which the FEC verified), it is also a political committee required to disclose detailed donor and expenditure information to the public. Yet by mid-

2009, none of the core issues of the case had been resolved. Presiding Judge Richard J. Leon held a status hearing and ordered a "fast track" schedule of cross briefs that could allow the court to make a final ruling by 2010. Plaintiffs have filed a draft motion for Judge Leon that would force AIPAC to disclose donors, funds, and activities influencing U.S. political campaigns (see appendix).

But delaying the premier campaign finance case against the largest foreign interest lobby in the U.S. for two decades had already produced a clear victor. Stealth PACs and donation coordination maintained Israel's status as the top recipient of U.S. foreign aid and other taxpayer-funded aid. Israel has received $104 billion from Congress since 1948.

U.S. Aid to Israel ($USD Million)[45]

Year	Total	Military Grant	Economic Grant	Immigrant	ASHA[vi]	All Other
1949-1996	68030.9	29014.9	23122.4	868.9	121.4	14903.3
1997	3132.1	1800	1200	80	2.1	50
1998	3080	1800	1200	80	?	?
1999	3010	1860	1080	70	?	?
2000	4131.85	3120	949.1	60	2.75	?
2001	2876.05	1975.6	838.2	60	2.25	?
2002	2850.65	2040	720	60	2.65	28
2003	3745.15	3086.4	596.1	59.6	3.05	?
2004	2687.25	2147.3	477.2	49.7	3.15	9.9
2005	2612.15	2202.2	357	50	2.95	?
2006	2534.53	2257	237	40	?	0.53
2007	2500.24	2340	120	40	?	0.24
2008	2423.8	2380.6	0	39.7	3	0.5
Total	103614.67	56024	30897	1557.9	143.3	14992.47

This statistic does not represent the total cost of Israel to the United States. According to the late Dr. Thomas Stauffer, who wrote and taught about the economics of energy and the Middle East both at Harvard University and Georgetown University's School of Foreign Service, the real cost is higher. Stauffer's opportunity-cost-based calculations capture "an estimate of the total cost to the U.S. alone of instability and conflict in the region—which emanates from the core Israeli-Palestinian conflict." This analysis was first presented at an October 2002 conference sponsored by the U.S. Army College and the University of Maine. "Total identifiable costs come to almost $3 trillion…About 60 percent,

---

vi American Schools and Hospitals Abroad multi-agency funding.

well over half of those costs—about $1.7 trillion—arose from the U.S. defense of Israel, where most of that amount has been incurred since 1973." Yet again, even this figure excludes the vast and generally unexplored loss the U.S. has been slowly accruing since the 1940s due to economic espionage, including losses from a severely compromised trade deal, perpetrated by Israel and its U.S. lobby.

Even if Judge Leon rules that AIPAC is a kind of "super PAC" subject to campaign laws, it may not have any material impact. In 2009, the Supreme Court made a sudden (and unusual) move to re-hear a case over whether corporations have a protected free speech right to directly engage in campaign-related activities. The case could render moot the two-decade-old drive to regulate AIPAC by rescinding the 1972 Federal Election Campaign Act (FECA) restrictions on corporate activities in political campaigns.

In retrospect, AIPAC continues to operate much like its parent organization, the AZC. It coordinates closely with the Israeli government to lobby on matters of critical importance, such as preferential trade matters. According to AIPAC's bylaws,[vii] the remaining Zionist organizations that were once under the AZC's umbrella group are all incorporated into AIPAC's executive committee through standing corporate invitations and preferential membership status. Over 50 established and newer organizations such as American Friends of Likud and Friends of the Israel Defense Forces are also now included (see appendix).[46]

AIPAC's bylaws are, at their core, denials of activities in which the Israel lobby routinely engaged, such as "[AIPAC] shall receive neither funding nor direction from the State of Israel...AIPAC is not a political action committee ("PAC")...it does not solicit funds for or contribute funds to political candidates or to political parties."[47] Though most of these assertions are easily debunked by history, AIPAC is uniquely isolated from regulation and oversight.

Conclusion

Operating on the principle that it is exempt from the Foreign Agent Registration Act and 1972 Federal Election Campaign Act has paid off handsomely for AIPAC. The assumption that U.S. laws should accommodate the lobby's activities, rather than the reverse, was most eloquently expressed by the Jewish Agency's Maurice Boukstein during his testimony before Senator J.W. Fulbright. Foreign agent registration was fine for disclosing the activities of Soviet-backed communists or German spokesmen for the Reich, he stated, but it did not, in his view, apply to Israel lobbying closely coordinated with Jerusalem. The AZC was explicit that Zionism was being existentially challenged by

---

[vii] Corporate and organizational bylaws are drafted by a corporation's founders or directors under the authority of its charter or articles of incorporation. Bylaws generally regulate the form, manner, or procedures by which a company or organization should be run.

Kennedy administration policies. In the end, it was the Kennedy administration that was brought down, by a series of assassinations. This crisis allowed the AZC to regroup while a more favorable administration took power.

The Israel lobby's continuous challenges to governance, though largely invisible to the American public, have slowly eroded the rule of law in the United States. Stealth PAC coordination has delivered the U.S. Congress into the de facto control of a foreign interest, rendering two decades of legal recourse sought by concerned Americans moot. The Israel lobby's successful challenges to the rule of law enabled massive and unprecedented wealth transfers from U.S. taxpayers to Israel and an unprecedented power grab in Washington. When any key component of the lobby (such as the AZC or the Jewish Agency American Section) was seriously challenged by law enforcement, it simply folded, evolved, and reemerged within new shell corporations with its values and intent fully intact.

"Israel is asking for a chance to compete fairly and openly, accepting the responsibilities and risks of two-way free market competition." **1984 AIPAC paper—U.S.-Israel Relations**[48]

Overthrows of 1979 and the Kenya Group

The Haganah relied heavily on Nicaragua's Anastasio Somoza García beginning in 1939. Somoza transshipped arms from the United States to Jewish fighters in Palestine, and in 1948, even issued Nicaraguan passports for Haganah agents.[49] Somoza's early support for Israel came in exchange for kickbacks. His family dynasty's hold on power guaranteed future business dealings as the regime became an asset to Israel. Nicaragua's strategic location on the isthmus of Central America had also long captivated U.S. interests, much to the dismay of locals, for more than a century.

Tennessee native William Walker led a band of mercenaries to Nicaragua on a mission to secure U.S. business interests in 1855. The Franklin Pierce administration even recognized Walker's sovereignty when he declared himself president of Nicaragua in 1856, but he was quickly displaced by competing American interests. Walker double-crossed the powerful magnate Cornelius Vanderbilt, who financed and dispatched a rebel force to depose Walker. He fled on a U.S. navy warship, but later made three more attempts to seize power. The last ended in failure when his Honduran-based invasion was thwarted by the British, and Walker was unceremoniously handed over to Honduran authorities for execution.

U.S. Marines landed in Nicaragua to protect U.S. property and business interests from social turbulence in 1894, 1896, 1898, and 1899. Nationalist Jose Santos Zelaya aggravated both the U.S. government and Wall Street investors which backed opposition candidates in 1909. When U.S. citizens laying mines in the San Juan River were executed by Zelaya's troops, it provided a convenient pretext for U.S. intervention and installation of a more compliant government.

As commodity production increased under U.S. and European foreign investments, the U.S. took over Nicaragua's customs collection and the national railroad, and even hand-picked functionaries of the government in order to guarantee prompt loan payments. Local resentment soon grew into armed opposition. Rebellion was put down by Marines in 1912. Major Smedley Butler reflected frankly in a letter to his wife that the victorious government troops and U.S.-supported rulers won "a victory gained by us for them at the cost of good American lives, all because Brown Brothers, bankers, have some money invested in this heathenish country."[50]

Butler helped install another U.S.-favored ruler, the only candidate permitted to run in the election, under orders from the Taft administration. The Marines stayed in Nicaragua almost constantly until 1933. Their very presence became self-justifying, since it provoked many uprisings, which then had to be suppressed. Continued social unrest also provided a pretext to create a more effective local military. But the newly chartered Guardia Nacional was unable to face down the greatest threat to the cozy system of clientelism yet to emerge: Augusto Sandino.

Augusto Sandino, the son of a well-to-do peasant farmer, returned to Nicaragua in 1926 after a stint working abroad for U.S. corporations. He was determined to forever eject the U.S. presence, but his tiny military forays were outclassed by U.S. Marine air attacks, and he was forced to adopt hit-and-run guerrilla tactics. Sandino's successes against the Guardia Nacional and U.S. Marines prompted a U.S. withdrawal in 1933. Sandino became a martyr to his movement when he agreed to lay down arms and come to terms. He was assassinated by Guardia Nacional members under the command of U.S.-appointed commander Anastasio Somoza Garcia.

The U.S.-trained Guardia Nacional repressed dissent and social movements as the Somoza regime's family, foreign investors, and sundry supporters locked down national production. The Somozas personally amassed one of the world's largest family fortunes, estimated at nearly $1 billion.[51] Somoza ruled Nicaragua with an iron fist and absolute authority until 1979. But Sandino's movement lived on through the foundation of the National Liberation Front in the 1960s. They enjoyed little success or popular support until the Somoza regime sowed the seeds of its own destruction by attempting to profit from a devastating natural disaster.

In 1972, a catastrophic earthquake leveled the capital city of Managua. It left 5,000 dead and a quarter-million homeless. The ruling Somoza family members misappropriated foreign and humanitarian aid, and little of it ever reached victims of the quake. As popular backlash grew, the Guardia Nacional attempted to maintain control over both the city and the press coverage. It bombed sections of Nicaraguan cities and murdered ABC correspondent Bill Stewart in front of his own cameraman. After that, the Carter administration dropped support for Somoza and his Guardia Nacional, though Israel continued to ship arms to Somoza through nocturnal El Al flights and other means after the Carter ban. Israel provided $250 million or 98 percent of total supplies during the regime's final months.[52] But it wasn't enough. When the Sandinista National Liberation Front took over in 1979, Somoza escaped abroad and Israel lost an important arms export market.

Guardia Nacional officers and the rank and file regrouped in Central American border countries as well as South Florida, soliciting support for retaking Nicaragua. They did not have long to wait. Ronald Reagan entered the presidency in January of 1981 committed to a Cold War strategy designed to challenge and roll back the Soviet Union. The "Reagan Doctrine" required supporting anti-Communist insurgents wherever they might be. Reagan saw the Sandinista acquisition of Russian arms, flows of Sandinista arms and ideology into El Salvador, and warming Soviet ties as unacceptable developments. Six weeks after his inauguration, Reagan approved covert action through a presidential finding—initially giving the Contras $19 million. By November 1981, CIA Director William Casey was laying down definitive plans for arming and retraining exiles capable of facing the ideologically motivated Sandinistas. Israel became a constant shadow of U.S. military efforts in Nicaragua and other key Latin American countries, even as it lost other lucrative markets for its military equipment and services.

As they had in Nicaragua, foreign interventions also played a motivating role in the 1979 Islamic Revolution in Iran. In the 1950s, American and British intelligence agencies became concerned when Dr. Mohammad Mossadegh was named Prime Minister of Iran. Mossadegh was committed to reestablishing democracy and nationalizing the Iranian petroleum industry, effectively removing it from British control. Although the U.S. had no direct stake in Iranian oil, Cold War calculations drove it into action. Fearing Soviet-backed intrigues toward Iran, the U.S. supported British removal of Mossadegh in a secret intervention code named "Operation Ajax."[53]

Subsequent coup attempts resulted in the installation of the U.S.-backed Iranian monarch Shah Mohammed Reza Pahlavi. The U.S. saw economic and military aid to Iran as means of securing a loyal anti-Communist friend that would not challenge Western oil interest in the region while acting as a buffer between the Persian Gulf and the U.S.S.R. But the repressive and brutal tactics of the SAVAK—the Shah's internal security force, which the CIA helped create in 1957—generated popular opposition and outrage similar to Somoza's Guardia Nacional. Savak's unit responsible for torture was trained by Israel in the dark arts of repression. [54] Yaakov Nimrodi, a longtime intelligence and military operative and arms merchant, was posted to Tehran in 1955 for 13 years. According to Nimrodi, "When one day we shall be permitted to talk about all that we have done in Iran, you will be horrified...It is beyond your imagination."[55]

The groundswell to overthrow the Shah started with 1977 strikes and marches by Shiite followers of Ayatollah Khomeini. When President Jimmy Carter grudgingly allowed the fleeing Shah into the U.S. for medical treatment in October of 1979, it triggered waves of immense anger across Iran's revolutionary movement. The Iranian revolutionary government, cognizant of covert U.S. support for the overthrow of Mossadegh, demanded that the U.S. extradite the Shah to stand trial in Tehran. The U.S. refused.

The resultant storming of the U.S. Embassy in Tehran, during which Iranian students took U.S. diplomats and military and intelligence personnel hostage, came to symbolize the impotence of the Carter administration. Futile attempts at negotiating their release, along with an abortive military rescue attempt, plagued the president until he left office. The dilemma of American hostages was a motivating factor in Reagan's later covert dealings with Iran. The 1979 Soviet invasion of Afghanistan and Iraq's invasion of Iran in 1980 presented strategic challenges to U.S. policymakers: should they undermine the regime in Tehran or attempt a diplomatic opening as a buttress against Soviet expansion? Israel was eager to provide input and recover its market.

In addition to the tumult in Nicaragua and Iran, 1979 was also a year of economic chaos for Israel. President Jimmy Carter's intensive hands-on efforts led to the March 26 peace treaty between Egypt and Israel. The termination of war led to the withdrawal of Israeli troops from the Sinai Peninsula, and the peace treaty mandated the two parties enter into negotiations toward trade and other mutually beneficial economic relations.

Boosting the economy was a prime concern to the Israeli government. Between 1948 and 1972, the Israeli gross national product (GNP) had increased 10 percent annually, but it slowed to 2 percent following sharp increases in military spending and soaring energy imports. Israel's imports constantly outpaced exports, creating chronic current account deficits, and its trade deficit, around 20 percent of GNP in the 1960s, ballooned to 35 percent in 1973.[56]

Israeli military spending reached the incredible ratio of 25 percent of GNP between 1970 and 1982. The lion's share of import spending was concentrated in military merchandise (17 percent of GNP), though a quarter of the cost was paid by U.S. foreign aid. Returning Sinai's oil fields to Egypt created $12 billion in losses to the Israeli economy between 1973 and 1982. Government outlays for social welfare programs in the 1970s for housing, education, and support to the urban poor came at the worst possible time for the economy—after it had already begun to stagnate.

The Islamic Revolution presented a deep threat to Israeli economic interests— in particular, access to a friendly supplier of petroleum—which had been guaranteed under the Shah's police state. Israeli exports to Iran had boomed from $33 million in 1973 to $225 million in 1978—7 percent of Israel's total. Leading Israeli corporations had profitable business dealings with the Iranian government in supply and construction contracts. Close relations, formalized in 1958 through a trilateral liaison established by the Israeli Mossad, in cooperation with the Turkish National Security Service (TNSS) and Iran's National Organization for Intelligence and Security (SAVAK), enabled ongoing intelligence exchanges and semiannual meetings by the chiefs of service.[57] Israel even signed a contract to build nuclear-capable missiles—Project Flower—for the Shah. In 1977, Israeli Defense Minister Shimon Peres signed a secret agreement for advanced development of an Israeli missile design that had been underway since the 1950s. This "turn-key" package included a special airport, a missile assembly plant, and a long-range test site in exchange for $1 billion in Iranian oil deliveries. Israel attempted to interest Iran in Israel's U.S.-funded Lavi[viii] jet fighter project,[58] but the Iranian Revolution swept away all such aspirations while devastating the Israel economy. Yaakov Nimrodi claimed he personally lost $6 million to the revolution.[59] The September 1980 Iraqi invasion of Iran provided an opening to restore Israel's economic role and influence in Iran through arms sales.[60]

Lebanon, as refuge to more than 100,000 Palestinian refugees expelled from their lands and homes with the creation of Israel in 1948, presented another challenge. The Palestine Liberation Organization (PLO) grew in power as refugees concentrated in Southern Lebanon expanded to 300,000 by 1975. Ongoing border raids and violence between the PLO and Israel began in 1968. In 1978, Israel invaded Lebanon up the Litani River and pushed the PLO forces north. The creation of the UN peacekeeping force UNIFIL[ix] led to a partial Israeli withdrawal.

After the 1979 peace treaty with Egypt, Israel's Likud government committed to a more aggressive policy against the PLO in Lebanon. On July 10, 1981, violence erupted between South Lebanon and Northern Israel. Israeli Air Force attacks on PLO buildings and more powerful tanks and artillery were partially neutralized by the PLO's dispersed munitions stockpiles and small mobile guerilla units. The renewal of costly conflict and spiraling military outlays meant securing ever higher levels of American aid and support for the economy. Palestinian weapons captured by Israel soon found their way to Central America via Israel as it maneuvered to broker sales of its own stockpiles of U.S.-provided weapons to Iran.

This segment of the Iran-Contra scandal at one time threatened to bring down the entire Reagan administration. President Reagan was as viscerally committed to ensuring that American hostages held in Beirut would not define his presidency as he was to supporting the Contras as a means for rolling back the spread of Soviet expansionism. President Reagan's national security staff engineered covert privately financed support for the Contras by tapping contributions from international donors such as Saudi Arabia and the arms cache captured by Israel.

Historian Sean Wilentz places ultimate responsibility for the scandal firmly on the back of President Reagan. "They stemmed directly from the administration's pursuit of the so-called Reagan Doctrine in Central America and the Middle East, and thus went to the heart of what the president had proclaimed as the central

---

viii After becoming a billion-dollar exposure for proprietary technology leaks, the Lavi was canceled on August 30, 1987. In many ways the Lavi resembled a previous "big dream"—the aborted attempt to purchase the USS Attu aircraft carrier to deploy in Israel's 1948 war—except that American taxpayers, rather than the Sonneborn network, bore the financial loss.

ix United Nations Interim Force in Lebanon

mission of his second term—to challenge the Soviet Union's military expansion on all fronts. Reagan's determination to sustain that mission led him to proceed covertly and in flagrant violation of the expressed will of Congress. Exceeding the secret operations of earlier administrations, a cabal of well-placed officials inside the White House, with the help of the president, perverted the constitutional rule of law. Their exploits were hair-brained and counterproductive as well as illegal. Once exposed, they led to a serious constitutional confrontation."[61]

But the mechanics of the fumbling U.S. approach to the Iranians, sold on the dubious prospect of freeing American hostages held in Lebanon without condemning other Americans to kidnapping, was solidified in earlier "for profit" Israeli arms deals. Three separate covert actions became one as proceeds from sales to Iran were diverted to fund the Contras in Nicaragua in violation of the Boland amendments, even as Israel sought favor on Capitol Hill for enhanced access to the U.S. market. Israel's Iran-Contra role suffered serious blows due to sheer incompetence and the Reagan administration's discovery of Israeli spy Jonathan Pollard in November of 1985. The Iran-Contra and Pollard scandals effectively overshadowed a third and equally embarrassing affair—Israeli economic espionage coordinated with AIPAC against U.S. industry interests.

The central role of Israeli economic and military objectives in Iran-Contra and Jonathan Pollard is not well documented; Israel refused to cooperate with U.S. investigators looking into the Iran-Contra bank accounts and information held by actors such as Yaakov Nimrodi and David Kimche stayed safely offshore and out of reach of official inquiries. The Israeli government's refusal to cooperate with FBI investigations into Israel's penetration of top U.S. trade secrets has never been reported, since the FBI didn't declassify the relevant files until July of 2009.

Two figures deeply involved in the Sonneborn network—and convicted of violating U.S. arms exports laws—in hindsight were exceedingly poor candidates for engineering U.S.-Iran policy. Adolph "Al" Schwimmer, the legendary U.S. Army Corps flight engineer whose "Service Airways" funneled purchased, reconditioned, and stolen U.S. arms to Haganah forces fighting in Palestine, clearly had the experience, but not the right motivations.[62] Schwimmer's lifelong friend Herman "Hank" Greenspun, who stole the 35 tons of surplus machine guns from under the watch of U.S. Marines in Hawaii, also knew the arms business. While Schwimmer left the U.S. for Tel Aviv, Greenspun—formerly a publicist for mobster Benjamin "Bugsy" Siegel's Flamingo Casino—became publisher of the Las Vegas *Sun* newspaper.

Many historical accounts of selling U.S. arms to Iran began with Israeli proposals involving Saudi arms dealer Adnan Khashoggi in the mid-1980s; however, an "end of career" interview with Al Schwimmer by the *Jewish Daily Forward* in 2001 confirms that plans leading to Iran-Contra were already well underway in the late 1970s. This is when Al Greenspun introduced Adnan

Khashoggi to Al Schwimmer, shortly before the 1979 Israel-Egypt peace agreement was penned. Schwimmer told the *Forward* that "Khashoggi was a great gambler, and he spent a lot of time in Nevada...Hank thought it would be a good idea if somehow we got him introduced to Israel." Al Schwimmer arranged for Khashoggi to meet his business partner Yaakov Nimrodi, the former Israeli military attaché to Tehran and arms dealer, as well as other highly influential Israelis. After Nimrodi left Tehran in 1968, his contacts and influence with the Iranian government continued to yield profits. Nimrodi was a vital rainmaker for Israeli businessmen in Iran. Large military vendors such as Schwimmer's Israel Aircraft Industries paid Nimrodi commissions to open doors for business.[63]

In Schwimmer's own words, "Menachem Begin was the prime minister at the time, at Camp David negotiating the treaty with Egypt along with [then-cabinet members] Moshe Dayan and Ezer Weizman." The Schwimmer group attempted to broker a meeting between a crown prince of Saudi Arabia visiting the U.S. for medical treatment and Begin, who was staying in New York after meetings in Washington and Maryland. Although the meeting fell through, Begin sent wishes via Schwimmer's group, welcoming the Saudi prince to visit and pray at Al-Aqsa mosque in Jerusalem.[64]

David Kimche,[x] Uri Lubrani, and General Yaakov Nimrodi appeared on the BBC program *Panorama* on February 8, 1982. Kimche made a public case for supplying equipment to the Iranian military and keeping it strong. The public relations blitz was both timely and self-serving. By then, Israel had already begun selling huge quantities of arms to the Khomeini regime. In July of 1981, Israel agreed to sell $135.9 million worth of ammunition.[65] In 1983, Israel signed another contract worth $21 million. But Israel could not provide what Iran needed most—state-of-the-art surface-to-air missiles, tanks, and anti-tank weapons.

Schwimmer held a secret meeting in May of 1982 at a Kenyan resort owned by Adnan Khashoggi. Yaakov Nimrodi, who had handled the ammunition sales to Iran, Foreign Ministry Director General David Kimche, and Defense Minister Ariel Sharon all attended. They discussed the possibility of Saudi Arabia financing a large stockpile of weapons in Africa, either produced by Israel or captured from Egypt. The stockpile, like Reagan's arming of the Guardia Nacional and Contras, would be targeted toward exiled Iranian generals interested in staging coup attempts against the Islamic revolutionary regime. Although the Mossad later nixed the plan, the germ of the idea—profitable internationally financed Israeli-brokered arms sales to counter-revolutionaries in Iran—was now firmly in place. It was later pitched to the Reagan administration by various members of the 1982 Kenya group with an irresistible but dubious hook: arms sales would be used to free U.S. hostages held in Lebanon.[66]

---

[x] Also a former Israeli ambassador to Iran

Ariel Sharon divulged Israel's $27 million in arms sales to Khomeini during a visit to the United States in May of 1982. In September of 1982, the Israeli Defense Forces under the control of Sharon in Beirut allowed Lebanese Phalangist militiamen to enter two refugee camps. The subsequent massacre of 328-3,500 Palestinian refugees and subsequent public outcry forced Sharon to step down in February of 1983. He would later resurface pushing trade pact negotiations with the U.S. as Israel's economic minister.

Moshe Arens, Israeli ambassador to the U.S., confirmed in October that Israeli military supplies were being coordinated with the highest levels of the U.S. government and that they were designed to keep open channels to the Iranian military in order to bring down the Khomeini government.[67] In 1983, the Israeli Defense Ministry floated an audaciously profitable plan to sell 500 American M-48 tanks to Iran, which was promptly nixed by the United States.[68] Israel then redoubled its efforts to sell U.S. weapons from its huge U.S.-taxpayer-funded pre-positioned stockpile in coordination with the Pentagon, which was by then eager to end-run around congressional bans on arms to the Contras.

CIA and Argentine intelligence collaborated to unify the disparate "Contra-revolucion" groups against the Sandinista Junta of National Reconstruction. Nicaragua's northern neighbor Honduras served as the base for former Guardia Nacional Colonel Enrique Bermudez. After President Reagan issued his "finding"[xi] authorizing CIA paramilitary operations against the Sandinistas, the Contras received initial direct U.S. military and financial support through the Central Intelligence Agency supplemented by the Argentine government. Businessman and anti-Sandinista politician Adolfo Calero established a more workable Contra joint political directorate in December of 1982. But that same month, the U.S. Congress cast what would become an inconvenient series of cascading votes against using U.S. taxpayer funds to "overthrow the government of Nicaragua." Reagan signed the legislation into law as part of a defense appropriations bill on December 21, 1982—but an extralegal plan for funding the Contras soon began to emerge, with Israel at its epicenter.

Early in 1983, Director of Central Intelligence William Casey asked Secretary of Defense Casper Weinberger if the U.S. Department of Defense could obtain some of the abundance of infantry weapons that Israel had confiscated from PLO forces in Lebanon. The Kenya group was delighted. Retired U.S. Major General Richard Secord and Israel's Major General Menachem Meron entered into negotiations. By May of 1983, Israel had provided several hundred tons of weapons on a grant basis to the U.S. Department of Defense.[69] This became known at the Pentagon as "Operation Tipped Kettle."

The illicit arms transaction that began end-running Congress and the surrounding climate of U.S. secrecy provided immense leverage over the Reagan administration to Israel. Not only was it being asked to secretly provide weapons

---

[xi] A presidential mandate for covert actions

for NSC-directed operations banned by Congress, it was positioned to shape and influence future Iran initiatives to its own advantage. Though Honduras, Taiwan, South Korea, and Saudi Arabia were all tapped for financial aid or covert assistance to the Contras, none demanded as significant a return as Israel. Negotiations for preferential Israeli access to the massive U.S. import market began secretly in 1982 with Pentagon guarantees that are to this day secret.

Conclusion

Recapturing markets for Israeli military-related industries after popular backlash sweeps allied dictators out of power has been a recurring challenge for Israel and its lobby. Economics was the major driver of Israel's attempts to influence U.S. policymaking within the Pentagon, Congress, and the U.S. National Security Council in the 1980s. The policies violated congressional mandates and common sense and involved actors with extremely questionable motives. Iran-Contra, Jonathan Pollard, and the lesser-known Israeli Embassy AIPAC economic espionage incident reveal Israel and its lobby's role as a force undermining congressional mandates made in the interest of all Americans, even as it sought unprecedented levels of aid and special status. Access to high-level (and non-public) information about presidential administration needs, concerns, and objectives has been critical to Israel's involvement and shaping of U.S. overseas initiatives.

"The U.S. Bromine Alliance provided very sensitive cost information to the Commission in response to the Commission's requests for confidential business data in connection with its report on a free trade agreement with Israel. The Alliance presumes that these data were quoted in the Commission's confidential report to the USTR, a copy of which was obtained by representatives of the American-Israel Public Affairs Committee..." **Max Turnipseed, U.S. Bromine Alliance**[70]

Memoranda to "Free" Trade Agreement

Israeli Prime Minister Yitzak Shamir met with President Reagan at the White House on November 29, 1983. Economic support for Israel was at the top of the agenda. Reagan agreed to commence "fast track" negotiations toward bilateral tariff-free access between the two markets. This was an unprecedented step in the history of U.S. trade. Although the office of the president had sole authority over penning such a treaty, the drive was also secretly underwritten by the Pentagon as recognition for Israel's services in the covert operation to supply the Contras. As part of the secret Operation Tipped Kettle, the "DoD assured Israel that, in exchange for the weapons, the U.S. Government would be as flexible as possible in its approach to Israeli military and economic needs, and that it would find a way to compensate Israel for its assistance within the restraints of the law and U.S. policy."[71] Israel's PAC-enforced influence in Congress meant that AIPAC only had to overcome U.S. worker and industry opposition to forever open the U.S. market to Israeli exports.

Empowered by its preemptive victory in the 1967 Six-Day War and the efforts of its U.S.-based lobby, Israel had already quietly insinuated itself into the U.S. military-industrial complex through a series of signed memorandums of understanding (MOUs)[xii] with the U.S. Department of Defense long before the USIFTA was formally negotiated in 1984. On December 22, 1970, the U.S. and Israel signed the Master Defense Development Data Exchange Agreement (MDDDEA). This facilitated the free exchange of technical data Israel could use to develop military systems for surveillance, electronic warfare, tanks, air-to-air

---

[xii] MOUs continue. The U.S. and Israel signed a MOU in August 2007 committing $30 billion in American military aid over the subsequent decade to be given in cash at the start of each fiscal year as "grant aid." Israel must spend 74 percent of the aid to purchase U.S. military goods and services.

and air-to-surface weapons, and other major integrated engineering projects. U.S. Defense Secretary Harold Brown and Israeli Defense Minister Ezer Weizmann signed a "Memorandum of Agreement" in 1979. In April of 1981, Secretary of State Alexander Haig established the Defense Trade Agreement (DTA) and later endorsed a 1983 "strategic cooperation" agreement.

The DTA was a massive boost to Israel's economy. The Pentagon sought to enhance the competitiveness of Israel's defense industry by procuring Department of Defense contracts totaling $200 million a year for Israeli-produced equipment, according to a Government Accounting Office (GAO) report. The program was justified as a way to strengthen Israel's economy while maintaining its military superiority against Soviet-backed regimes in the Middle East. The DTA also expanded cooperation through joint research and development projects, equipment evaluation toward potential procurement, and competitive R&D allowing Israeli contractors to compete against U.S. vendors for contract awards. The DTA extended the 1970 MDDDEA with a Scientist and Engineer Exchange Program, and also provided an open-ended list of U.S. military items and service contracts that Israeli firms could bid on.

An interagency Defense Trade Task Force established to implement the DTA quickly discovered that the United States could not procure enough Israeli military equipment on a competitive basis to achieve the target $200 million goal. In looking for alternative means for enhancing Israeli military industries, the Defense Trade Task Force then expanded the number of Pentagon contracts Israeli firms could competitively bid on without the application of congressionally mandated "buy-America" restrictions. Israel was made eligible to bid on 560 Pentagon contracts under the Brown-Weizmann agreement of 1979. In 1981, Israeli firms sold between $50 million and $100 million worth of goods to the Pentagon or its contractors. The DTA continued despite the suspension of the 1981 MOU, while the total number of contracts Israel could bid on was expanded.

AIPAC led the charge by lobbying Congress and published 10 public relations booklets in its "Papers on US-Israel Relations" series in the early 1980s. Half of the series dealt with the US military. "The Strategic Value of Israel" (1982), "Israel and the US Air Force" (1983), "Israel and the US Navy" (1983), "Israeli Medical Support for the US Armed Forces" (1983), and "US Procurement of Israeli Defense Goods and Services" (1984) outlined strategic rationales for not just alliance, but full economic integration. The first AIPAC booklet argued for allowing Israel the permanent right to bid on U.S. defense contracts in terms similar to those permitted to NATO[xiii] allies. AIPAC asserted that such integration would help control American defense costs, widen procurement options available to the Pentagon, and "strengthen the defense industrial base by

---

[xiii] North Atlantic Treaty Organization, a system of collective defense under which European member states and the U.S. agreed to mutual defense against the Soviet Union after 1948.

linking Israel's defense industry to other parts of the West's military production capability." AIPAC also wanted permanent, rather than negotiated, direct Israeli rights to sell military equipment to the U.S. Department of Defense. The lobby argued for enhanced integration through the licensed production of military hardware by corporations from either the U.S. or Israel, joint development projects between private U.S. and Israeli military contractors, and more extensive subcontracting in both countries. AIPAC also demanded that the U.S. give Israel contracts to maintain and overhaul U.S. armed forces equipment that was being serviced in Europe.

In 1984, according to the GAO, Israel even sought to have the U.S. government formally mandate that "major U.S. military equipment exporters conclude 'buyback' arrangements with Israeli manufacturers whereby U.S. suppliers offset or buy-back goods and services from Israel; encourage Pentagon contractors to involve Israeli manufacturers as subcontractors; exercise a liberal policy with regard to reciprocal transfer of advanced technologies; and assist in the modernization of Israeli maintenance and refurbishing services to U.S. forces stationed overseas."[72]

Early MOUs were primarily focused on providing immediate economic support or financial opportunities for Israeli vendors, but enabled few meaningful joint U.S.-Israeli military exercises aimed at impressing U.S. adversaries. The early Pentagon-managed agreements intertwined Israeli and U.S. industry through joint ventures and expanded commercial trade that had no basis in competitive market advantage. These somewhat contrived military-industrial interdependence ventures also never had much to do with Cold War military calculations. Israel's early leverage through the Pentagon sought a favorable structural integration of the two countries' economies whereby the United States became dependent to some degree on Israeli-made specialty products. The 1984 AIPAC report "U.S. Procurement of Israeli Defense Goods and Services" boasted that "U.S. corporations either own or have substantial interests, either directly or through holding companies or subsidiaries, in Tadiran, Elbit Electronics, Motorola Israel, Elisra, El-Op, and numerous smaller firms. This includes virtually all Israeli corporations involved in electronic warfare development."[73]

AIPAC touted such forced interdependence as a means for reducing outright U.S. economic assistance, though such outlays have never diminished. Most importantly from Israel's perspective, such ties limited the ability of changing political winds in Washington to cut or condition aid to Israel, while making the broader American business community support Israel lobby initiatives as the easiest choice, or a "no-brainer" in business school reasoning.

U.S. Defense Secretary Caspar Weinberger and Israeli Defense Minister Yitzhak Rabin signed a memorandum of agreement in late 1984. Building on the 1979 DTA and 1983 strategic cooperation agreement, the pact allowed Israel to sell into the American military hardware procurement market. In a precedent-breaking move, the Defense Department waived both customs duties on merchandise sold to the U.S. armed services and buy-America requirements that had garnered heavy congressional support by producing jobs across congressional districts.

The five-year MOA extended military exchange programs through cooperation in R&D, data exchange, and scientist-engineer exchange programs. The U.S. was also required to purchase $100 million worth of Israeli merchandise in 1985 to "offset" Israeli purchases of U.S. military equipment, and U.S. contractors were mandated to buy Israeli goods worth 15 percent of Israeli military purchases in the United States. The Weinberger-Rabin pact also unfettered Israeli merchandise sales to U.S. military bases in Europe and across the Mediterranean.

The public U.S. military rationale behind the MOUs was confronting the Soviet Union. Tactically, they did reduce Syria's influence on Lebanon. Four days after President Reagan and Prime Minister Shamir signed the MOU, U.S. and Israeli warplanes attacked Syrian positions in Lebanon. Though the bombing raids were only 24 hours apart, the appearance of unity was achieved.

The U.S. received very little in return for its massive taxpayer-funded concessions that subsidized Israel's transformation into a top global arms merchant. The Reagan White House hoped Israel would become more responsive to U.S. initiatives in the Arab world, but Israel's U.S. lobby continued to mobilize Congress against administration proposals for weapons sales to friendly Arab states while Israel entrenched its own occupation of captured West Bank and Gaza territory. Israel would later lobby for legislation that vastly reduced U.S. corporate access to the surrounding Arab import market. Israel's ability to "burrow" into the U.S. defense establishment, which jump-started its own capacity for building advanced weaponry through joint production of sophisticated military systems, also presented unprecedented opportunities for espionage. When the moment was right, Israel began independently selling ever more sophisticated copycat weapons to markets of its own choosing, with little regard for U.S. national security concerns.

Such heavy investment and development of the Israeli military-industrial complex, with an emphasis on securing tightly held foreign intellectual property, reflects David Ben-Gurion's vision of the primacy of military force in foreign policy. "Success in the international arms market is as much as matter of foreign policy as commercial considerations. That is why the buying and selling of weapons—or, as it came to be known, 'Uzi diplomacy'—became early on a major consideration in Israel's overseas relations."[74]

America's first ever bilateral trade agreement with Israel was an unprecedented gift in the modern international trading system that began at the postwar July 1944 Bretton Woods conference. Although the conference was most noted for establishing the World Bank and International Monetary Fund, the foundation for the General Agreement on Tariffs and Trade (GATT) also sprang from Bretton Woods.

After World War II, the United States dominated the world's economy. After Bretton Woods, U.S. trade policy and foreign policy became highly intertwined, and opening the world to American business became a strategy for winning the Cold War. Trade policy was advanced as a tool for fighting communism that was every bit as important as direct deterrents like ballistic nuclear missiles and conventional military forces. This sprang naturally from the American belief in markets, enterprise, and promoting the business interests that were rebuilding Europe and Japan. A new drive under the label of "free trade"[xiv] proceeded—even though many trade counterparties such as the "Asian Tigers" (South Korea, Singapore, Hong Kong, and Taiwan) successfully engaged in export promotion while protecting their industries behind high import barriers.

The GATT was originally only a provisional negotiating body intended to give rise to a final global trade institution that would stand alongside the World Bank and IMF. Fifty countries participated in negotiations that might have led to the formation of this "International Trade Organization" (ITO). However, a draft ITO charter revealed ambitions far beyond the technicalities of tariffs and barriers. It not only encompassed rules on employment, restrictive business practices, and international investments, but also trade in services. The creation of the ITO faltered under serious opposition from Congress and U.S. business interests. Provisionally negotiated GATT tariff reductions and periodic "trade rounds" regulated world trade from 1948 through the creation of the World Trade Organization (WTO) in 1995.

The highest GATT membership benefit was "most favored nation" (MFN) status, which allowed every member to receive the tariff reductions extended to any other member. Other arrangements emerging during the reign of GATT allowed for free trade agreements, common markets, customs unions, and economic unions. All were mechanisms for achieving closer regional economic integration. The Kennedy Round of GATT during the 1960s launched anti-dumping provisions. The Tokyo Round during the seventies tackled non-tariff barriers. The Uruguay Round of 1986-1994 was the GATT's last and most

---

[xiv] Adam Smith, who documented the value of trade in his seminal 1776 book *The Wealth of Nations*, and economist David Ricardo, who later modeled relative productivity between nations, would not likely recognize the present-day initiatives made under the banner of "free trade agreements" as true free trade. Their pure thesis envisioned exchanges based on comparative advantage without interference from government. Modern free trade agreements are negotiated between governments, which favor key domestic industries and lobbying interests through subsidies (particularly agro and military industries in the U.S.) and other interventions including tariffs, taxes, quotas, and most importantly, whom they chose as FTA partners. Honestly marketed, most present-day "free trade agreements" would at best qualify as "inter-government managed trade agreements," and quite possibly as a form of protectionism.

comprehensive.[xv] It led to the formation of the WTO and an entirely new set of trade rules.

There were few "restraints of the law or U.S. policy" (as expressed in the DOD Operation Tipped Kettle guarantees to Israel) to prevent President Ronald Reagan from signing a trade deal with Israel that would open up the U.S. market, despite the alarm in American industry and worker associations. Under an FTA, Israel could theoretically burrow in and gradually take over high-value-added U.S. import markets where it held, or could create, comparative advantages, including locking out competitors. In the 1980s, USIFTA had to pass muster on Capitol Hill, since the U.S. Constitution gave Congress exclusive authority to set tariffs and enact legislation governing international trade. But the president retained constitutional authority to negotiate international agreements, so only organized popular or industrial opposition threatened Israeli market access.[xvi]

One important prelude to the USIFTA was the U.S.-Israel Binational Industrial Research and Development (BIRD) Foundation. Created by the U.S. and Israeli governments on March 3, 1976, BIRD was endowed with $60 million. Though it was publicly positioned as an equal partnership, BIRD's endowment was 100 percent U.S.-taxpayer-funded. Fifty percent of the funding derived from an Economic Support Fund provided by an act of Congress, and Israel's paid in shares were actually repayments of loans already owed to the U.S. government.[xvii] BIRD's charter was to "generate mutually beneficial cooperation between the private sectors of the U.S. and Israeli high tech industries, including start-ups and established organizations."[75] BIRD provided "matchmaking" services between Israeli and American companies, both established organizations and startups. BIRD would provide up to 50 percent of project and product development costs. It took no equity stake, but expected future repayments to build the endowment.[76] USIFTA would provide an enormous market for BIRD projects and existing Israeli companies.

Congress and the president had long recognized that negotiations and implementation of trade agreements required levels of cooperation only possible with strictly defined roles, rules, and procedures. A closer working relationship on tariff negotiations was first envisioned in the Reciprocal Trade Agreements of 1934, but nothing like what was being proposed with Israel had ever been

---

[xv] "Trade Rounds" continue. The Doha Round commenced in 2001 and seeks to lower trade barriers world wide, but stalled along a North-South split over agriculture subsidies and tariffs.

[xvi] When the office of the president negotiates trade agreements that change tariffs or other related domestic laws affecting trade, the implementing legislation must be submitted to Congress for approval, or the president can obtain advance approval for changes.

[xvii] Derived from accelerated payments to the United States of Israel's Public Law 480 debts according to Article VII of the BIRD agreement.

attempted. Regulations over product content, health, and consumer safety also factored in alongside numerical tariff schedules as primary concerns in trade negotiations. The Ford administration and Congress created the "fast track" precisely to address the much broader scope and detailed investigations necessary for comprehensive binding treaties. The Trade Act of 1974 enabled "fast track negotiations" in the Tokyo Round of the General Agreement on Trade and Tariffs (GATT). Until relatively recently, this gave U.S. presidents the authority to negotiate using fast track almost continuously.[77] But by the time of USIFTA negotiations, the Israel lobby had already used its power in Congress to pass legislation restricting U.S. trade promoting the Jackson-Vanik amendment, named after co-sponsors Charles Vanik and Henry "Scoop" Jackson. The amendment denied most favored nation status to countries restricting emigration to Israel and targeted the Soviet Union. Israel's foreign policy favored population growth through expedited emigration of Soviet Jews; Jackson-Vanik was an easy Cold War victory for the lobby which also worked to oppose Arab restrictions on imports from U.S. corporations doing business in Israel. Fifteen hundred U.S. firms, including Ford and Xerox, were placed on Arab country blacklists for trading with Israel. Legislation prohibiting U.S. companies from complying with the boycott passed in 1977. With the end of the Cold War and collapse of the Soviet Union, such legislation gradually came be seen as interventions in trade policy that had little to do with U.S. national security or long-term economic interests.[78]

Under fast track, congressional consideration of trade agreements is both expedited and limited. Congress can only vote an agreement up or down, and cannot reopen or change any section of its numerous provisions. Fast track requires the administration to consult and coordinate with Congress throughout the process to avoid any "deal breakers" or unacceptable provisions. The president must also specify how the administration will use its regulatory authority across different agencies to implement the agreement.

Private sector advisory committees are invited to give their views to both Congress and the president about whether a proposed agreement meets U.S. negotiating objectives. All bilateral agreements require that Congress be given advance notice of the president's intent to begin negotiations, at which time they have 60 days to vote to deny fast track.[79] Israel tentatively sought such a free trade zone with the United States in the late 1970s,[80] but didn't have enough overall leverage to compel the U.S. The mid-1980s were an entirely different era in Israel lobby power and U.S.-Israel political relations.

On January 31, 1984, the ambassador of the U.S. Trade Representative (USTR)—the agency responsible for developing and recommending trade policy to the president and coordinating trade policy within interagency committees— swept into action on President Reagan's authority. He issued an order to the United States International Trade Commission (ITC), a quasi-judicial federal agency charged with measuring the impact of imports on U.S. industries and directing enforcement actions against dumping, patent, trademark, and copyright infringement, to begin industry consultations and development of a comprehensive written analysis to be used in fast track negotiations with Israel.

Industry participants had no way of knowing about the Operation Tipped Kettle guarantees already given to Israel. Most understood the power of AIPAC, but not the lengths to which it was willing to go in order to achieve preferential market access. Their only clues were the hints of espionage targeting their trade secrets—exposed by the *Washington Post*, protested by industry, investigated by the FBI, and ultimately swept under the rug by the Department of Justice. Reviewing the formerly classified details of how Israel managed to achieve the USIFTA in the midst of two other major scandals reveals that the values and ethics governing pre-state weapons acquisitions by the Sonneborn network in the U.S. were still in place.

Negotiations entered their advice and consent phase in 1984. The strictly regulated and choreographed fast track processes formally commenced on January 1, when USTR ambassador William E. Brock formally requested that the U.S. International Trade Commission perform a detailed investigation into the effects of a free trade area with Israel on U.S. industries.[81] [xviii] American industry and the public were notified on February 15, 1984 via a Federal Register notice soliciting industry input for a written report to be completed by May 30, 1984.[82] The notice also announced that public hearings in Washington, DC were scheduled for April 10-11, 1984, with the deadline for requests for appearances and testimony before the ITC set no later than noon, April 3, 1984.

Businesses were told to submit their most closely held (and potentially damaging) information in confidence to the ITC: "In lieu of or in addition to appearances at the public hearing, interested persons are invited to submit written statements concerning the investigation...by the close of business on April 3, 1984." The International Trade Commission underscored its commitment to properly handling industry trade secrets by stating that "commercial or financial information which a submitter desires the Commission to treat as confidential must be submitted on separate sheets of paper, each clearly marked 'Confidential Business Information' at the top."[83] But the ITC and USTR's ability to keep such secrets from a country eager to build its own economy was about to be severely tested by operatives working out of the Israeli embassy in Washington, DC and AIPAC's own public relations and lobbying team members.

The formality and tight structure of the ITC investigation masked the reality of three tracks in the USIFTA process: one in the National Security Council armed with guarantees from the president to top-level Israeli insiders in exchange for

---

[xviii] He specifically ordered ITC to "Conduct an investigation pursuant to section 332(g) of the Tariff Act of 1930, and to advise the President, with respect to each item in the Tariff Schedules of the United States as to the probable economic effect of providing duty free treatment for imports from Israel on industries in the United States producing like or directly competitive articles and on consumers."

Iran-Contra assistance, another for U.S. commercial and public interests, and a third for AIPAC with its links to foreign diplomats and—allegedly—Israeli intelligence.

The public record reveals advice and consent leading to a bona fide USTR negotiation and treaty passed unanimously by Congress. The secret history reveals the interplay of Israel facilitating clandestine support for the Contras and arms for hostages in collusion with the office of the president. The USIFTA is revealed as a prize that Israel determined it simply could not be denied by any public protest or advice and consent. But AIPAC's covert activities, investigated by the FBI under suspicion of espionage and theft of government property, could never be publicly known until they were declassified in April of 2009 and released on July 31, 2009.[xix]

On the national security track, Operation Tipped Kettle II was launched in February of 1984. Israel had already secretly provided several hundred tons of weapons to the DOD for the Contras in May of 1983, according to declassified summaries of the operation used in judicial proceedings: "In February, 1984 the CIA again asked the DOD if it could obtain additional PLO weapons from Israel at little or no cost for CIA operational use. After negotiations between March 1984 and July, 1984, Israel secretly provided additional weapons to the DOD in Operation Tipped Kettle II."[84] The DOD's guarantee that it would "compensate Israel for its assistance within the restraints of the law and U.S. policy" was now clearly operative.

During the period for public comment, a strong coalition of individual experts, associations, and corporations provided highly negative feedback to the ITC. Seventy-six were strongly opposed to the proposed USIFTA, while only 17 organizations—mostly small and obscure with few direct economic stakes in U.S.-Israel trade—were in favor (see appendix). On April 10, 1984, public testimony was heard.[xx] The large Arkansas delegation was committed to opposing unlimited amounts of Israeli bromine flowing into the U.S. market.[xxi]

[xix] The Federal Bureau of Investigation released 82 pages of internal investigation records under the Freedom of Information Act after a one-year process involving two formal appeals, the final to the FBI director.

[xx] From the U.S. Bromine Alliance, the Arkansas Industrial Development Commission, the California Tomato Growers Association, Inc., the University of California at Berkeley, tri/Valley Growers, Hunt-Wesson Foods, the American Dehydrated Onion and Garlic Association, Sun Garden Packing Company, the Western Growers Association, Monticello Canning Company, Inc., the National Milk Producers Federation, the California Olive Association, Florida Citrus producers, and Sunkist Growers, Inc.

[xxi] Bromine is a chemical element vital to the production of fine chemicals, extracted from bromide salts accumulated from sea water. The U.S., Israel, and China are the world's primary producers of bromine in a market worth

The delegation from Arkansas, led by then Governor Bill Clinton, was given preferential scheduling for the hearing. Clinton argued against the undue burden USIFTA would create for his state: "So I would just plead with you to consider the enormously concentrated adverse economic impact of including bromine in this FTA, because 85 percent of the production is concentrated in two small rural counties..." U.S. Senator Dale Bumpers railed against state involvement in Israel's bromine industry: "All of us are concerned about the potentially serious consequences that an FTA could have upon the United States bromine industry, a small but vital sector of the American economy... The Israeli bromine industry enjoys a series of subsidies and other special advantages...To begin with, the Israeli bromine industry is government-owned."

On April 11, the ITC heard public testimony on behalf of the American Israel Commerce and Industry Association and AIPAC. Thomas A. Dine, then executive director of AIPAC, testified on the mutual benefits of the agreement while lobbying against any special exemptions by economic sector: "Because of Israel's small size and limited production capacity relative to the U.S., there is little reason to fear major short term negative effects from increased Israeli imports into the U.S....The proposed Free Trade Area is therefore a two-way gain—both countries will reap the benefits from the pact..." [85]

The AIPAC executive also argued for "keeping the proposed FTA as 'clean' as possible and avoid[ing] gutting the agreement by carving out exception after exception."[86] AIPAC's formal testimony for the agreement and coordinated lobbying for Israeli Dead Sea bromine suggested access to proprietary information. How much proprietary inside information AIPAC had obtained soon became publicly known—though its impact was never fully appreciated.

In April of 1984, Robert McFarlane secretly directed Howard Teicher of the NSC staff to discuss additional aid to the Contras with Kenya Group member David Kimche from the Israeli government. They proposed that the U.S. government facilitate an Israeli point of contact in Honduras. The Israelis would later return in September of 1986 with a proposal for sales of Israeli-built Kfir fighter jets to Honduras, bundled with Israeli military advisors to train the Contras. President Nixon had allowed the Israelis to license a more powerful General Electric engine for the Kfir. Though Israel gave assurances that it had no intention of exporting the plane, it proposed sales to Ecuador in 1976. Al Schwimmer personally traveled to Washington to respond to an arms ban on the Kfir imposed by Jimmy Carter, declaring, "It is not that we seek to become a merchant of arms; we need military exports for our defense capability." Carter gave an extra $285 million in economic aid but did not lift the ban.[87] However, President Reagan later allowed the Kfir sales to Ecuador.

---

approximately $2.5 billion today. Modern applications also include gasoline additives, pesticides, and commercial flame retardants. Israel's bromine reserves are extracted from the waters of the Dead Sea, while U.S. production is centered in two counties in Arkansas.

AIPAC ramped up its public relations effort to build support for the USIFTA in an April 30, 1984 memorandum to members and stakeholders. In a "benefits to the U.S." section, AIPAC pitched USIFTA as a way for the U.S. to compete with the European Community's duty-free trade deal with Israel. An AIPAC memo forecast expansion of U.S. exports, noting that the U.S. already enjoyed a "six-to-one surplus in agricultural products and textiles in its trade with Israel." A section titled "Cause few problems to domestic industries" noted that "Israel's ability to increase exports is restricted by its limited amounts of land and water and the expensive costs of shipping perishable products long distances."[88]

On April 4, 1984, 20 copies of an ITC "prehearing report" for the USTR were made and circulated in the ITC. Word soon spread that AIPAC was handling the classified material. Early access to this classified information was critical in AIPAC's drive to counteract U.S. industry exemptions and effective opposition to the USIFTA. This was important because some concerned U.S. companies were already raising major red flags about potential intellectual property theft based on their previous trade experiences in Israel. On May 2, 1984, Monsanto International voiced concerns that "a local concern has been able to take advantage of the procedural shortcomings in the Israeli 'patent opposition system,' [and] the granting of a patent to Monsanto has been blocked." The heavy state involvement in Israel's economy was also raised as a concern: "Three fourths of Israel's chemical industry is owned by the government and it receives substantial export subsidies....In the decade ahead Israel will become an increasingly active exporter of these products and may cause some market discontinuities in the U.S."[89]

Echoing many other industry expert petitions in the public fast track process, Monsanto questioned the overriding wisdom of signing a bilateral trade agreement with such a small, developing economy: "Our government should make the distinction between the advanced developing and developed countries with a strong current account position (such as Taiwan, Hong Kong and Japan) and those with severe balance of payments problems..." But Monsanto's concerns about intellectual property were sent on May 2 (just after the April 3, 1984 comment filing deadline) and were rejected by the ITC.[90] Curiously, the ITC committee chair accepted a late filing from Israel's Dead Sea Bromine Company, LTD on May 11, 1984.[91]

A Department of Commerce (DOC) delegation participated in formal U.S.-Israel negotiations the week of May 14, 1984 in Jerusalem. A DOC employee who stayed a week after the meetings made a disconcerting discovery: on May 21, in a meeting with the Israeli delegation and diplomats from the Washington DC embassy, an Israeli announced he had received a cable from Israel's Washington, DC embassy "and then proceeded to read from this cable what appeared to be a full summary of the report, including the conclusions regarding sensitive products."[92]

The House Ways and Means Committee reviewed draft USIFTA legislation on May 22, 1984, publicly assuring that both the Senate and the president backed the measure. The Heritage Foundation, a conservative think tank, quoting the Israeli Manufacturers Association as a source, calculated that "if the U.S. does not negotiate the FTA, it not only will forego potential exports but could lose some of its current sales, now valued at between $1.5 billion and $1.8 billion a year. This is because the Israelis are phasing in a trade agreement with the European Economic Community (EEC)." Heritage also consoled U.S. companies by echoing AIPAC talking points, stating that "because the Israeli share of the American market is very small, the complete elimination of tariff barriers would be no threat to American industry."[93]

Troubling reports of leaks of the classified ITC report continued to pour in. On or around May 30, a member of the Trade Sub-Committee notified the USTR that "after a conversation with an employee of the American Israel Public Affairs Committee (AIPAC) in WDC, this member was left with the impression that AIPAC had a copy of the subject report." The unidentified AIPAC member was familiar with the report's contents and conclusions.[94] But it was too late to delay the final report.

On May 30, 1984, Chairman of the ITC Alfred Eckes transmitted the final 300-page report, derived from both public and confidential business information. The classified final report, titled *Probable Economic Effect of Providing Duty Free Treatment for U.S. Imports from Israel, Investigation No. 332-180,* was sent to the office of President Ronald Reagan, giving the deal a green light but warning of industry consequences in a cover letter. "Based on the information gathered in the U.S. International Trade Commission's investigation of the proposed free trade area, the Commission does not expect duty-free treatment for U.S. imports from Israel to have a significant adverse effect at the aggregate level for any of the major sectors examined; however, at the less aggregated commodity level, significant adverse effects are likely in seven different product areas as discussed in the report."[95]

Organizations formally petitioning from the ITC "advice and consent" track in opposition to the agreement outnumbered parties in favor by three to one (see appendix), and thousands of individual Americans also submitted signatures on petitions opposing the deal. Only AIPAC, the American Israel Chamber of Commerce, and organizations such as a tiny, recently chartered bank operating out of Bethesda provided supporting testimony to the ITC.

USTR ambassador William Brock became aware of the report leak during a June 7 luncheon with the Israeli Trade Ministry. Brock heard not only news of the circulation of the report, but analysis of its contents, while seated at the table. News that "certain members of Congress could acquire copies of the ITC report through AIPAC" filtered into the USTR office on June 12 and 13.[96] A congressional staffer advised the USTR that "the Israelis were offering copies of this document to members of Congress because the United States Trade Representative was slow in delivering them."[97] On June 15, 1985, USTR General Counsel Claude Gingrich called Ester Kurz and demanded to know whether AIPAC possessed the classified ITC report. Kurz admitted it did. [98] Gingrich told her the document was classified and demanded that AIPAC return it. [99] Thomas Dine, AIPAC's executive director, immediately contacted the USTR to "claim no knowledge of the report himself and to disassociate himself from such activities."[100] Dine promised that the material would be returned and they would cooperate in every way in any investigation to determine how they received a copy of a classified document.[101] On June 19, the USTR referred the matter to the FBI, which began a formal investigation.[102] But AIPAC's massive public relations campaign to push USIFTA soon eliminated the possibility of any meaningful industry exceptions or advice and consent feedback.

Thomas Dine and Douglas Bloomfield, AIPAC's chief lobbyist, issued a legislative update directed to "officers, executive committee, national council and key contacts" on June 30, 1984 (see appendix). The update trumpeted AIPAC's success in winning $2.6 billion in foreign aid for 1985, a resolution calling to move the U.S. embassy from Tel Aviv to Jerusalem, meetings on a proposal to fund "joint U.S.-Israel development projects in the third world," opposition to proposed U.S. sales of Stinger missiles to Saudi Arabia, and hearings on the USIFTA. An attached action alert urged supporters to contact their representatives "at their district offices" to sponsor the USIFTA. The inside track in the National Security Council was also heating up.

The National Security Council had settled on an audacious plan to continue Contra funding via third-country contributions.[103] In June, the Saudi government was successfully lobbied to provide $1 million in financial support to the Contras. Attorney General William French Smith studied the National Security Council's plans for financing the Contras via Saudi, Israeli, and other third-country support in July. He rendered his opinion to the president that U.S.-managed third-country funding—even in the face of congressional bans on U.S. support to the Contras—would not be an impeachable offense.

The growing irrelevance of the advice and consent track soon became evident to unwitting participants on August 30, 1984, when the *Washington Post* reported that the FBI had launched its investigation of the American Israel Public Affairs Committee. The *Washington Post* was frank in its damage assessment that the report "contains proprietary data supplied by American industries and other sensitive information for the negotiations, which began early this year...Trade officials said the report would give Israel a significant advantage in the trade talks because it discloses how far the United States is willing to compromise on contested issues. Some of the proprietary information, moreover, could help Israeli businesses competing with U.S. companies, officials said."[104] But the USTR also privately worried about the impact on the sanctity and "effectiveness of the ITC to solicit data from the U.S. business community," according to FBI files released in 2009.[105]

An AIPAC spokesman publicly acknowledged that AIPAC had obtained a copy of the classified ITC document, but brashly stated that "the lobbying group did nothing illegal" and had "returned" the report.[106] It claimed it had returned the classified report to the USTR by "AIPAC messenger."[107] The classified FBI incident report noted that AIPAC returned a "copy of the final report" that "had no identifying mark on the outside cover which was clearly stamped confidential." The FBI went on to observe that "this indicates that this copy was probably made prior to the May 30 delivery to USTR. USTR officials advised the significance of the unauthorized disclosure of the contents of the ITC report is that the bargaining position of the United States was compromised."[108] The FBI noted that the copy probably came from the ITC, since "all internal copies kept at the United States Trade Representative...would have an internal document control number in the upper right hand corner of the cover page. The document identified as having been returned from AIPAC had no such number."[109]

The Israeli government was by then so intimately intertwined in Iran-Contra activities that it was politically well positioned to weather public exposure of its role in covert information gathering in the US—for the time being. The Department of Justice Internal Security Section and General Litigation and Legal Advice Section, under the permissive Attorney General William French Smith, promptly quashed the FBI espionage investigation into AIPAC on August 24, 1984. They determined that "this matter did not represent a violation of the espionage statute as it was reported that no national defense information was utilized in the preparation of the report." But the DOJ did believe that a violation of the Theft of Government Property statute had occurred, and it referred the matter to Assistant United States Attorney Charles Harkins "for a prosecutive opinion."[110] The largest Israeli espionage scandal of the decade, the Jonathan Pollard affair, had not yet broken. But when it did, it would refocus the DOJ's attention toward unearthing an Israeli Embassy-AIPAC connection.

In September, Ester Kurz, Martin Indyk, and Steven J. Rosen issued a densely written, highly detailed 46-page booklet for AIPAC's public relations series, titled "A U.S.-Israel Free Trade Area: How Both Sides Gain," under Peggy Blair's byline. It rebutted U.S. industry concerns about the USIFTA with optimistic job creation and opportunity forecasts that, while widely echoed in establishment media in 1984 and 1985, proved to be wildly inaccurate.[xxii] The report listed "Thirteen U.S. Exports that Will Gain," but did not mention sensitive industries such as bromine. AIPAC's public relations and lobbying nucleus had little to fear about its acquisition of the classified ITC report. On September 19, 1984, DOJ prosecutor Charles Harkins "opined that this matter lacked prosecutive merit" and declined to pursue Theft of Government Property indictments against AIPAC.

[xxii] The two editors of the report, Martin Indyk and Steven J. Rosen, had subsequent involvement with classified information. In September of 2000, Indyk had his security clearance suspended by the U.S. State Department while acting as U.S. ambassador to Israel. Rosen was indicted in 2005 under the Espionage Act over an incident involving national defense information and was subsequently fired by AIPAC. In 2009, he sued AIPAC for defamation.

The U.S. Bromine Alliance was incensed about the leak and demanded action. Unaware of the immense gravitational pull of the inside track, it gathered together legal counsel for a high-level confrontation. Accompanied by lawyers Will E. Leonard and Edward R. Easton from the law firm of Busby, Rehm, and Leonard, P.C., the Bromine Alliance director met with ITC Chairwoman Paula Stern on November 1, 1984. They requested a detailed confirmation that confidential Alliance business information had been disclosed to AIPAC in the classified report.[111] The Bromine Alliance would not receive an answer until after Ronald Reagan was reelected in a November 6, 1984 landslide.

In October of 1984, Reagan met with Israeli Prime Minister Shimon Peres to discuss "early opportunities" for more U.S. aid to address Israel's ongoing economic crisis. Peres was David Ben-Gurion's young protégé in 1947 and became a liaison to the Haganah's underground arms procurement and smuggling network in New York in 1950. That early Sonneborn-financed mission had been semi-covert because the U.S. abided by the 1950 Tripartite Agreement with Britain and France to regulate arms sales to the Middle East. When Peres returned to Israel in 1951, Al Schwimmer lobbied to place him in charge of starting up an Israeli aerospace industry, which eventually grew into Israel Aircraft Industries. Over the decades, Peres molded and shaped the Israeli military-industrial complex.[112] Reagan confirmed delivery of $2.6 billion in aid passed by Congress to help Israel's economic development and "divert undue attention to its balance of payments problems."[113] An official involved in the meeting verified that the United States had given Peres firm commitments that it would provide as much support for Israel's overall economy as it had for the Israeli military.[114]

But within the ITC, the aftermath of the AIPAC classified document incident continued to reverberate. After considerable internal consultation about whether the ITC could even publicly respond to industry queries about what secret data from the classified report had been obtained by AIPAC, on November 29, 1984 ITC Chairwoman Paula Stern formally confirmed that all of the Bromine Alliance's most confidential business data had been contained in the report. "Specific business confidential numbers extracted from the Alliance's letter and shown in the report included: (1) the production cost for bromine, (2) production cost, raw material cost, depreciation or manufacturing cost, by-product cost, and shipping cost for the compound TBBPA and (3) the length of time that sales of domestic TBBPA could be supplied from inventory."[115] Stern confirmed that 15 copies of the confidential information were made and circulated, and stated, "You may be assured that we place a high priority on safeguarding sensitive data and we are currently preparing detailed internal procedures."[116] For its part, the FBI concluded that "this report was likely leaked while being prepared at the International Trade Commission (ITC). A review of security procedures at ITC disclosed the fact that there are no security procedures in place that would prevent the outright theft or the printing of an 'extra' copy of a report."[117]

Conclusion

The Israel lobby's influence over Congress was strong enough to pass laws such as Jackson-Vanik and treaties such as USIFTA that undermined U.S. economic interests. USIFTA extended Israel's economic integration with the U.S. beyond the renewable agreements concentrated in military-related industries that were justified on the basis of U.S. defense interests.

This permanent transformation in economic relations diminished Israel's accountability for meeting U.S. foreign policy expectations and the expectations of the global community concerning Middle East peace. U.S. industry and worker advice and consent during USIFTA trade negotiations was strictly cosmetic; not even the theft of confidential industry information had any impact on the "fast track" process moving through Congress and the executive branch. The U.S. Department of Justice demonstrated that it was politically incapable of providing relief to victimized parties despite incontrovertible evidence of AIPAC wrongdoing uncovered by the FBI.

Iran-Contra, AIPAC, and Jonathan Pollard

When arms dealer Manucher Ghorbanifar approached retired CIA officer Theodore Shackley in Hamburg, Germany in November of 1984 with an incredible proposal, violating the Boland Amendments was probably not on his mind. Ghorbanifar, a former officer in the Shah's notorious security service (Savak) and later an arms merchant and middleman, was a survivor. Ghorbanifar switched sides and became close to the Revolutionary Guard, the Iranian Ministry of Intelligence and National Security and to various officials in Tehran following the Islamic Revolution in 1979.[119] Ghorbanifar put himself forward as a middleman for Israel (and more specifically, for the Kenya Group) who was able to secure the release of American hostages held in Beirut. The U.S. Central Intelligence Agency had issued a "burn notice" warning all U.S. personnel against working with him. The U.S. State Department had also rebuffed his advances.

New York financier Roy Furmark, a former private-sector client of CIA director William Casey, helped Ghorbanifar gain the backing of a major Saudi financier and Kenya Group member Adnan Khashoggi. Khashoggi, Furmark's former employer, in turn, urged Ghorbanifar to work through Kenya Group member Al Schwimmer, the arms merchant and close advisor to Israeli Prime Minister Shimon Peres. Israel's interests in repairing economic ties to Iran and keeping the Iran-Iraq war going in order to maintain rifts in the Arab world and divert attention away from itself would ultimately position Israel for a post-Khomeini alliance with Iran.[120] Reagan national security advisor Robert McFarlane was persuaded by his consultant Michael Ledeen to allow Ledeen to approach Peres, ostensibly to leverage Israeli intelligence toward formulating America's own post-Khomeini policy. As a friend of Ledeen, Peres expressed interest, and an unofficial study group composed of Israeli defense officials and Kenya Group members Al Schwimmer and Yaakov Nimrodi worked on the proposal.

Schwimmer and Nimrodi's interests were highly conflicted. They promoted themselves as conduits for a larger volume of U.S. weapons sales under the auspices of securing the release of U.S. hostages held in Lebanon, but if the hostages were released, U.S. arms sales would likely stop. As sponsors of Ghorbanifar, Ledeen and Israeli diplomats in Washington gradually drew McFarlane into what has became known as the "arms for hostages" scheme. In early July 1985, Schwimmer and David Kimche, who was posted as a senior officer in the Israeli foreign ministry, visited Washington to press the Ghorbanifar proposal on Ledeen and McFarlane again.[121]

Attorney General William French Smith, who gave Reagan the legal opinion that he could circumvent the Boland Amendment restrictions by raising funds overseas, remained in office until February 25, 1985 and presided over the department's decision to stop the AIPAC investigation. In December 1984, a final act of Congress absolutely prohibited CIA and DOD funding of the Nicaraguan Contras. Despite ongoing U.S. industry concerns over the classified AIPAC document release, on January 7, 1985 the ITC secretary formally brought the fast-track U.S.IFTA negotiation process to a close.[122]

In March, Dan Halpern, the economic minister of the Israeli Embassy in Washington, went on a U.S. public relations blitz for USIFTA. "This is going to help the Israeli economy in the long run." Halpern ignored the existing U.S. trade surplus with Israel, stating that "with a rising American trade deficit, it was essential for the U.S. to maintain a twenty percent share of the Israeli import market." Reading from the new AIPAC-supplied USIFTA booklet, the Israeli stressed the looming threat to U.S. exporters of the decade-old Israeli-European Common Market free trade agreement. The *New York Times* summarized that "from the American viewpoint, the most sensitive Israeli exports include cut roses, gold jewelry, leather goods, footwear, bromines (a sulfur derivative), olives, citrus juices and dehydrated garlic. Israel regards as sensitive American-made refrigerators, radio navigation equipment and aluminum bars." The *New York Times* positioned the deal positively. "For the United States it represents a further refinement of the use of trade to help countries that it considers strategically, and politically, important."[123]

On the other hand, the *Providence Journal* viewed the deal as an "insurance policy" for Israel. Under the international trade General System of Preferences then in place, 90 percent of the merchandise sold by Israel to the U.S. was already duty-free, but the deal was a potential life preserver if global trade regimes collapsed. "It gains duty-free status for the remaining ten percent, plus confidence that what it now gets under the system will not be lost if the system should ever collapse." But the *Providence Journal* made no allusions that USIFTA was anything but aid for Israel: "Over time, Israel's trade balance likely will benefit more than America's. Any time such a strong economy makes it easier for such a weak economy to penetrate its markets, an element of generosity exists. Thus the free-trade pact can be seen as further U.S. aid to Israel."[124]

In April, Kenya Group member Ariel Sharon, now Israel's Minister of Industry and Commerce, and USTR ambassador William Brock signed the USIFTA agreement. President Reagan praised the deal as "an important milestone in our efforts to liberalize trade," and pledged to "continue to help Israel achieve its great potential."[125] The Israeli Cabinet approved the formal agreement in August of 1985, expecting the pact to add an additional $200 million in exports over the next two years.[126] The Senate Finance Committee also approved the measure, agreeing to "make clear in a report accompanying the bill that it should not be viewed as a precedent for dropping trade barriers with Mexico, Canada and other nations."[127] The U.S.-Israel Free Trade Agreement went to Congress for an up or down vote, passed 422-0, and took effect on September 1, 1985.

Meanwhile, the Kenya Group pledged to the NSC that they trusted Ghorbanifar when he said that high-level Iranians would help free seven American hostages in exchange for a new dialogue with the U.S. Kimche told McFarlane that the question of U.S. weapons sales from Israel's stockpile would proceed only later, if the U.S. gave a go-ahead. McFarlane briefed President Reagan on the Kimche proposal, including arms sales, on July 18, 1985, and received the president's verbal approval to proceed in the presence of chief of staff Donald Regan.

President Reagan was now on the hook. He had expressed to McFarlane during the summer his desire to find ways to free the hostages, and had been inquiring into their welfare almost daily. At this moment of vulnerability, David Kimche pressed McFarlane for approval of military equipment sales to Iran from Israel's stockpiles of advanced U.S. weaponry. On August 6, 1985, McFarlane presented Kimche's proposal that Schwimmer and Nimrodi be allowed to sell the Iranians antitank missiles and other equipment. Secretary of State George Shultz and Defense Secretary Caspar Weinberger both advised against it, but the president announced no final decision at the National Security Council meeting. Several days later, Reagan verbally approved the sale in a telephone call to McFarlane, and also granted permission to replenish stocks depleted from the Israeli arsenal.

McFarlane passed the information to Kimche, and on August 30, Schwimmer shipped 96 wire-guided TOW anti-tank missiles from Israel to Iran. A second consignment two weeks later brought total TOW sales up to 504. Within days, Reverend Benjamin Weir, a Presbyterian missionary who had been held hostage for more than a year, was released in Lebanon.

Robert McFarlane had originally requested that kidnapped CIA station chief William Buckley be released first. According to the Israeli newspaper *Haaretz*, the intellectual author of that shrewd trade was Al Schwimmer, "who came up with the idea of 'arms for Buckley.'"[128] However, the U.S. later learned that Buckley had died under torture in June of 1985. Ledeen continued to meet with Ghorbanifar, Kimche, Schwimmer, and Nimrodi in September, October, and November of 1985. But with no further hostage releases forthcoming, McFarlane began considering whether to shut down the entire arms-for-hostages operation.

Israel, however, took the original arms sales as an open-ended U.S. approval to sell as much of its U.S. stockpile as possible. In November of 1985, Israeli Defense Minister Yitzhak Rabin contacted McFarlane for help arranging a transshipment of Hawk surface-to-air missiles through a third country. Since McFarlane was at that time working at a U.S.-Russian summit in Geneva, he directed Contra point man Oliver North to assist from Washington.

McFarlane advised President Reagan, George Shultz, and chief of staff Donald Regan of the plan. Israeli aircraft chartered by Schwimmer and Nimrodi were to fly 100 Hawk missiles to Iran upon the release of four hostages. Israel would then be allowed to buy replacements from the U.S. George Shultz again protested, but the highly conflicted deal was approved.

However, Israeli covert initiatives began to unwind on two fronts: espionage and incompetence. In November of 1985, Israeli spy Jonathan Pollard was recorded stealing classified national defense information under active video surveillance by U.S. Navy investigators. Pollard, a former civilian intelligence analyst for the Navy, was arrested by the FBI in November of 1985. The vast volume of documents stolen by Pollard, his receipt of cash payments, and his divulgence of the identities of U.S. agents in the Soviet Union who were coldly traded by Israel in exchange for Jewish émigrés enraged the Secretary of Defense. Caspar Weinberger later delivered classified memoranda and a public supplement to the judge presiding over Pollard's sentencing, arguing that they all weighed against leniency. Weinberger accused Pollard of treason and recommended a life sentence, which Pollard received.

The agent in charge of counterintelligence for the Naval Investigative Service at the time of Pollard's arrest believes the incident was "one of the most devastating cases of espionage in U.S. history" and that Pollard stole over "one million classified documents."[129] The Pollard espionage case is also unique in that it was the first instance of an Israeli handler with diplomatic immunity being criminally indicted in the United States.[130] The day after Pollard's arrest, Israel quietly recalled two of its diplomats from the United States: Yosef Yagur, a science attaché at the Israeli mission in New York, and Ilan Ravid, deputy science attaché at the embassy in Washington. The Pollard affair also had a direct tie to the BIRD Foundation, raising questions about whether the U.S. had inadvertently funded espionage against its own military.

Pollard delivered his stolen documents a few hundred yards from the Israeli embassy to the apartment of Irit Erb, an Israeli embassy employee and unindicted co-conspirator who fled the U.S. after Pollard's arrest. A second apartment in Erb's building served as the alternate drop for classified documents stolen by Pollard; it was also where he met his controller every month to be paid in cash, obtain feedback on the quality of documents stolen, and receive new instructions. This apartment housed key photocopying and photographic equipment and was owned by Harold Katz, an American attorney living in Israel who served as an adviser to the Israeli Ministry of Defense and legal counsel to the BIRD Foundation. Katz admitted knowing Erb and giving him a key, but claimed he thought the apartment was "unoccupied" during the incident. Katz denied involvement in the operation, but only agreed to answer U.S. prosecutor questions in Israel.[131] Pollard's handling by the LAKAM[132] network of accomplices and the wide-ranging Justice Department investigation had an immediate impact on the aborted investigation of AIPAC, though it was never publicly revealed.

The DOJ and FBI clearly related Pollard's activities to the 1984 AIPAC investigation. The Washington Field Office had earlier noted an "allegation that a member of the Israeli Intelligence Service was a staff member of AIPAC."[133] The FBI quietly reopened its previously aborted investigation of AIPAC under the direction of Assistant Attorney General Stephen S. Trott. The Public Integrity Section of the DOJ met on November 15, 1985 with representatives of the FBI to "outline investigative strategies." They settled on hitting the fading trail anew by simultaneously interviewing the AIPAC employees known to have had first contact with the ITC report in order to finally determine how they obtained it. The FBI sought to determine whether AIPAC's Ester Kurz and Peggy Blair had violated Theft of Government Property and Disclosure of Confidential Business Information statutes.[xxiii] [134]

On December 11, 1985, as the deep impact of Pollard espionage was cascading through the administration; Deputy Assistant Director Phil Parker from the Intelligence Division at FBI headquarters contacted the special agents in charge of the AIPAC investigation at the Washington Field Office. Parker notified the agents that "this investigation had come to the attention of Director [William] Webster," "asked for an explanation of [the] investigation thus far," and told them the case was being "studied" at FBI headquarters and the Washington Field Office would soon be contacted about its renewed investigation.[135]

Ester Kurz and Peggy Blair were less than forthcoming during their separate December 19, 1985 interviews with the FBI.[xxiv] In the presence of a lawyer, Kurz detailed her employment status at AIPAC and the explosive news that she had received the classified ITC report from Dan Halpern, the economic minister at the Israeli Embassy who had been so active in public relations for USIFTA. She described it as being 50-80 pages in length, but denied being aware of the document title, though she did confirm it was marked "confidential." Kurz claimed she couldn't recall who was at the AIPAC meeting about USIFTA where Halpern passed the secret document.

Kurz said that about a week after receiving the document, she passed it to Margaret [Peggy] Blair, the author of the special USIFTA lobbying booklet, but "did not recall any specific instructions" she gave to Blair. Kurz said she also received a duplicate copy of the secret report from AIPAC employee Douglas Bloomfield. She claimed she "paid no attention to" the classified ITC report until she received a phone call "several weeks later" from USTR General Counsel Claude Gingrich, seeking to "ascertain if AIPAC had this trade report in their possession." After Gingrich called, Douglas Bloomfield told Kurz to destroy the

---

[xxiii] 18 U.S.C. 641 and 18 U.S.C 1905

[xxiv] The records of AIPAC staff interviewed by the FBI were submitted to headquarters on FD-302 forms. These are used for noting interviews that may become testimony.

duplicate copy of the report, which she claimed she did by "throwing it down the garbage" chute at her residence. She told the FBI the original report was returned to the USTR. Kurz wouldn't speculate about who else at AIPAC had the document or what use they made of it, but claimed it was "floating around town" and that the contents were common knowledge to those interested in these matters. What Kurz couldn't explain, if the report was all but blowing like tumbleweed throughout Washington, was why she had to acquire it from the Israeli embassy, and who provided it to them. Her lawyer then stepped in and advised the FBI that it should submit any further questions for Mrs. Kurz to him, but that otherwise she "did not wish to furnish any additional information regarding this matter."[136]

Margaret "Peggy" Blair had even less to say when she met with the FBI in the presence of her lawyer from the firm Frank, Harris, Shriver, and Jacobson. She confirmed that Ester Kurz had passed her the classified ITC report, telling her to "keep it in a safe place," but claimed no specific direction about how to use the report in AIPAC's lobbying campaign or who initially gave the report to AIPAC. Blair confirmed that some time in July, the general counsel for the USTR had asked her if she'd seen a copy; she advised him she had, but passed him off to AIPAC's general counsel. Like Kurz, Blair claimed she "did not see a title to this report," but described it as being an ITC document "examining the different product sectors in America and the possible impact [on] these sectors if duty free imports from Israel were allowed." Blair claimed she did not "utilize any of the information gleaned from this report" and that she "could not recall" whether the report was classified or not. Blair also confirmed that there was "general discussion of the report at AIPAC but that this was not considered an especially significant matter." Like Kurz, she ended the interview by asking the FBI to direct any future questions about the affair to her lawyer.[137]

The FBI was unable to interview Douglas Bloomfield, AIPAC's head of congressional relations and lobbying on Capitol Hill, until February 13, 1986. Bloomfield claimed he first become aware of the secret ITC report when Ester Kurz "advised him that she received a call from the USTR General Counsel Gingrich." According to the FBI transcript, "Bloomfield advised that Kurz stated to Gingrich that she had the document and at that point Gingrich asked that she return it to the USTR. Bloomfield asked Kurz if that was true that she had this report and she advised that she did have it." Bloomfield's account of when a copy of the secret document was made differed substantially from the Kurz account. Kurz claimed that Bloomfield came into possession of it and copied it to her before the USTR call, but Bloomfield outlined a private and lawyerly review of the ITC document with AIPAC director Thomas Dine following the USTR call, after which a duplicate was made for imminent AIPAC lobbying on the USIFTA.

> Dine immediately called Gingrich at the USTR to make arrangements to return the document. The report was subsequently returned to the USTR by a member of the AIPAC office staff. Prior

to returning this document, UNKNOWN asked to have a duplicate copy of the document made so that the staff of the AIPAC could further examine the report. Bloomfield advised that he saw no "secret classifications"[xxv] on the report and there were no indications that this was a report pertaining to United States National Security. He further believed that AIPAC had not acted improperly or illegally in having this report in its possession and thereafter asked UNKNOWN to examine the document regarding the free trade issue between the U.S. and Israel. He stated that Kurz retained the duplicate copy of the report and that the original report was returned to the USTR. Bloomfield advised that he did not consider this report to be especially important and thought that any controversy regarding the report had ended. [138]

Bloomfield said he followed up with Ester Kurz about the duplicate ITC report in November of 1985, confirming that she had "eventually thrown it away." Bloomfield claimed no firsthand knowledge of "the individual who provided the report to AIPAC, but advised he was told that Dan Halpern at the Israeli Embassy originally passed the report to AIPAC."[139] The FBI was soon on a trail that, like the Pollard affair, led directly to the Israeli embassy.

Israel's reputation in Washington began to unravel. Disaster struck again when Israeli arms merchants failed to obtain clearance for missile transshipment from the designated European transit country to Iran and were turned back. Oliver North sent retired General Richard Secord to convince the appropriate officials to allow the shipment through, but met with no success. North also unsuccessfully appealed for logistics help to CIA European operations directorate Dewey Clarridge, a transferee from Latin America who was heavily involved in the Contra supply effort. North notified McFarlane's deputy John Poindexter that five hostages would be freed in exchange for a November 22 shipment of 80 Hawks (already purchased with an $18 million payment). North also advised the DOD that it would need to quickly resupply depleted Israeli stocks. However, Israel only delivered battered first-generation Hawks of limited range that were stenciled with the Star of David. Insulted, the Iranian counterparties rejected them on the basis of obsolescence and uselessness against high-flying Iraqi aircraft.

Under North's direction, the Iran and Contra operation resources soon fully merged. To deliver the Hawks to Iran, Richard Secord chartered two 707 aircraft through the same Swiss front company he used to finance Contra arms purchases.

On December 5, a National Security Planning Group in the White House concluded unanimously that the Iranian negotiations had gone "badly off course" and that any future dealings should begin with a declaration that the U.S. would

---

[xxv]The United States government has three levels of classification: confidential, secret, and top secret. The ITC report was marked "confidential."

not permit any further arms sales. McFarlane then traveled to London and met with Ghorbanifar, Nimrodi, Schwimmer, Kimche, and Oliver North to discuss how to put the operation back on track. McFarlane relayed the order that arms sales were off the table, but Ghorbanifar refused to communicate this key tidbit to his contacts in Iran.

McFarlane then reported to President Reagan in the Oval Office with Regan, Casey, Weinberger, and Shultz and presented his frank assessment that Ghorbanifar seemed primarily driven by potential profits from further arms sales, and that he was "not a trustworthy person." Although McFarlane recommended ending the arms-for-hostages maneuvers, both a Shimon Peres advisor on terrorism and Oliver North advised Reagan that the hostages would probably be murdered if the administration suddenly cut off communications.

Poindexter soon replaced McFarlane as national security advisor and immediately dismissed Michael Ledeen. The NSC also dropped the Israeli supply intermediation in favor of direct U.S. sales from the CIA to Iran, with Ghorbanifar still involved. In a memo about the renewed arms-for-hostages dealings in 1986, Oliver North specified that sales to Iranians of missiles costing only $3.6 million would generate $13.4 million in net revenue to supply the Contras and cover administrative overhead. On the diplomatic front, North also planned to pressure Iran to end its assistance to the Sandinistas.

After receiving a clearance from the U.S. State Department, the FBI interviewed Dan Halpern, the economics minister at the Israeli Embassy in Washington, DC on March 7, 1986. Halpern admitted "having a report which was prepared by the U.S. Trade Representatives in early 1984 and subsequently turning it over to representatives of the American Israel Public Affairs Committee." In his opinion, the report contained "little, if any sensitive or confidential information" and it was of "little or no interest to his government."[140] Halpern then claimed diplomatic immunity from prosecution.

When the FBI pressed him for information about who gave him the classified ITC report, Halpern stated it would be "impossible within the professional ethics of his diplomatic position" to identify the individual who gave it to him. But Halpern then assured the FBI it was not a U.S. government official or employee. He clarified his interpretation of Operation Tipped Kettle, Tipped Kettle II, and the DOD doctrine that gave rise to Iran-Contra and the inside track of USIFTA, and stated he was given the report because "somebody on the U.S. side had an interest in Israel knowing [that the] U.S. [was] falling short on [its] commitments."[141] Echoing the Sonneborn/Jewish Agency delegation to J. Edgar Hoover, Halpern assured the FBI investigators that "the fact that Israel had the report caused no economic damage to any U.S. business or interest and that the entire issue seems to have received more attention than it deserved."[142] But only time would tell if Halpern's assessment proved correct.

Subsequent U.S. arms missions to Iran failed to produce large net hostage releases. A single hostage had been freed by July 26, 1986. Vice President George H. W. Bush then met in Israel with Amiram Nir, Israel's advisor on terrorism, who lobbied for a package of serial weapons sales in exchange for potentially sequential hostage releases. On July 30, President Reagan approved the delivery of a second shipment of Hawk parts. After the shipment, U.S. officials dropped Ghorbanifar as an intermediary. Ghorbanifar's replacement, identified as a former officer in the Iranian Revolutionary Guard, negotiated the release of an additional hostage who, at the cost of 500 TOW missiles, was freed on November 2, 1986, two days before the U.S. midterm elections. Spurned, Ghorbanifar began talking to the press about murky American arms-for-hostage deals with revenues diverted to the Contras. On November 3, the Lebanese magazine *Al Shiraa* published an exposé on the arms sales that was confirmed by Iranian parliament Speaker of the Majlis Ali Hashemi Rafsanjani. The news exploded into the U.S. media, and by December 2 a Gallup public opinion poll measured Reagan's approval rating at 46 percent—a 21 percent drop from the previous month.

A drawn-out criminal investigation into what became known as the Iran-Contra affair commenced, but was ultimately of very little consequence. After George H.W. Bush was elected president, he pardoned six administration officials convicted for their roles in the affair.[xxvi] Oliver North was criminally indicted on multiple charges and found guilty on three minor counts. These were later overturned on appeal that earlier testimony he gave to Congress with immunity was improperly used in his prosecution.

The early and guiding role of Israeli tactical and economic interests was barely explored in the establishment U.S. news media when it mattered most—the late 1980s and early 1990s. The Israelis refused to turn over their Swiss bank account records or government documents related to Iran arms sales to U.S. investigators, just as Halpern's diplomatic immunity stopped the FBI AIPAC investigation cold. A book about Israeli arms sales published in 1987 by Andrew and Leslie Cockburn is unequivocal about the origin of arms sales to Iran: "The Iran-Contra affair grew out of earlier Israeli deals with Iran and the continuing contact since 1979, maintained with American knowledge and approval. Israel had the connections with Iran, and the intelligence. The Israelis came up with the idea of encouraging 'moderate elements'—that is, the military."[143] A 2009 analysis by John Limbert delivers a harsh analysis about Ghorbanifar and the Israelis as intermediaries: "They were talking to people who were not only misrepresenting their own position but they were misrepresenting themselves both to the Iranians and to the Americans, and promising more than either side could deliver."[144]

Carefully scouring relevant contemporary sources reveals that the date of Israel's formative role in the scandal continues to recede in time—Al Schwimmer's firsthand account of the May 1982 "principals meeting" in Kenya to plan the accumulation of arms caches and covert sales in the interest of toppling the Iranian government wasn't published until 2001. The intertwined USIFTA

[xxvi] Elliot Abrams, Duane R. Clarridge, Alan Fiers, Clair George, Robert McFarlane, and Caspar Weinberger.

and Iran-Contra timeline reveals how meeting Pentagon "commitments" undermined advice and consent. A still unknown Israeli passed the classified ITC document to Halpern at the Israeli embassy, who then relayed them on to AIPAC. The agent's motives were clear—U.S. commitments weren't being met. But despite FOIA requests, even in 2009, those secret commitments and their justifications still aren't publicly known. The DOD refuses to declassify and release[xxvii] [145] the full texts of Operations Tipped Kettle and Tipped Kettle II.[146]

In the end, only Israel emerged as a clear winner in the Iran-Contra affair. Two more American hostages were seized in Lebanon after earlier promising releases, numerically negating any net U.S. benefit for all of the costly arms shipped to Iran in the short term. In the medium term, Sandinista leader Daniel Ortega was never deposed by armed Contra forces. He lost the 1990 elections to an anti-Sandinista alliance led by Violeta Barrios de Chamorro, but was back in power by 2006. President George W. Bush made a congratulatory phone call to Ortega, even as Iran renewed foreign aid proposals for civilian housing and industrial cooperation.

Tariff-free access to the U.S. market from behind Israel's own protective wall of tariffs, quotas, non-tariff barriers, and shifting regulatory regimes was an incredible, though ill-gotten, prize for Israel. Stymied, disenfranchised, and disunited American industries have never stopped opposing it. Meanwhile, Israel continued overtly and covertly pursuing U.S. military technology, commercial intelligence, and the know-how to build its own competing export base. The U.S.—constantly urged to provide for Israel's defense—wound up subsidizing a competing industrial complex. Israel soon won a well deserved reputation for selling weapons to any regime with ready cash, particularly those off-limits to U.S. vendors. The elite Israeli spy network that in the 1960s forcibly extracted uranium from U.S. company NUMEC and stole plans for the Mirage jet fighter from the French was turned fully against the U.S., with devastating impact. Opposition to USIFTA intensified when Israel jump-started entirely new export-oriented industries, such as generic and counterfeit pharmaceutical production, through unauthorized access to U.S. innovations.

Although the DOJ did not pursue theft of government property or espionage charges, the USTR and ITC with proper backing of the president could have fought harder for the U.S. industry and worker rights they claimed to advance under existing treaties. AIPAC and the government of Israel abrogated the Treaty of Paris[xxviii] (in effect before and after the negotiations) by obtaining and

---

[xxvii] During the 1991 criminal trial of ousted Panamanian dictator Manuel Noriega, a federal judge ordered the release of Operation Tipped Kettle. Noriega was convicted, but Tipped Kettle did not become public.

[xxviii] The core foundation for expanded and productive trade is the protection of intellectual property. This was encapsulated in the July 21, 1969 Paris Convention for the Protection of Industrial Property. Signatory countries including the United States and Israel pledged to avoid "breach of contract,

leveraging the confidential business information provided by corporations and associations most concerned about the FTA against them. Beginning in 1984, the Israeli government, industry, and AIPAC acted in concert with this highly sensitive market and industry information—unobtainable from any legitimate market research or data service provider. This insight touched off a string of intellectual property rights violations, empowered by purposeful regulatory changes in Israel and economic espionage generating billions of dollars of losses to the United States.

In Congress, the Senate Finance Committee's assertions that USIFTA would not be a springboard to further managed trade pacts proved hollow. NAFTA negotiations were soon underway, along with the spiraling U.S. trade deficits that soon followed. Decades later, Martin Indyk, the deputy director for research involved in AIPAC lobbying for USIFTA and its booklet advancing the deal, would claim that AIPAC's "wedge" in Congress was what made agreements like NAFTA possible.

The director of the FBI closed[xxix] the AIPAC investigation on January 14, 1987.[147] There were further avenues open for criminally pursuing the source of the classified report, including interviews with ITC employees. But the Washington Field Office was unequivocal: "Due to the fact that Dan Halpern has claimed diplomatic immunity in this matter, active investigation in this matter will be discontinued..."[148] The report *Probable Economic Effect of Providing Duty Free Treatment for U.S. Imports from Israel, Investigation No. 332-180* is still classified by the ITC and USTR. It is considered so highly sensitive that almost three decades later, neither agency will release it under the Freedom of Information Act or Mandatory Declassification Review.[149]

---

breach of confidence and inducement to breach, and includes the acquisition of undisclosed information by third parties who knew, or were grossly negligent in failing to know, that such practices were involved in the acquisition."

It was subsequently expanded in the Agreement on Trade Related Aspects of Intellectual Property Rights (TRIPS), ratified by the United States and Israel. The Uruguay Round of the General Agreement on Tariffs and Trade (GATT) negotiated TRIPS in 1994. TRIPS is an international agreement administered by the World Trade Organization (WTO). It is binding on the U.S. and Israel, and establishes even more highly defined regulations and standards for many varieties of intellectual property (IP) than the Paris Convention.

Under TRIPS, trading nations' laws must meet strict requirements covering copyrights, industrial designs, patents, monopolies for the developers of new plant varieties, and trademarks, as well as undisclosed or confidential information. TRIPS also establishes enforcement procedures, remedies, and dispute resolution procedure.

[xxix] Acting FBI Director John Otto asked for an update in October of 1987, after former Director William Webster left the FBI to lead the Central Intelligence Agency.

Conclusion

Because the USIFTA economic espionage incident was overshadowed by the Iran-Contra scandal and the Jonathan Pollard affair, it never received the attention it deserved—despite vast consequences for the economy and advice and consent governance. FBI interview files documenting tight coordination between AIPAC and the Israeli Ministry of Economic Affairs on USIFTA, to the point of passing purloined U.S. government property in complete confidence, were kept secret until 2009. But the declassified files contribute to the growing body of evidence that AIPAC (like its parent organization, the AZC) operates as a de facto stealth foreign agent of the Israeli government.

The secrecy surrounding this "third scandal" means that it was never publicly debated or allowed to influence public awareness or news coverage about later FBI investigations into AIPAC—which tended to be portrayed more as anti-Semitic persecutions or thuggish forays against freedom of speech than legitimate counterespionage actions launched in the interest of all Americans.

"People sometimes refer to Israel as an ally... Israel is not an ally. One becomes an ally through a treaty of alliance, and allies take special pains to try to co-ordinate their policies as much as possible. I don't think the Israelis have ever wanted that kind of obligation. They prefer to take their chances on going their own way and expecting Jewish support in this country to force the United States to go along." **Dean Rusk,** [150] **secretary of state under Presidents John F. Kennedy and Lyndon B. Johnson**

Military-Industrial Espionage

The murky origins of Israel's Kfir jet fighter foreshadowed challenges the U.S. would face in military research and development exchanges and trade with Israel. In 1968, French president Charles De Gaulle imposed a total arms embargo after Israeli commandos attacked the Beirut airport and destroyed 13 parked Lebanese aircraft as a reprisal to a Palestinian attack on an El Al airliner in Athens.[151] Israeli dependence on French-built Mirage jet fighters was absolute, and their numbers were heavily depleted in the 1967 Six-Day War. The Mossad stole more than 250,000 Mirage III blueprints weighing three tons from Switzerland's Sulzer Engineering Corporation which was building fighters under contract with Dassault. Israel then secured a license to build General Electric J79 turbojets and was soon test-flying Mirage- based fighters that became the copycat Kfir fighter by September of 1970. Israel, the U.S., and France were all signatories to a July 21, 1969 treaty pledging mutual respect for the protection of intellectual property and trade secrets. [xxx] But such treaties had little impact on Israeli espionage.

Israel slowly became a top-10 arms exporter by tapping U.S. military know-how, shadowing U.S. overseas military deals, and adopting extremely loose export controls. According to data from the Stockholm International Peace Research Institute, Israel will soon occupy a top-five slot in global arms exports. But the cost paid by the U.S. for Israel to reach this position is little understood.

[xxx] The Paris Convention for the Protection of Industrial Property

Israel Global Arms Export Rank[152]

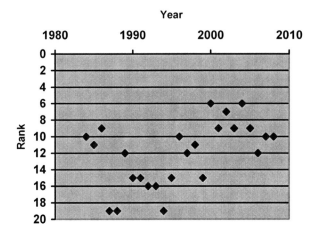

As a descendent of the pre-state Sonneborn weapons smuggling network, Israel's Military Purchasing Mission in New York now openly procures weapons for the Israeli Defense Forces, paying with a yearly aid earmark granted by Congress. The Military Purchasing Mission has had numerous run-ins with the U.S. Department of Justice over economic espionage, including a 1981 incident involving intellectual property theft of industrial processes for chrome-plating tank barrels. The Reagan administration granted the Military Purchasing Mission full diplomatic immunity in October of 1988, over the strong objections of the FBI and Justice Department. Both law enforcement agencies felt that this would encourage illegal export of critical military technology while making corruption prosecutions almost impossible.[153] This prediction has proven to be largely correct.

The primary focus of the U.S. Foreign Military Sales program is managing responsible weapons sales to allies that further U.S. national security concerns. Its secondary purpose is to provide vetted customers for American military firms, particularly foreign customers receiving aid from Congress. But the Israeli Military Purchasing Mission's direct relationships with U.S. military contractors have led to massive fraud and abuse. The potential for structuring kickbacks and fraud through shifting shell corporations was rife in 1983. According to the General Accounting Office the Military Purchasing Mission was making 30,000 purchases a year—100 for more than $1 million each, but 85 percent for less than $5,000 apiece.[154]

One case that didn't escape criminal prosecution was the "Dotan Affair." In 1991, retired Israeli general Rami Dotan was indicted for embezzling $40 million in U.S. foreign military aid in collusion with Herbert Steindler, an official at American aircraft engine manufacturer Pratt & Whitney. Dotan and Steindler were both imprisoned for their actions. In July 1992, parent company General

Electric paid $9.5 million in criminal penalties and $59 million in civil damages in a settlement with the U.S. Department of Justice over the incident.

Israel continued the tradition begun under David Ben-Gurion of quietly and secretly handling such corruption cases away from the public eye. General Accounting Office Director of Special Investigations Richard C. Steiner commented in congressional oversight testimony that GAO "requested to meet with government of Israel officials to discuss information they have regarding the diversion of U.S. funds and other abuses of the assistance program. However, the government of Israel declined to discuss the issues or allow our investigators to question Israeli personnel."[155] Israel had many reasons to maintain such secrecy.

The objectives of LAKAM, an Israeli economic espionage unit founded in the 1950s, were to obtain useful technology and protect Israel's secret nuclear weapons program. As a "technology penetration and acquisition network," LAKAM operated globally but focused on the most developed economy in the world: the United States. With diplomatic immunity, Israeli intelligence agents had many advantages over the Sonneborn network. Working under cover as scientific attachés in consulates near sensitive regions such as southern California, LAKAM began to spy on the aerospace industry and other high-tech targets.[156] Many other LAKAM operations flourished. LAKAM's most famous industrial espionage to date may have been securing highly enriched uranium via a U.S. front company. The means and outcomes of its operations bear uncanny resemblances to pre-state smuggling operations behind the archipelago of Sonneborn network front companies.

Zalman Shapiro, an Israel sympathizer who led a Zionist Organization of America (ZOA) chapter, also headed the Nuclear Material and Equipment Corporation (NUMEC) of Apollo, Pennsylvania after 1956. A private corporation, NUMEC obtained government contracts to convert highly enriched uranium into fuel for nuclear submarines. The Atomic Energy Commission (AEC) discovered that stocks of uranium delivered to NUMEC for fuel conversion were never returned to the government. Shapiro could not account for it. This soon touched off congressional, counterintelligence, and FBI investigations.

Carl Docket, a CIA executive, stated during an investigation of NUMEC that "the clear consensus in CIA...was that indeed, NUMEC material had been diverted and had been used by the Israelis in fabricating weapons."[157] Rather than covertly smuggling the material out of the United States welded into boilers or large generators, NUMEC likely shipped it by air in sealed containers that were not even subject to U.S. Customs inspection. As with the Sonneborn network's "black" materials smuggling, a special purpose entity was formed to provide cover and plausible deniability for the operation.

Four Israelis visited NUMEC on Sept. 10, 1968 to "discuss thermoelectric devices" with Shapiro.[158] The Atomic Energy Commission (AEC) gave approval for Avraham Hermoni, Ephraim Beigon, Abraham Bendor, and Rafael Eitan to visit NUMEC. NUMEC and FBI files listed Hermoni as an Israeli Embassy scientific counselor, Beigon and Bendor as members of the Israeli defense ministry's electronics department, and Eitan as a chemist in Israel's defense ministry. At the time of the visit, Eitan[xxxi] was an acting agent for Mossad, on special assignment to LAKAM on a mission to acquire nuclear technology by any means necessary.[159] Shortly after his visit, up to 587 pounds of weapons-grade uranium was registered as missing.

Federal agents believed that Israel smuggled the enriched uranium out of the country under the cover of NUMEC's civilian food irradiation partnership with Israel. A NUMEC employee interviewed by FBI agents in November 1968 confirmed that the losses occurred at about the same time that NUMEC was involved in developing and manufacturing at least one large irradiator and several smaller units called "howitzers" and shipping them to Israel. The employee stated that "it would have been a simple matter of placing the material in these food irradiator units in large quantities and shipped to Israel with no questions asked." There was a notice printed on the side of the food irradiator containers indicating radioactive material contents. Irradiator shipments were legal, and no customs official could have opened the "howitzers," according to the FBI report.[160]

The Israeli embassy also informed the U.S. State Department that if any effort were made to inspect containers being shipped from NUMEC to Israel under the "food irradiation" project, it would place them under diplomatic immunity. After the State Department communicated that potentially serious consequences would follow any breaches of diplomatic immunity, FBI agents monitoring El Al shipments of NUMEC lead-lined containers out of Idlewild Airport[xxxii] took no action.[161]

NUMEC later paid nearly one million dollars in fines to the AEC for the lost uranium. Shapiro was subsequently unable to renew his security clearances at the insistence of the White House. He repeatedly denied participating in any diversion of highly enriched uranium to Israel, and it is quite possible that Shapiro had no overt role in the uranium disappearance, just as Nathan Liff's invitation for Hank Greenspun to visit his Hawaii military surplus scrap yard only presented the entrepreneurial Greenspun an opportunity to steal machine guns from under the noses of U.S. Marines. But the modus operandi of Israeli smuggling operations, the large amount of missing uranium, and the timing of the loss when NUMEC opened its facilities with the unknowing approval of the

---

[xxxi] Eitan was also involved in the case of American Jonathan Pollard. Arrested in 1985, Pollard is still serving a life prison sentence for selling classified material to Israel while he was a U.S. naval intelligence analyst.

[xxxii] An airport in New York City, now John F. Kennedy International Airport

U.S. Atomic Energy Commission to LAKAM's top operative all point to espionage.[xxxiii]

NUMEC's founder went on to file 15 promising patents on revolutionary new technologies potentially worth millions of dollars.[162] The government has also been conducting a $56 million taxpayer-funded cleanup of nuclear contamination at the NUMEC site that has plagued the health of area residents for decades.[163] A former CIA station chief in Tel Aviv, John Hadden, stated that NUMEC as a whole was essentially a front, "an Israeli operation from the beginning."[164] But neither Israel, LAKAM, nor Zalman Shapiro has taken responsibility for the theft or cleanup, even as Israel pressures the U.S. for its own civilian reactor build out—under the condition that it not be forced to sign the nuclear nonproliferation treaty that would require immediate declaration of its clandestine arsenal.[165]

Despite unprecedented access to the American military-industrial complex through MOUs and the ratification of USIFTA, Israel continued its espionage programs to acquire proprietary test data, designs, and other information needed to leapfrog onto the world stage as a major weapons seller. A 1983 General Accounting Office report noted that "Most [Israeli] exports [contain] an import component of about 36 percent" and "almost every Israeli production effort includes a U.S. input." Although military-industrial espionage is usually considered a U.S. national security issue, the commercial and governance impact is onerous.

Israeli economic espionage violated the Treaty of Paris and the superseding WTO rules covering trade-related aspects of intellectual property rights (TRIPS), but no enforcement measures have ever been taken by the USTR, which considers violations to be "export control issues." Espionage not only denies direct compensation to American rights holders for their sunk development costs, licensing, and related royalties, but forces U.S. taxpayers to ultimately foot the bill for stolen and replacement technologies. The structure of the domestic market U.S. arms manufacturers serve means few can ever productively seek civil damages against Israel in court as compensation for losses. Congress, which controls the Department of Defense purse strings as well as military aid to Israel, discourages parties from seeking redress in the courts system or formal USTR remediation processes. AIPAC could raise congressional opposition to attempts to embarrass "America's strong ally." Those corporations that have tried working through various agency channels for redress have encountered serious roadblocks that served as a deterrent to others.[xxxiv] It is also well documented

---

[xxxiii] For an alternative theory that NUMEC uranium was lost to absorption in the plant facilities and dissipation into the surrounding environment, see *The Samson Option: Israel's Nuclear Arsenal and American Foreign Policy* by Seymour Hersh.

[xxxiv] This is not the case for every industry. The pharmaceutical lobby, which has diverse markets and large current and future potential losses from Israeli violations, began to actively pursue Israel in formal USTR disputes in 2005.

that few of the thousands of privately reported suspected espionage incidents ever generated DOJ criminal complaints or indictments.

The 2008 criminal case of Ben-Ami Kadish underscores the difficulty of seeking redress. From 1963 through 1990, Kadish worked as a mechanical engineer at the Army's Armament Research, Development, and Engineering Center at the Picatinny Arsenal in Dover, NJ. Kadish held a security clearance and between August 23, 1979 and July 15, 1985 signed out classified documents on varied U.S. weapons systems. After he was accused of spying and arrested in April 2008, a criminal complaint filed by U.S. government prosecutors documented that between 1980 and 1985, he delivered 50 to 100 classified U.S. national defense files about nuclear weapons, fighter jets, and missiles to Israeli agent Yosef Yagur. Yagur allegedly photographed the documents at Kadish's residence.

One document Kadish obtained covered a modified version of an F-15 fighter jet manufactured by McDonnell Douglas. Yet another covered the Patriot missile air defense system manufactured by Raytheon Company, Hughes, and RCA. Mr. Kadish testified that he neither solicited nor received anything of value for the documents.[166] Kadish fared much better than Jonathan Pollard, the other Israeli spy simultaneously handled by Yosef Yagur. Kadish was permitted to plead guilty to the trivial charge of acting as an unregistered foreign agent and pay a $50,000 fine in May of 2009.

Prosecutors could have pressed for grand jury indictments of Kadish under the much harsher Economic Espionage Act of 1996 or even the 1917 Espionage Act. U.S. District Judge William Pauley was incredulous during sentencing: "It is clear the [U.S.] government could have charged Mr. Kadish with far more serious crimes."[167] Corporations could have pushed damage claims forward. Yet none of this occurred. Kadish's claims of "no harm to the U.S." for his actions in the 1980s persevered—like the Sonneborn network's earlier appeal to the FBI director. While such delayed justice for Kadish provided no deterrent to espionage, by the mid-1990s the Department of Defense was taking active countermeasures.

In January of 1996 the Pentagon's U.S. Defense Investigation Service (DOD/DIS) based in Syracuse, New York dispatched an urgent three-page memo about Israeli industrial espionage in the United States to 250 facilities and defense contractors conducting sensitive American military projects (see appendix).[168] According to an April 1996 report from the Interagency Operations Security Support Staff titled *Operations Security Intelligence Threat Handbook*:

> Israel has an active program to gather proprietary information within the United States. These collection activities are primarily directed at obtaining information on military systems, and advanced computing applications that can be used in Israel's sizable armaments industry. Two primary activities have conducted espionage activities within the United States: the Central Institute for Intelligence and Special Activities (MOSSAD), and the Scientific Affairs Liaison Bureau of the Defense Ministry LAKAM.

> The Israelis use classic HUMINT techniques, SIGINT, and computer intrusion to gain economic and proprietary information.

Despite existing treaties protecting against U.S. intellectual property theft and the potential of the USTR and ITC to place the USIFTA on the table through established enforcement mechanisms, Congress felt compelled to pass the Economic Espionage Act[xxxv] in 1996, specifically making theft or misappropriation of a U.S. trade secret a federal crime. Though prosecutions of Asian and European economic espionage have proceeded, no prosecutions of Israeli violations under the Economic Espionage Act have ever been attempted. The Economic Espionage Act has forced some Israeli economic intelligence collection activities offshore, further away from jurisdiction of U.S. courts. Even discriminatory U.S. countermeasures were pushed by the DOD in order to stem espionage and blackmail.

In 2006, an administrative judge at the Pentagon defended harsh new denials of security clearances for Americans with family in Israel over their high potential blackmail risk. "The Israeli government is actively engaged in military and industrial espionage in the United States. An Israeli citizen working in the U.S. who has access to proprietary information is likely to be a target of such espionage."[169] While this sort of broad-brush treatment is lamentable, detailed information about how Israeli manufacturers have serially violated U.S. intellectual property by copying and selling patented American technology are so well documented by private organizations that serious countermeasures are clearly called for.

The American Society for Industrial Security reported 1,100 incidents of economic espionage and 550 suspected incidents that could not be fully documented in 1997. Estimated losses totaled $300 billion. An FBI agent involved in investigating such cases said that France, Germany, Israel, China, Russia, and South Korea were top offenders.[170] Larry Torrence, deputy assistant director for the national security division at the FBI, described the vulnerability of U.S.

[xxxv] The first section of the Economic Espionage Act allows prosecution for misappropriation of trade secrets and the subsequent acquisition of such misappropriated trade secrets with the knowledge or intent that the theft will benefit a foreign power. This statute covers precisely the type of activity involved in the AIPAC/Israeli government misappropriation of confidential U.S. business information in 1984. The second section of the law criminalizes the misappropriation of trade secrets related to or included in a product that is produced for or placed into interstate (including international) commerce, with the knowledge or intent that the action will injure the owner of the trade secret. Penalties include imprisonment for up to 10 years for individuals and fines of up to US $5 million for organizations. But the law is silent about sanctions for countries launching economic espionage networks.

industry. "The odds are not favorable for any American company when it is targeted for clandestine action by some country's intelligence service."[171]

Fortune 1,000 companies alone lost an estimated $59 billion in 2001, according to a survey by the American Society for Industrial Security, PricewaterhouseCoopers, and the U.S. Chamber of Commerce. According to the 2007 Defense Security Service report, the FBI had opened 89 economic espionage cases and was pursuing 182 active cases by the end of 2005. *Air Force Magazine* revealed in 2007 that the top five "collecting countries" were responsible for 57 percent of all technology espionage activity. They reported an increase of 43 percent over 2005 and 971 suspicious contacts, indicating that theft "eroded the U.S. military advantage by making dangerous technology available to adversaries." The leading state sponsors included Israel, India, Pakistan, Iran, Japan, and France, with China and Russia leading the list.[172] A 2007 report referenced a California FBI field office investigating espionage cases, which estimated that in Silicon Valley, the rate of trade secret theft rises 30 percent each year.[173]

The national security threat is also relevant, since the transfers directly and indirectly provide the latest technology to countries that are off-limits to U.S. vendors because they are considered potentially hostile. These are markets Israel can serve with knockoffs or weapons with integrated U.S. components. Such "Uzi diplomacy"—selling military goods to virtually any customer—was described by Shimon Peres in 1958: "By not selling an Uzi to a certain country, we are not implementing an embargo against that country, but against ourselves. It is absolute nonsense to embargo ourselves on an item that can be acquired elsewhere."[174] Israeli espionage has altered the strategic and tactical military balance of power between the U.S. and China. Whether the Israelis leaked sensitive data on the Patriot anti-ballistic missile defense system or other less significant systems, U.S. taxpayers again became the economic victims as they funded next-generation military hardware. Tactically, U.S. Marines were already facing U.S. optical technology illicitly provided by Israel and mounted on Iraqi tanks.

Israeli Military-Industrial Espionage Incidents[175]

U.S. Weapon/IP	Israeli Violation	Outcome
HAVE-NAP missile system	POPEYE	By reverse engineering the Martin-Marietta HAVE-NAP, an Israeli manufacturer avoided millions in development costs as well as warranted license fee payments. Israeli sales staff admit, "95 percent of the Popeye is U.S. technology."
U.S.-developed cruise missile technology.	STAR Cruise Missile	The CIA found Israel to be marketing the STAR, which incorporates sensitive U.S. technology, to China.
Sidewinder air-to-air missile	Python-3, Shafrir-2	Israeli versions of the Sidewinder were sold to South Africa, Chile, Thailand, and China. China then developed its own version of the Israeli copy (PL-8) and sold it to Iraq.
TOW-2 anti-tank missile	Mapatz	Israel's unauthorized copies of the Hughes Aircraft company's TOW-2 missile have been sold to apartheid South Africa, Venezuela, and China.
Patriot snti-missile system	Israel leaked technical information on the system to China in exchange for sensitive IP.	Former defense secretary Dick Cheney concluded that Israel had leaked IP about the Patriot to China in exchange for information on China's M-9 and M-11 ballistic missiles. The leak would enable Chinese modification of the M-9 and M-11 ballistic missiles to avoid intercept by U.S. systems.
Patented U.S. thermal imaging technologies	Israeli and Dutch firm Delft integrated U.S. IP into tank sights sold to countries including China.	China installed Israeli tank sights on MOD-2 tanks, then sold 69 of them to Iraq. U.S. Marines faced and captured some of the tanks, seizing evidence of the illegal transfer during the first Gulf War.

U.S. corporations face market disincentives for alerting their shareholders to security breaches that threaten their economic livelihood. An American Bar Association study found that companies reporting economic espionage suffered an immediate punishment from investors in the form of stock price declines.[176] They have an added obstacle: Israel lobby political appointees in government thwarting the enforcing U.S. arms export controls. Many private industry calls for investigations and law enforcement are deterred as soon as the complaint rises in the chain of command.

Barrington, Illinois military contractor Recon-Optical learned this the hard way. In 1984, the company won an Israeli air force contract valued at $40 million to be paid out of U.S. foreign military aid. Recon-Optical normally sold aerial reconnaissance systems direct to the U.S. military. The Israelis demanded a 40 percent "offset" on the contract, meaning Recon Optical had to spend $16 million with Israeli contractors. Some worked on site within the Barrington plant.

The contract soon soured. Recon Optical intercepted Israelis carting away 10 boxes of technical notes and blueprints of the company's core intellectual property. Recon-Optical's chief executive flew to Washington and was advised by his senator to take the matter up with Stephen Bryen, who had become deputy assistant secretary at the Pentagon under the recommendation of Richard Perle. In 1979, Bryen had been investigated by the FBI for disclosing classified information to the Mossad when he worked as a Senate aide, but this prior incident didn't prevent him from receiving a top secret security clearance at the Pentagon. Soon after Bryen was briefed about the Recon-Optical complaint, news stories based on documents and Recon-Optical testimony appeared in the Israeli press, denying espionage charges and chastising the company for bias against offsets. As in other cases involving Israel, Recon-Optical's efforts to achieve accountability were thwarted. In 1988, another scandal erupted when Bryen individually approved a license for the export of klystrons[xxxvi] to Israel, despite a DOD panel vote in opposition to the sale.[177]

Such incidents are rarely mentioned in U.S. establishment media. But Uzi diplomacy and the long track record of Israeli technology theft are sometimes frankly discussed in the Israeli press as misbehavior that could jeopardize the country's access to top-shelf U.S. military hardware. In 2009, Israel was on track to receive $37.5 million in U.S. funding for development of the Arrow-3 missile. Although Israel requested American F-22 Raptor fighter jets with the support of some members of Congress, others worried aloud about whether an "export version" of the airplane should ever go to Israel. As quoted in the *Jerusalem Post,* Barry Watts, a senior fellow with the Center for Strategic and Budgetary Assessments, said the feeling in the Air Force was that "it'll make a lot of people nervous...Japan isn't busy selling military hardware all over the planet Earth like the Israeli military is."[178] In mid-2009, the Pentagon issued new regulations governing the way Israel could use the almost $3 billion in military aid it receives from the U.S. It informed Israel's Defense Ministry that the foreign military financing (FMF) needed to be used strictly for weaponry and defense-related projects rather than nonessential items such as covers for trucks, uniforms and food for soldiers, and other exceptions previously granted by the Pentagon.[179] But despite a toughening stance from Washington, embedded commitments to Israel coupled with the Israel lobby's value system continue to undermine American industry and national security.

Pervasive secrecy and limited declassification and release of U.S. government documents limit Israeli accountability, particularly concerning nuclear smuggling and its weapons capability. The nonprofit National Security Archive at George Washington University has doggedly pursued public release of key CIA files about Israel's nuclear weapons programs under the Freedom of Information Act (FOIA). It has so far obtained "only a small fraction of a large body of documents...that remain classified."[180] Even after the Obama administration issued an executive order calling for a new "presumption of openness,"[181] government agencies thwart the release of sensitive information about Israel, possibly fearful of retaliation. In 2008, the FBI's most frequent

---

[xxxvi] A highly sensitive technology used in ballistic missiles.

response to Freedom of Information Act (FOIA) requests was that it could not locate records (57 percent of the time), and it only provided documents in 14 percent of cases.[182] The CIA proactively denies even the existence of relevant records.[xxxvii] The U.S. Department of State frequently denies Israel-related FOIAs under broad exceptions "protecting from disclosure national security information concerning the national defense or foreign policy." The Department of Defense is perhaps the most restrictive of all. Unless filers seeking Israel-related documents can prove they are a "scientific research organization" exempt from fees for FOIA searches,[xxxviii] researchers must agree to pay $44 per search hour to an institution not known for its thrift.[183]

Such U.S. government secrecy creates an information deficit. This in turn fuels a vicious cycle that thwarts governance, leaving stakeholders and accountability organizations completely in the dark as they try to research whether the vast benefits granted under U.S.-Israel policy are actually warranted.

Conclusion

U.S. counterintelligence and government agencies—along with private industry associations—have documented widespread and ongoing efforts by Israel and the Israel lobby to obtain sensitive, commercially valuable military-industrial technology. The prosecutorial immunity of offenders, or light sentences for major violators such as Ben-Ami Kadish, indicate that in spite of massive economic losses and negative impact on U.S. national security, the criminal justice system faces institutional barriers in regulating the Israel lobby. Political pressures—and the threat of systemic risk—render law enforcement incapable of properly executing its public interest mandate to defend and uphold the Constitution. Because the U.S. government refuses to declassify many of its most sensitive reports about Israeli activity, including espionage, there has been no widespread outcry from industry and the public for more criminal prosecutions or sanctions under treaties.

---

xxxvii This is referred to as a "Glomar" response, in reference to CIA responses to FOIAs seeking information about the Glomar Explorer, a now retired CIA sea vessel built to find and recover a lost Soviet nuclear submarine.

xxxviii A status granted to less than 10-15 percent of organizational filers

"The free-trade area is simply another form of aid, but the cost of the aid will be borne unequally by the American worker who loses his job." **Mark A. Anderson, economist, AFL-CIO**[184]

USIFTA and the American Economy

After the USIFTA threw open the U.S. market to Israel in 1985, difficult questions about U.S. agricultural exporter access to Israeli consumers were postponed for future negotiations. USIFTA permitted import restrictions based on quotas and fees determined by each party. Israel quickly imposed both.[xxxix] Far from following "free trade" principles, Israel engaged in straightforward mercantilist policies of expanding exports while limiting imports.

Israeli promoted economic development by protecting infant industries. USIFTA gave Israel the unilateral right to impose a floating 20 percent ad valorem[xl] customs duty on merchandise imports of its choosing. This helped Israel protect infant industries that weren't major exporters at the time of USIFTA's signing.[xli] USIFTA also allowed Israel the flexible application of "corrective" measures in the form of surcharges, import deposits, and restrictions on import quantities to assuage Israel's constant balance of payments problems. Israel could suddenly impose sweeping duties or charges in the event that the value of its currency decreased more than 20 percent against the U.S. dollar.

Though the U.S. and Israel did not (and still do not) have any formalized mutual defense treaties, USIFTA mandated coordination between the Israel Ministry of Defense and U.S. Department of Defense—a reminder of the treaty's origins in the DOD MOUs and Operation Tipped Kettle.[xlii] Both parties waived their "buy national" government procurement restrictions: the U.S. fully, and Israel with caveats. In USIFTA, Israel gained permanent preferential access to procurement from the entire U.S. government, as opposed to only DOD, avoiding the reciprocal and performance-based pressures of temporary MOUs.

[xxxix] Article 6

[xl] Based on the assessed value

[xli] Article 10

[xlii] Article 15

Minor trade disputes and accusations erupted when Israeli rose vendors were effectively shut out of the U.S. market, but most complaints were from U.S. exporters. In 1989, Israel's Magam United Rubber Industries Ltd. was found guilty of violating anti-dumping laws and fined for conveyor belt exports. The ITC, in its enforcement role, found that Magam incorporated subsidized components in order to beat American prices.[185] Magam then called for "Industry Minister Ariel Sharon to make a personal call to the U.S. trade secretary."[186] U.S. Ambassador to Israel Bill Brown charged that "Israel was continually violating the spirit of the FTA by making it hard, if not impossible, for American goods to be sold in Israel at competitive prices...not only were these unfair trade barriers harming American exporters, but they were also souring Israel's relationship with the U.S."[187]

But the longest-standing public rift involves food and agriculture exports from the U.S. to Israel. Given the power of the U.S. grain lobby and farm-subsidy-fueled agro industry, it is not surprising that Israel limited a flood of cheap imports by putting forward "differing interpretations" about its own agricultural trade rights and obligations. The U.S. and Israel signed a separate annex to USIFTA clarifying treatment of agricultural products, but the November 1996 Agreement on Trade in Agricultural Products (ATAP) was only meant to be temporary; it was set to expire on December 31, 2001. Israel rarely upheld its commitments.

The ATAP divided U.S. agricultural exports to Israel into three categories: products exempt from tariffs; products exempt from tariffs, but under numerical quotas; and products levied at a "preferential" import tariff rate. Most Israeli agricultural products entered the U.S. duty-free. As an incredibly generous additional concession, the U.S. unilaterally lifted all quota allocations governed by its WTO commitments.[188] Israel could export as many agricultural products as it could produce.

As in the 1984 fast-track negotiations, U.S. agricultural interests were formally invited to submit public and "business confidential" comments to the USTR via the ITC toward renegotiating ATAP on December 1, 2000. From the perspective of American natural and processed food sellers, their experience accessing the Israeli market was portrayed as limited, governed by arbitrary rules, and far from "mutually beneficial."

The California Pistachio Commission quickly uncovered new Israeli-Iranian intrigues. It argued that while "Israel is the largest per capita consumer of pistachios in the world and imports annually around 9 million pounds," American "industry has not been successful in increasing its pistachio trade" since "most of Israel's pistachio imports are Iranian in origin, even though the country has a ban against trade with Iran." Israel categorized re-exports of Iranian pistachios to the U.S. as originating in the European Union. But U.S. exporters only experienced spikes in Israeli demand in 1997, when aflatoxin (a fungus) temporarily halted Iranian exports to Europe. University scientific tests and data confirmed the pistachio origins in Iran. One Israeli importer was indicted for such practices, but later acquitted of charges for trafficking Iranian pistachios.[189]

The Northwest Horticultural Council, representing apple, cherry, pear, and stone fruit growers, charged that "Israel utilizes a complex and confusing combination of tariffs, duty free quotas, and 'cost of production prices'…to limit market access." Sunkist Growers, representing U.S. citrus fruit producers, noted a disparity in reciprocity: "While the U.S. seems to strictly adhere to the provisions of this agreement in providing duty free U.S. market access for Israeli fresh citrus fruit, U.S. citrus exporters nevertheless continue to be denied access to the Israeli market…Israel maintains a Tariff Rate Quota[xliii] (TRQ) that limits the volume of American-origin citrus that may enter Israel and imposes a very high 30 percent duty on imports outside their TRQ limits." Sunkist recommended that the USTR return to the original vision of the USIFTA by "reduction of Israeli's tariffs on U.S. citrus to zero, or in the absence of such elimination by the Israelis, the harmonization of U.S. tariffs with Israeli tariffs." However, the USTR pursued neither.

The National Sunflower Association complained that TRQs led to significant losses: "U.S. exporters have sold product to Israeli importers late in the year, only to have the Israeli officials declare that the quota had already been filled. The exporter was then forced to reroute these containers into another country at a significant loss."[190]

Kosher winemaker Royal Wine charged that Israeli delays and the original ATAP punished its wine and grape juice exports while allowing duty-free entry of Israeli products: "Israel agreed to substantially reduce import duties it imposes on these products, these reductions are not meaningful, as they did not result in the import duties being lowered to levels which would permit either wine or grape juice to be sold in Israel at competitive prices….The FTA has now been in existence for fifteen years, more than enough time for the Israeli government to phase out import duties on wine and grape juice."[191] Non-kosher winemaker JBC International stated flatly that "U.S. wines have not benefited from the U.S.-Israel FTA, but Israeli wine exports to the U.S. have increased greatly…In 1998 Israeli wine exports to the U.S. totaled $2.58 million, while U.S. exports to Israel totaled only $313,000…A tariff rate of 40 percent on wine imports, sixteen years after the original FTA in which Israel agreed to lower its tariffs to zero, is unacceptable….Israel is growing their market at our expense and that violates the principles of the Free Trade Agreement."[192]

[xliii] A trade tactic used to protect a domestically produced product or commodity from competitive imports. The tariff rate quota (TRQ) quota component sets a specified tariff level to provide the desired degree of import protection. Imports entering a country during a specific time period under the quota component of a TRQ are usually subject to a lower tariff rate or no tariff. Imports above the quota's quantitative threshold face a much higher (and usually even prohibitive) tariff.

The Grocery Manufacturers of America faulted Israel's punitive and arbitrary administration of its TRQ system: "The quota is allocated on a lottery-style basis so that applicants with no history or capacity to import product stand as much chance of obtaining a license as those with historical trade flows."[193] Kraft Foods noted with alarm the "disappearance" of unfilled quotas and general chaos: "Under the current Israeli system of TRQ administration, licenses for importing cheese are allocated arbitrarily. Consequently, some importers fill quota, others don't. As a result, distributors are unable to estimate how much will be available at the in-quota rate, so are reluctant to buy at full duty of 133.2 percent....The result is that Kraft can only import a small fraction of the quota for cream cheese and is unable to grow its business. The current duty on fresh cheese is 148 percent. Imports from the U.S. pay no duty but are subject to a 90 percent surcharge, so the effective rate U.S. suppliers pay is 133.2 percent ad valorem."[194]

Many American ATAP petitioners expressed suspicions about Israeli regulatory agencies. An association representing 90 percent of U.S. chocolate and confectionary products and $23.5 billion in sales worried about product formulas: "Our members have expressed concern over requests by the Ministry of Health Food Control Administration for proprietary ingredient and food additive information in order to obtain a license to import a product into Israel."[195] In isolation, the candy makers' complaint may seem overly suspicious—until the Ministry of Health's record of channeling pharmaceutical clinical dossiers to Israeli generic drug makers is examined.

In 2004, Israeli and U.S. delegations hammered out a temporary understanding over treatment of agricultural products that was to be binding through December 31, 2008. The agreement established import quantities and applicable tariffs for a number of categories identified by standard five-digit classification codes and scheduled consultations aimed at replacing the agreement by December 31, 2008.

The ITC received a renewed flood of U.S. private sector complaints about quota abuse and lack of reciprocity during a subsequent round of ATAP public comments in late 2007. The Corn Refiners Association reminded the ITC that the ATAP was discriminatory as "the only bilateral trade agreement that is not based on a general model of eventual elimination of trade barriers in agricultural products. The ATAP restricts many U.S. products through tariff-rate quotas and maintains permanent duties on numerous agricultural products. The United States should have an objective of aligning this agreement with other U.S. bilateral trade agreements that will result in elimination of all tariffs and quotas."[196] Blue Diamond Almond growers were blunter still: "The fact that the U.S.–Israel Free Trade Agreement is twenty-two years old and still maintains high tariffs on almonds is a clear indication of its failure."

Blue Diamond went on to allege that Israeli almond production wasn't economically viable, even as U.S. production was shut out under $1,800 duties: "Although Israel claims to be an almond producer, it is not considered a commercial producer. It cannot supply its own market with almonds. Although Israel has tried to increase almond production, it has failed. It simply does not have the land to accomplish this successfully....Our understanding is that Israel has 3,500 acres of irrigated bearing almonds and 625 acres of irrigated new plantings. It also has 2,250 acres of un-irrigated bearing and 625 acres of un-irrigated new plantings. This is not commercially significant. Israel should not be allowed to protect a few selected growers to the detriment of U.S. growers. This is particularly true when one considers that the duty in the U.S. on Israeli almonds is zero."[197]

The California Dried Plum Board, representing 900 growers and 22 packers in California, slammed Israel's 91.8 percent tariffs on prunes and import licensing regime: "Israel offers excessive protection for its very small domestic dried prune industry. It allows importation of prunes only by import license holders, but the required licenses are often distributed through favoritism to companies that are not even prune importers, who then resell them at a profit to legitimate prune importers. There is no transparency to the licensing system, and its efficiency limits access for California Prune exporters. It is difficult for importers to arrange retail promotions in advance; since they are not sure they will be able to get a license to import California Prunes."[198]

The touchy Iranian pistachio issue resurfaced as Paramount Farms cited the endemic Israeli refusal to prosecute violations: "Israeli national law prohibits the importation of goods and services—including pistachios—from Iran. Under Israel's Trading with the Enemy Act...any form of trading, direct or indirect, with Iran is prohibited. If Israeli customs authorities believe that goods are imported from Iran, they may block the import(s), and the importer(s) may be subject to certain penalties." Paramount estimated the Israeli pistachio market potential at $20 million per year, but stated that Turkish re-exports of Iranian pistachios held 83 percent of the market compared to the paltry U.S. share of 5 percent.[199]

The Distilled Spirits Council (DISCUS), which submitted protests in earlier ATAP negotiations, called again for reciprocity for liquors: "...the United States imposes *no* tariffs on imports from Israel of *any* beverage alcohol product, including beer, wine, brandy, and other spirits." DISCUS also sought elimination of 10.2 percent tariffs on brandy and recognition of both bourbon and Tennessee whiskey as distinctive products of the United States.[200]

The Western Growers Association lamented the continuing existence of quota and tariff schedules on fresh U.S. vegetables: "Western Growers requests USTR to negotiate the elimination of all tariffs on imports of U.S. fresh fruits, tree nuts, and vegetables. These tariffs should be zeroed immediately. In addition, duty free import volumes must be expanded to allow Western Growers members to benefit fully from this twenty-two-year-old FTA. It seems just to expect an FTA with a trading partner as mature as Israel to provide U.S. fresh fruit, nut, and vegetable interests with the opportunities and benefits afforded to us under the more recently concluded high quality FTAs."[201]

Although most ATAP submissions during the year 2007 process criticized ongoing tariff and quota barriers, the U.S. Grain Council praised ATAP's progress and alluded to its own inside track. "U.S. grain producers have benefited significantly from the U.S.-Israel FTA. Import duties on corn, barley, sorghum and related products are set at zero under the agreement, and we are not aware of any significant non tariff barriers to Israeli feed grain imports. As a result, U.S. exports of feed grains to Israel totaled just over 1 million metric tons (MT) in 2006, valued at $124 million." The council then referenced a secret agreement obligating Israeli grain purchases: "It is our understanding that Israeli government officials at some point engaged in an exchange of letters with the United States committing to import no less than 1.6 MT annual of U.S. cereals and oilseeds. As we understand it, this letter may have been a side letter to a U.S.-Israel Support Funds Agreement. We strongly encourage U.S. negotiators to incorporate this commitment into the AFTA, as it would have significant value to the U.S. grains industry. Moreover, we believe it is in Israel's interest to reaffirm a strong feed grains trading relationship with the United States through such a commitment."[202]

The U.S. Grain Council was unsuccessful in having a purchase quota formally written into ATAP, though other U.S. supports for U.S. agriculture remain high. In 2008, Congress passed a five-year, $289 billion U.S. farm bill replete with loan guarantees, crop subsidies, and tax credits. Although controversy over Israeli food import barriers was still raging, in December of 2008 President George W. Bush signed a one-year extension to ATAP, allowing the highly contentious negotiations to continue.

USIFTA was the first bilateral trade agreement ever signed by the United States. The exploding U.S. trade deficit with Israel, while small compared to the overall U.S. trade deficit, is an anomaly among other bilateral free trade agreements (though not for the multilateral, intergovernmental managed trade pact known as NAFTA). Israel's ongoing violations of the spirit of rules-based trade threaten American workers and intellectual property of U.S. businesses. Unpunished violations could also signal to other trade partners that WTO enforcement mechanisms are not functioning as designed. USTR and ITC enforcement mechanisms similarly do not appear to be used when warranted. Visible violations that are not seriously investigated or punished by the United States undermine the confidence of U.S. industry in USTR-negotiated bilateral treaties. Quantitatively reviewing the result of USIFTA is illustrative.

Although the total loss to American businesses from stolen defense, pharmaceutical, and other IP is largely unquantifiable, the economic impact of the USIFTA-generated deficit can be precisely calculated in terms of job creation.[xliv] According to the U.S. Census Bureau's last survey of export manufacturing establishments published in 2006, total direct U.S. export-related jobs numbered 5,070,900.[203] U.S.-manufactured merchandise exports during that

---

[xliv] Job creation calculations have most frequently been used by lobbies pushing trade agreements before they are signed, but are rarely used to measure actual performance after several years under managed trade treaties.

year totaled $818 billion. Dividing export revenue by jobs yields one direct export-related job supported by every $161,300 in export revenue in 2003. International Commercial Diplomacy Inc., a consultancy, estimates that two additional indirect jobs[204] are supported by each direct export manufacturing job. By factoring in yearly worker productivity gains from the Bureau of Labor Statistics (each worker produces more export revenue as manufacturing productivity rises), by 2008, the estimated revenue required to sustain one direct export related manufacturing job and two indirect jobs grew to $187,000. We can use this input-output data to see how the deficit impacts the U.S. in terms of jobs.

AIPAC originally argued job loss avoidance as a factor for promoting USIFTA. The widely quoted 1984 AIPAC report "US-Israel Free Trade Area: How Both Sides Gain" by Peggy Blair predicted that a 10 percent decline in U.S. exports to Israel would generate 20,000 export-related jobs. She predicted that bringing the U.S. market share up to 40 percent via USIFTA would generate 40,000 U.S. jobs.[205]

However, shortly after its inception, USIFTA reversed the formerly balanced trading relationship, producing an ever-widening United States trade deficit. Translating this into American jobs by the input-output method, the USIFTA has been highly negative for American workers. Using the formerly balanced trade as the relevant benchmark, the $7.8 billion U.S. deficit with Israel in the year 2008 was equivalent to 125,663 lost American jobs.

American Jobs Lost to USIFTA

Year	Nominal U.S. Trade Deficit with Israel ($Billion)	Revenue per Direct Manufacturing Job	Manufacturing Labor Productivity Gain	Direct Jobs	Indirect Jobs	Total American Jobs Loss
1999	-$2.2	$132,500	6.40%	-16,604	-33,208	-49,811
2000	-$5.2	$141,500	7.10%	-36,749	-73,498	-110,247
2001	-$4.5	$152,400	1.10%	-29,547	-59,094	-88,641
2002	-$5.4	$154,000	4.50%	-35,065	-70,130	-105,195
2003	-$5.9	$161,300		-36,578	-73,156	-109,733
2004	-$5.3	$169,700	5.20%	-31,232	-62,463	-93,695
2005	-$7.2	$178,200	5.00%	-40,404	-80,808	-121,212
2006	-$8.2	$185,300	4.00%	-44,253	-88,505	-132,758
2007	-$7.8	$192,200	3.70%	-40,583	-81,165	-121,748
2008	-$8.0	$187,000	-2.70%	-41,888	-83,775	-125,663

The fact that USIFTA mainly benefits Israel is also revealed in market share. Even discounting that U.S. military sales are taxpayer-subsidized, the U.S. share of the total Israeli import market declined from 27.1 percent in 1985 to 12 percent in 2007, as Israeli trade barriers kept U.S. agricultural products out while Israel's intellectual-property-fueled exports grew. The CIA World Factbook lists the U.S. as the number one destination for Israel's exports (receiving 35 percent of the total). The U.S. is Israel's number one import partner, followed by Belgium, [xlv] Germany, China, Switzerland, the UK, and Italy.[206]

U.S. Share of Israel's Import Market [207]

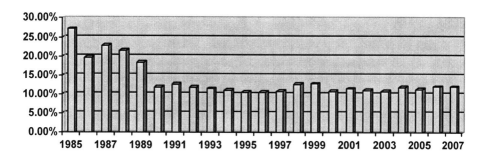

The stated purpose of the 1984 U.S.-Israel Free Trade Area, like those of most other trade agreements, is "mutual benefit" derived through cooperation.[208] But the U.S. clearly never achieved the potential share of Israel's market outlined by AIPAC. From 1985 to 2007, the U.S. share dropped from 27.1 percent to 12 percent of the Israeli import market. If the deficit generated by the USIFTA (-$7.8 billion) were eliminated, the surplus from bilateral FTAs signed by the United States would have been $29.4 billion, sustaining the equivalent of 471,850 direct and indirect jobs in the American economy. Because USIFTA delivers most benefits only to Israel, it differs substantially from subsequent intergovernmental bilateral managed trade deals. In the year 2008, all ratified[xlvi] bilateral FTAs produced a cumulative $21.6 billion surplus, while none of the other countries had histories of systemic espionage across high-technology and high-value-added U.S. industries. This extreme deficit anomaly is quantitatively revealed in a comparison of the other subsequent U.S. bilateral agreements.[xlvii]

[xlv] Selling uncut diamonds to Israel's polishing industry.

[xlvi] As indicated on the USTR website on 12/31/2008.

[xlvii] Data is from the U.S. Census Bureau TradeStats Express database.

2005 U.S.-Australia FTA

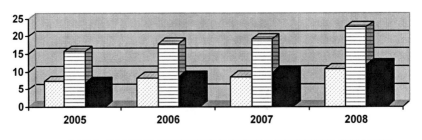

The U.S.-Australia FTA substantially improved U.S. access to the Australian market while rectifying conflicts over Australia's complex drug listing system. U.S. exports of industrial machinery and passenger vehicles expanded under the FTA, while Australian food and beverage exports blossomed. The formerly stagnant bilateral trade relationship experienced double-digit growth averaging 12 percent since 2005, and reached $33 billion in 2008.

2006 U.S.-Bahrain FTA

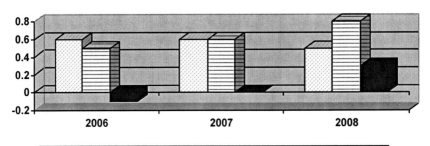

Though it is a small economy, Bahrain enjoys strong competitive advantages in aluminum and fertilizer production. Exports of both grew under the FTA, while diversified U.S. exports to Bahrain of aircraft, vehicles, and machinery boosted a minor trading relationship. Bilateral trade in 2008 amounted to $1.37 billion.

2006 U.S.-Chile FTA

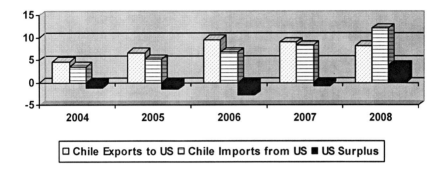

U.S.-Chile bilateral trade reached $16 billion in 2008. Copper, fruit, and seafood dominate Chilean exports to the United States. U.S. exports are concentrated in heavy machinery, fuel, passenger vehicles, and aircraft. Over the past 15 years, Chile and the U.S. have held thin but temporary "surplus" positions in the relationship during alternating five- to six-year periods.

2006 U.S.-Jordan FTA

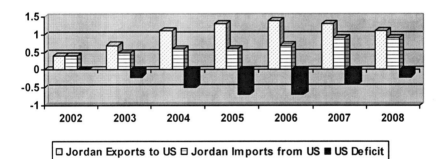

Bilateral trade between the depressed Jordanian economy and the U.S. reached only $2 billion in 2008. Implementation of the FTA failed to deliver the robust job opportunities sought by Jordanian government for its workers or resolve longstanding disputes between Jordan and Israel over Palestinian refugees. Jordan's new sweatshop apparel industry instead employs many temporary Bangladeshi contract workers brought in to manufacture for export, drawing condemnation from international human rights organizations. The U.S. deficit with Jordan has narrowed from $0.7 billion to $0.2 billion since the pact was implemented in 2006.

2006 U.S.-Morocco FTA

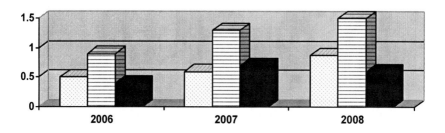

Trade relations have been on a sound footing since Morocco became the first country to recognize the newly independent United States in 1777. Morocco exports raw materials for cement, as well as machinery, apparel, and fuel, to the U.S. The U.S. exports cereals, aircraft, and other agricultural commodities in exchange. Bilateral trade reached $2.38 billion in 2008. The U.S. has enjoyed a trade surplus with Morocco in all but one year since 1989.

2004 U.S.-Singapore FTA

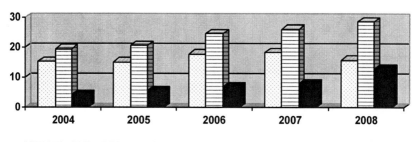

Bilateral U.S.-Singapore trade reached $44.7 billion in 2008. Major U.S. exports to Singapore include electronics, heavy machinery, aircraft components, and optical and surgical instruments. Singapore exports include heavy machinery, electronics, and pharmaceutical products. After a long period of deficits with Singapore, the U.S. has won a growing surplus since the year 2001, but neither holds artificial systemic advantages.

1985 U.S.-Israel FTA

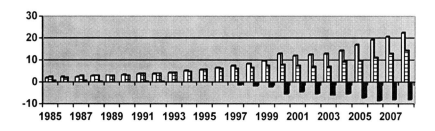

Only with carefully chosen numbers and qualifiers can a positive case for USIFTA be made. Mitchell Bard[xlviii] wrote in the *Los Angeles Times* that "the financial benefits to the states from bilateral agreements can also be substantial, considering that seventeen states exported at least $100 million worth of goods to Israel in 2006, and three exported more than $500 million, with New York leading the way with $4.6 billion."[209] While U.S.-Israel bilateral trade totaled $36.8 billion in 2008, the U.S. trade deficit with Israel reached $7.8 billion. Precious stones, metals, and coins account for almost half of Israeli exports to the U.S., followed by pharmaceutical products, which grew from less than $57.1 million in 1995 to $2.6 billion (12.4 percent of total exports) in the year 2007. A U.S. trade deficit with Israel has occurred every year since 1994. Since 1985 when USIFTA was signed, the cumulative U.S. trade deficit with Israel has grown to $63 billion.[210] When inflation is factored in, the value of the cumulative deficit through 2008 totals U.S. $71 billion. The unprecedented agreement may also have touched off global market segmentation and contributed to less successful trade rounds under the WTO.

In 1985, Sidney Weintraub, one of the most prominent American members of the post-Keynesian school of economics, foresaw that the USIFTA would halt general lowering of trade barriers by kicking off a global segmentation into isolated trading blocks.

> This free-trade area (FTA) agreement raises 2 types of issues: 1. whether the principle of nondiscrimination will be abandoned for bilateralism, thus undermining most-favored-nation (MFN) agreements, and 2. whether this particular FTA is more likely to be trade-diverting than trade-creating. It is uncertain whether the inherent discrimination of an FTA would lead to an improvement or deterioration in world welfare. Actually, the struggle against bilateralism has long been lost. The trade-policy issue is essentially

---

[xlviii] Director of the America Israel Cooperative Enterprise and former editor of AIPAC's *Near East Report*.

the question of compatibility between FTAs and the General Agreement on Tariffs and Trade (GATT). The Israel-U.S. FTA is merely an episode in the evolution of international commercial policy. It is, however, another step in the segmentation of the world into preferential trading areas, and the long-term consequences of this discrimination are hard to predict. [211]

An earlier *New York Times* editorial hypothesized that the deal would actually lower tariff barriers worldwide:

A U.S.-Israel zone won't threaten the world's trade patterns. Their trade last year totaled only $3 billion. Full realization of any agreement will take years. But the deal is important in three respects:

First, it aims to be a bold stroke, a formal commitment to open all trade. That will surely increase the two nations' commerce and assist Israel in significant ways.

Second, it will signal America's interest in widening trade in services as well as goods - things like engineering, insurance and banking. Even as tariffs and quotas against products have been progressively slashed, there's been no broad relaxation of licensing and regulations that discriminate against service industries. Such balance is long overdue.

Finally, this initiative puts the United States on the side of liberalization at a time when contrary pressures are rising everywhere. Washington has been trying for two years to get another multilateral negotiation started. Western Europe and Japan have persistently balked.[212]

USIFTA did pave the way for a major multilateral intergovernmental managed trade area (the North American Free Trade Agreement with Canada and Mexico) in 1994 and subsequent bilateral agreements. Weintraub's prediction of "segmentation" and "discrimination" seems to have come true, in contrast to the *New York Times* editorial stocked with AIPAC's USIFTA talking points.

Even while WTO "rounds" have gone nowhere as the U.S. trade deficit explodes, the Israel lobby has slowly cut off U.S. export access to natural trading partners across the 22-country Arab League, particularly Gulf oil producer states. AIPAC-driven legislation drives such as the Syrian Accountability Act, the annual attempt to pass a Saudi Accountability Act, embargoes, and even blockades have sought to condition and cut commercial ties between U.S. exporters and Arab trading nations. Periodic lobby-fanned conflagrations, such as the 2006 drive to keep Dubai Ports World, a company backed by a UAE sovereign wealth fund, from acquiring and managing U.S. port facilities, have also driven many Arab investors and importers away from the U.S. market fearful of discrimination and unmanageable legal exposure.

Yet this "Israel lobby boycott" has been partially masked by AIPAC's long-term efforts to condition trade under the banner of a "Middle East Free Trade Area" initiative through bilateral agreements amalgamated into a larger managed trade area. While the proposal is portrayed as multilateral free trade, its effect would subjugate U.S. regional trade policy to an Israel-centric model.

In 1994, House Majority Leader Richard A. Gephardt urged President Bill Clinton to expand the USIFTA to include all Middle East countries if they would normalize relations with Israel.[213] The wife of Speaker of the House Newt Gingrich was later put on the payroll of Israel Export Development Corporation to seek corporate tenants for an export-related business park in Israel.[214] In 1998, in exchange for Jordan's peace agreement with Israel, the U.S. launched the Qualified Industrial Zones (QIZ) program. It gave Jordanian products that sourced at least 8 percent of their content from an Israeli manufacturer duty- and quota-free access to the U.S. market. During the George W. Bush administration, the United States and Israel tried to replicate the model in other trade deals in the Arab world, but President Bush's plan to create the MEFTA "tying all 22 Arab states with the U.S. and Israel in a trade deal by 2013" largely stalled. The Jordanian QIZs degenerated into sweatshops using imported labor at two cents per hour to supply U.S. retailers such as Wal-Mart, Target, Gloria Vanderbilt, and Kohl's. The QIZ climate of 24- to 72-hour shifts, physical abuse (including rape), and near imprisonment for workers has been named in numerous human rights reports. In 2005, 54 companies registered in QIZ, rising to 203 as exports reached a total U.S. $1.3 billion by 2007.[215]

The U.S.-Oman FTA, which AIPAC lobbied for as a way to break the Arab boycott of Israeli goods, didn't roll up the larger boycott effort, although Bahrain did close down its boycott office in 2005 just ahead of signing its free trade agreement with the United States.[216] Meanwhile, earlier lobby attempts to control U.S. trade continue to face critical review. Although Russia has still not attained WTO ascension, it began agitating for the U.S. to drop the punitive Jackson-Vanik amendment as an irrelevant Cold War relic standing in the way of increased U.S.-Russian trade. Israel's influence over U.S. trade policy has been disastrous for U.S. exporters searching for opportunities in fast-growing Middle East markets.

Arab Import Market Growth and Declining U.S. Share

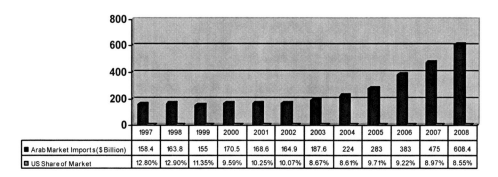

	1997	1998	1999	2000	2001	2002	2003	2004	2005	2006	2007	2008
■ Arab Market Imports ($ Billion)	158.4	163.8	155	170.5	168.6	164.9	187.6	224	283	383	475	608.4
◙ US Share of Market	12.80%	12.90%	11.35%	9.59%	10.25%	10.07%	8.67%	8.61%	9.71%	9.22%	8.97%	8.55%

Natural U.S. trading partners such as Saudi Arabia and other Gulf oil-producing states have increasingly sourced merchandise and industrial goods imports from Asia. The U.S. share of Saudi imports declined from 24.75 percent in 1997 to 11.6 percent in 2008. The overall U.S. share of the import market in the 22-country Arab League declined from 12.77 percent in 1997 to 8.55 percent in 2008. Antagonism of consumers and industrial partners to U.S. trade and regional foreign policy accelerated the decline after the year 2001.[217] For U.S. exporters, this is significant. Arab merchandise import demand reached $609 billion in 2008, after doubling every three years. If U.S. exporters had maintained market share momentum in the region, capturing a reasonable 25 percent, it would have added over 800,000 export-related jobs to the U.S. economy in 2008.[xlix]

By limiting such competition and taking advantage of trade preferences, Israel increased its share of total U.S. import demand from .97 percent in 1997 to 1.06 percent in 2008, an amazing feat for a country with a population of less than eight million. Even as AIPAC continues to push for policies that could trigger enormous economic consequences for Americans, such as U.S. economic and military blockades on Iran, the dark underside of a trade deal forged in a crucible of espionage is becoming apparent.

Since the period when USIFTA was inked, U.S. trade policy has generally followed the broader principles that underpin USIFTA, throwing open the U.S. market, disregarding industry and worker concerns, and inevitably generating record deficits financed only by the willingness of foreigners to invest in the United States.

[xlix] Using the previously referenced input-output model.

Annual U.S. Trade Deficit ($ Billion) [218]

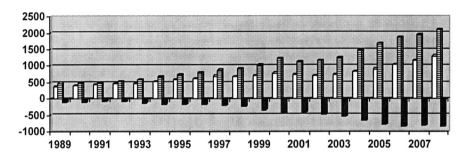

The negotiation of USIFTA was a true turning point in U.S. trade policy. From the end of the Civil War through the 1970s, the international share of the U.S. economy was relatively small. Exports and imports were generally either in balance or delivering a small U.S. surplus. In the last quarter-century, foreign trade has risen 700 percent, more than doubling as a share of U.S. gross domestic product to 28 percent. The U.S. trade deficit explosion put the excess of imports over exports at almost $900 billion in 2006, roughly equivalent to 7 percent of GDP.[219] America's drive to implement intergovernmental managed trade policies began with USIFTA, then proceeded to stitch a patchwork of similarly flawed multilateral deals, including the massive North American Free Trade Agreement (NAFTA). Trade policy mismanagement has not only led to unsustainable trade deficits, but undermined the nation's competitiveness, job security, and income distribution. [220]

While the lion's share of benefits from trade policy and globalization have been concentrated among those at the top rungs of the wealth ladder, they have been paid for with wealth transfers from working families at the middle and bottom. Benefits and real wages for the majority of U.S. workers remained stagnant as high-wage jobs were destroyed and industries producing secure living incomes were broken up—even as remaining worker productivity increased. While this horrifying trend is usually only observed from 30,000 feet, a close examination of USIFTA's impact on military, food, and pharmaceutical products (along with counterfeits, illegal drugs, and diamond-related issues) reveals how corrupted policy can threaten not only workers, but highly innovative U.S. industries.

During its 1984 lobbying push for USIFTA, AIPAC invited the American pharmaceutical industry to step up its presence in the Israeli market. "Tariffs range from 2 percent for antibiotic preparations which are not produced in Israel to 18 percent for those medicines competing with Israeli goods. If U.S. companies were to step up their advertising to increase brand name recognition, and take advantage of duty-free treatment, it is likely that American firms could greatly increase their current 16 percent share of the import market."[221] In reality, increased presence by the American pharmaceutical industry has been a trap.

Just as American businesses indirectly gave Israel their trade secrets via the ITC's classified report, drug manufacturers have faced systematized violations of their intellectual property rights.

The USIFTA has fueled an Israeli regulatory and manufacturing collusion that feeds American drug innovations into Israel's new export-oriented generic drug industry. This is enabled by the Israeli government's legally mandated access to sensitive American drug company innovations. However, unlike the military contractors, U.S. pharmaceutical industry representatives have fought back, insisting that Israel remain on the USTR's Priority Watch List for intellectual property violations between 2006 and 2009.

Under the auspices of approving drugs for its domestic market, the Israeli Ministry of Health (MOH) solicits patented drug data and formulas. MOH then delays the approval process while data is reviewed by Israeli drug-makers. The drug makers subsequently challenge the patents while seeking rushed commercialization of cutting-edge U.S. drug innovations worldwide. Israel is obligated by TRIPS to protect clinical dossiers against unfair commercial use.[1] But in March of 2005, Israel purposefully enacted the weakest data exclusivity regulations in the developed world. Under the weaker regime, American clinical dossiers quickly became a data source that Israeli generic drug exporters came to rely on for manufacturing and accelerated exports of generic versions based on U.S. drug patents.

USTR's 2005 annual intellectual property violations report (called Special 301 after the relevant section of trade law) to the U.S. Congress details the protection of IP rights and financial incentives at the core of pharmaceutical innovation:

> The United States is firmly of the conviction that intellectual property protection, including for pharmaceutical patents, is critical to the long term viability of a health care system capable of developing new and innovative lifesaving medicines. Intellectual property rights are necessary to encourage rapid innovation, development, and commercialization of effective and safe drug therapies. Financial incentives are needed to develop new medications; no one benefits if research on such products is discouraged.

> Israel's intellectual property protection deteriorated over the last year. The recently-enacted patent term extension (PTE) and data exclusivity (DE) legislation, taken together with Israel's continued pre-grant opposition and its attempts to exclude intellectual property infringement from the scope of its unjust enrichment doctrine, guarantees that Israeli generic producers will be free to manufacture in Israel for export, primarily to the United States.

---

[1] Known as "data exclusivity."

U.S. pharmaceutical companies allege that Israeli intellectual property laws have been purposely weakened and placed out of sync with major industrial countries that permit much longer time periods before market exclusivity given by patents expires. Israel seems to agree. Developed country regulators don't count the regulatory approval process time period against patent term expiration the way Israel does. The chairman of the Knesset's Constitution, Law and Justice Committee confirmed during consideration of the Patent Term Extension Legislation that cutting the patent term was a protectionist measure to boost generic exports, saying, "We have a local industry that we want to protect." The short periods left to recoup investments have left U.S. pharmaceutical manufacturers at a major disadvantage compared to Israeli generic drug manufacturers such as Teva.

Teva's global sales are premised upon preferential access to the U.S. market, commercial data leaks, and purposely weakened IP protection in Israel. U.S. consumers and taxpayers subsidize research and development that Israeli generic drug manufacturers then monetize—in the U.S. PhRMA, the U.S. industry lobby, observed the following:

> Under Israeli law, patents are thoroughly examined by technically competent examiners. It normally takes four to six years until the examination is completed. The duration of a patent is twenty years from the date of filing the application. As a result of the examination, the patentee "loses" a significant part of the period of exclusivity to which it is entitled. After examination and acceptance of the application, it is published for possible oppositions in the Patent Gazette. One would have assumed that, once the examiner deems that the invention is worthy of patent protection and accepts the application, the patent will finally be granted. However, under Article 30 of the Israeli Patents Act, any competitor may block patent grant simply by filing an opposition to the patent application.

> The resolution of the opposition may take many more years so that the patentee is actually deprived of the remainder of the period of exclusivity to which it is entitled. During the opposition proceedings the patent is not registered and not yet valid. The legal situation in Israel is diametrically opposed to the legal situation worldwide. In most (if not all) OECD countries, any opposition proceedings are conducted post registration (e.g., in the EPO) and it is not possible to block the registration of the patent. The deeply flawed pre-grant opposition system applicable under Israeli law has been rejected in the vast majority of developed countries, including in the EU and the United States. Third parties can be given an opportunity to challenge the validity of the patent, but as recognized elsewhere, any such action should be done post-grant. Indeed, the Patents Act already provides a system for post-grant challenge. Additionally, a potential infringer is also entitled to

challenge validity in infringement proceedings. However, a system of pre-grant oppositions, which blocks patent grant for many years, actually nullifies patent protection. Such a system has been rejected worldwide.[222]

American pharmaceutical companies and associations seeking redress in Israeli courts found that governing laws had been undermined by Israeli Ministry of Justice enforcement policies:

> The Ministry of Justice has recently revived a 2003 recommendation of the now disbanded Patent Advisory Committee to exclude the principle of unjust enrichment from litigation concerning IP issues. Since the unjust enrichment principle has been the only enforcement tool available to PhRMA member companies for use against generic infringers when faced with pre-grant opposition, the exclusion has been high on the wish list of Israeli generic manufacturers. Revival of a recommendation of an advisory committee, whose recommendations had not been accepted by the then Minister of Justice precisely because it had been demonstrated at the time that the Committee had been under the influence of the Israeli generic industry, is a cause of concern for PhRMA member companies, especially when coupled with enactment of the recent PTE and DE legislation and the continued maintenance of pre-grant patent opposition.[223]

A quantitative analysis of Israel's pharmaceutical exports and imports reveals how pharmaceuticals became yet another high-margin export business (like weapons) derived from misappropriated U.S. innovations and preferential access. According to WTO data, in 1990 Israel exported only $80 million in pharmaceuticals while importing $180 million—a category trade deficit of $100 million. Weaker IP regimes were mandated in 2005, and by the year 2007 Israel was exporting $3.51 billion (74 percent destined for the United States under the USIFTA) and importing only $1.11 billion—a net category surplus of $2.4 billion. Israeli pharmaceuticals accounted for 10 percent of all Israeli industrial exports, reaching more than 120 countries.[224]

Israeli Pharmaceutical Imports, Exports, Surplus[225]

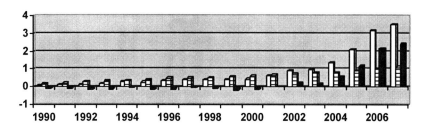

☐ Israel Pharmaceutical Exports ⊟ Israeli Pharmaceutical Imports ■ Surplus

U.S. pharmaceutical innovations that are detached from U.S. rights holders by the Israeli legal regime and MOH to be monetized by "free riding" Israeli manufacturers and marketed in the U.S. have a special designation—an "at risk" product launch. Despite Israel's placement on the USTR watch list in 2009, Teva Pharmaceutical Industries showed no sign of slowing its aggressive production and marketing of generic versions of U.S. patent-protected formulations, taking advantage of U.S. regulatory jurisdiction conflicts. On July 7, 2009, Teva was forced to stop shipping a generic version of the birth control pill Ortho Tri-Cyclen after Johnson & Johnson filed a patent infringement lawsuit. Teva had already received FDA approval for its generic version, shipping under the name of Tri-Lo Sprintec, in an "at risk" launch into a $400 million American market held by Johnson & Johnson.

The Israeli government has been unapologetic toward American industries, innovators, and workers. In March of 2008, in response to the USTR's third sequential placement of Israel on the "Priority Watch List," the Ministry of Foreign Affairs highlighted the USTR's weakness:

> The Government of Israel maintains that its intellectual property law regime, including acquisition, maintenance and enforcement of intellectual property rights, is modern, effective and exceeds uniform minimum standards set forth in multilateral treaties regulating large aspects of intellectual property standards. Intellectual property law provides for monopolies limited in time and scope with respect to, inter alia, inventions, trademarks, and works of copyright, such as computer software, films and recorded music....Despite Israel's 2007 ranking on the watch lists, no claim has ever been commenced against Israel by USTR alleging failure to maintain a treaty obligation, and it is the position of the Government of Israel that its intellectual property regime fully conforms to its treaty obligations. Accordingly, maintaining Israel on any of the watch lists is unjustified.[226]

Israel's hardened stance against the rights of U.S. producers and disdain for the USTR indicate that little progress will likely result from USTR efforts to create "positive dialogue," promised "preparatory" work to change regulations, and periodic treaty reviews, which make no attempt to obtain damages for past misappropriation of U.S. intellectual property.

In Israel, U.S. patent regimes are depicted as "overly generous to U.S. companies." In the U.S., pharmaceutical companies have been portrayed by Israeli legal experts as "bullies" trying to block cheaper generic drugs from reaching U.S. consumers.[227] In 2008, Israel attempted to get off the USTR watch list not by harmonizing or rolling back its controversial laws, but by mobilizing the Israel lobby to enlist 28 members of the U.S. Congress to write letters in protest. This effort failed to secure watch list removal.[228] Teva's CEO refers to drug innovators as "monopolies…trying to stop the exports of our generic medicines abroad through so-called legal means."[229] Teva has deployed an army of lawyers across the U.S. that rivals the Sonneborn network and LAKAM in its ability to win IP for Israeli production.

Israel first passed patent laws in 1967 allowing Israeli companies to copy any drug if foreign patent holders didn't actively market it in Israel.[li] Early on, Teva Pharmaceutical Industries Ltd. received domestic approval to copy drugs and carved out a market in Israel by becoming the most efficient copycat manufacturer.[230] Currently, although 10 percent of the estimated $250 billion the United States spends on pharmaceuticals each year goes for generics, Teva's strategy is to take over production of $92 billion worth of U.S. branded drugs with the assistance of its multitude of lawyers deployed in Israel and across the United States.[231]

After Congress passed the 1984 Hatch-Waxman legislation[lii] loosening rules for launching generic drugs, Teva transformed itself into a legal powerhouse by building a vast network of international subsidiaries devoted to "at risk" launches and legal challenges to drug innovators. Under the Hatch-Waxman Act, the first company to file a patent challenge wins 180 days of market exclusivity. This legal maneuver is Teva's main source of competitive advantage. Teva reports that between 2003 and 2006, it won eight cases, settled eight, and lost

---

[li] According to Teva and Israeli regulators, such a law was necessary to counteract the Arab Boycott, which discouraged multinational pharmaceutical companies from dealing with Israel.

[lii] The Drug Price Competition and Patent Term Restoration Act of 1984 promoted generics while attempting to sustain the financial incentive for research and development. It allows generics to seek FDA marketing approval by submitting "bioequivalence studies" rather than much costlier clinical trial data, eliminating the requirement for extensive human testing of generics. The law allowed generic companies to market drugs if they convinced a court that their products didn't violate any patents while proving that their copies were equivalent to the original drug.

two, while being involved in 50 patent challenges. It is a numbers game; the Israeli generic manufacturer realizes that if it files enough challenges, it diversifies its risk enough to reap huge profits. One law firm estimated Teva can capture "80 percent of the innovators' market—sometimes within two months" through huge numbers of patent challenges.[232]

Around the world Teva operates in 50 markets, with 44 manufacturing sites, 15 generic R&D centers, and 18 facilities that generate active pharmaceutical ingredients aimed at producing 36 billion tablets and capsules in 2006.[233] Of 250 patent lawyers in Israel, half work in pharmaceuticals, and Teva alone demands the services of 100. Teva trains its in-house lawyers to "look at other people's patents, assess them, and decide when to attack and when to challenge them." If Teva can't disqualify patents on drugs with significant markets, it opts for "bypass" by using substitute compounds (such as magnesium for calcium) to launch a "bioequivalent" generic version of a patented drug. U.S. innovators have been forced to devote more resources to defending patents at the cost of innovation and R&D.[234]

As employment in generic pharmaceuticals in Israel grew to 7,000 by 2007, global pharmaceutical innovators faced an unpleasant tradeoff. They could invest in manufacturing in Israel, while facing accelerated commercialization of their patents from Ministry of Health leaks, or stay out of the market entirely and be publicly chastised for "never investing a penny" in Israel.[235]

The unique regulatory framework that is the basis of Israel's pharmaceutical industry has fed another serious challenge to the rule of law—counterfeit Israeli pharmaceuticals and illegal narcotics trafficking. In 2008, Israel ranked as the eighth largest pharmaceutical counterfeiter in the $75 billion world market. Counterfeit pharmaceuticals kill thousands around the world each year due to poor quality and lack of active ingredients and physician oversight. A Knesset member insisted that "pharmaceutical enforcement manpower should be doubled, and entities beyond the police, such as the Health Ministry and the Tax Authority, should be authorized to deal with the problem…The emphasis should be on immediate sanctions rather than extended legal proceedings, so that this trade won't pay."[236] But Israeli law enforcement seems to be unaware of how the overall climate of a renegade regulatory regime degrades the entire industry.

Nowhere is this more apparent than in the trafficking of illegal narcotics. In 2003, the U.S. State Department placed Israel at the center of international Ecstasy trafficking. "Israeli drug-trafficking organizations are the main source of distribution of the drug to groups in the U.S, using express mail services, commercial airlines, and recently also using air cargo services." A Drug Enforcement Administration (DEA) report found that "Israeli drug traffickers, perhaps thanks to their long-standing ties in Antwerp, continue to be the major elements in the transfer of large shipments of Ecstasy from Belgium [to the United States]." The DEA believes that Israeli mobsters operating in the Belgian diamond smuggling trade became Ecstasy traffickers when Antwerp became the drug's major export hub to the U.S. The common estimate was that Israeli criminals controlled 75 percent of the Ecstasy market in the U.S.[237]

From a historical perspective, the Israeli government's practices strongly resemble the Sonneborn smuggling ethic, transforming illicit acquisition of U.S. industrial munitions and weapons-making machines into more legitimate "joint projects" funded by the U.S. Israel's pharmaceutical innovation acquisition process also bears an uncanny resemblance to the mistreatment U.S. industries received during the 1984 leak of confidential U.S. business secrets during the USIFTA negotiations. But in pharmaceuticals, Israel and its U.S. lobby face a unified and well funded American industry willing to fight for control of sensitive American patents, the U.S. market, and its future of innovation.

Israeli access to the immense U.S. market has facilitated other activities that run contrary to American economic and national security interests in the Middle East. One primary U.S. import from Israel, gem diamonds, finances the construction of illegal colonies in Israeli-occupied West Bank territory. The revenue from such "settlement diamonds" further destabilizes the Middle East by radicalizing and rallying opposition to the United States.

Tariff- and quota-free access to the U.S. market massively increased the Israel exportation of pearls, precious stones, and metals. The category grew 13 percent per year between 1989 and 2007. Over the same period, revenues grew from $1.5 billion to $9.8 billion per year. Israel supplied half of total U.S. import demand ($19 billion) for such precious objects in 2008. The Israel Diamond Controller's office of the Ministry of Industry, Trade, and Labor reported that total 2008 diamond exports reached $6.2 billion. LLD Diamonds Ltd., owned by Israeli-American Lev Leviev, topped the list of exporters at $417 million.[238]

Leviev constructs Israeli settlements in the occupied West Bank through Danya Cebus, a subsidiary of the Africa-Israel company that subcontracted the construction of two settlements—Mattityahu East—to Shaya Boymelgreen. Danya Cebus is also constructing part of the huge settlements of Har Homa and Maale Adumim, which bisect the West Bank and weaken the longstanding U.S. foreign policy objective of peace negotiations leading to the creation of a viable Palestinian state. In 1999, Danya Cebus announced plans to build new homes in the settlement of Ariel through the subsidiary corporation LIDAR. Leviev also appears to be the sole realtor/developer of the settlement of Zufim.

The United Nations Children's Fund (UNICEF) advised Leviev that it would no longer partner with him or accept any contributions because of his ongoing illegal activity.[239] Leviev's retail outlets in Manhattan have been picketed and celebrities have been urged to refuse endorsements of his jewelry products. But the effect of Leviev's highly visible access to the U.S. market, which finances settlements, may rub off on U.S. industries doing business in other parts of the Middle East and Muslim world. When viewed alongside AIPAC's legislative activities that limit U.S. industry relations with these markets, Leviev's flagrant activities might seem purposefully provocative as a way to taint America's image in the region, except that illegal settlement financing from the United States is a much larger issue than Leviev.

Despite U.S., UN, and world opposition to illegal settlement building, in 2005 Shimon Peres estimated that "Israel has spent about $50 billion since 1977...Other former finance ministers and government officials don't discount a price tag— commonly floated but never documented—of $60 billion."[240] David Newman, a political scientist at Israel's Ben Gurion University who researches settlement finance, pointed to ongoing misuse of U.S. tax-exempt donations by the Jewish Agency (which had its American Section shut down by the Kennedy/Johnson administration) and World Zionist Organization (which formed a U.S. shell corporation to replace the Jewish Agency in New York in 1971). Instead of financing startup lobbying groups in the U.S. as they did during the 1960s, the quasi-governmental organizations expropriate or purchase lands for illegal settlements with laundered donations.[241] The U.S. Treasury Department, which has the most visibility into financial flows between the U.S. and Israel, has done nothing to stop illegal settlement finance or the misuse and laundering of charitable tax-exempt donations.

The Israel lobby has long maintained preferential access to the U.S. Treasury. Henry Morgenthau Jr. fought to wrest control of the resettlement of displaced persons in Europe from the U.S. State Department during WWII. When President Roosevelt dragged his feet over policy takeover demands, Morgenthau threatened to turn the State Department into an election year scandal. Anti-Semitism at State, he threatened, was a charge that would "require little more in the way of proof for this suspicion to explode into a nasty scandal." Morgenthau's aides facilitated the European movements and communications of Irgun (a pre-state militant Jewish terrorist organization fighting in Palestine) with U.S. government resources.[242]

In 1959, Fred Scribner, a U.S. Treasury undersecretary, confidentially recommended during a meeting with top Zionist organizations that they needed to restructure their operations in order to avoid problems with the Eisenhower administration, the IRS, and the U.S. Department of Justice.[243] When the effort failed to stave off Kennedy's later effort to register the Israel lobby as foreign agents, AIPAC and other members redoubled their efforts to influence the U.S. Treasury Department. By 2005, at least one U.S. Treasury unit was under "regulatory capture" of the lobby, which helped deter its use as a tool against illegal settlement finance.[liii]

[liii] Regulatory capture occurs when an agency created to act in the public interest instead acts in favor of the interest of the sector it is charged with regulating. This occurs because groups with high-stakes interests in the outcome of enforcement, policy, or regulatory issues can be expected to focus their resources and energies on achieving the policy outcomes they prefer. Members of the general public, each with only a tiny (though often quite consequential) individual stake in the outcome, usually ignore the issue altogether, or mount inconsequential protests.

In early 2004, AIPAC and its associated think tank, the Washington Institute for Near East Policy (WINEP), were instrumental in lobbying President George W. Bush to create the new Office of Terrorism and Financial Intelligence (TFI) by executive order.[244] The Israel lobby vetted Stuart Levey, whom President Bush then approved to lead the new unit. TFI claims to be "safeguarding the financial system against illicit use and combating rogue nations, terrorist facilitators, weapons of mass destruction (WMD) proliferators, money launderers, drug kingpins, and other national security threats." TFI has delivered numerous briefings to AIPAC's think tank and contracts its employees as consultants. However, despite numerous taxpayer-financed trips to Jerusalem, the TFI leadership has taken no visible steps to stem illegal settlement financing by charitable or private organizations—a core issue driving conflict in the Middle East, according to the statements of former U.S. presidents.

The U.S. Treasury and U.S. trade treaty enforcement agencies (such as USTR and ITC) have never been effectively deployed to prosecute systematic violators. Some of this inaction can be attributed to "regulatory capture," which not only undermines the U.S. economy, but lays tripwires for future wars that are not in the American interest.

Conclusion

The USIFTA is an anomaly among other bilateral intergovernmental managed trade pacts negotiated by the U.S. USIFTA offers benefits to only one party while presenting threats to major industries. The core drivers of USIFTA trade policies, which sacrifice U.S. worker income and wealth creation along with the nation's competitiveness, have subsequently been imbedded in much larger multilateral treaties such as NAFTA.

The lack of coordination by U.S. enforcement and regulatory agencies places American firms at a disadvantage against "at risk" pharmaceutical launches that violate patents. The USTR refuses to treat Israeli espionage as an intellectual property or treaty violation issue, instead referring it to agencies enforcing arms and other export controls.

At the regional level, the Israel lobby has used its influence to successfully undermine and thwart greater U.S. export access to the Arab market while financing illegal activity—from settlement construction to counterfeit pharmaceuticals—that is only possible due to Israel's preferential access to U.S. consumer markets and proprietary American innovations.

"The fact is that the U.S.-Israel Free Trade Agreement served as a wedge that opened up the Congress to Free Trade Agreements throughout the world, including the NAFTA agreement." **Martin Indyk, Brookings Institution Saban Center for Middle East Policy**[245]

"The first such treaty between America and another nation, it [USIFTA] provides the impetus for explosive growth in trade and investment and sets a precedent for future agreements between the United States and other nations." **1998 AIPAC "Fifty Years of Friendship" brochure**[246]

The Möbius Strip of Immunity

The Israel lobby was the critical factor behind the Bush administration's disastrous 2003 invasion of Iraq.[247] Although the long-term human and economic fallout of this unnecessary war has not yet been entirely accounted for, one outcome could have been predicted even before the invasion began: none of the authors or influencers who had pushed for the war since the mid-1990s would ever face any consequences. The mechanics of such immunity can be traced at the individual level along the career path of Martin Indyk, AIPAC's former deputy director of research, who edited the 1984 promotional booklet "A US-Israel Free Trade Area, How Both Sides Win" in the months following AIPAC's acquisition of the classified ITC report. Indyk made a mundane analysis of the USIFTA legacy in 2006:

> The whole free trade agreement process was started with the U.S.-Israel Free Trade Agreement. Why? Because that was the only way the…Reagan administration, could get it through Congress was with AIPAC's help. And once they established the free trade agreement with Israel it became possible to get free trade agreements and that was the precursor to NAFTA and so on.[248]

AIPAC's objective, as stated in "A US-Israel Free Trade Area, How Both Sides Win," was to stitch the U.S. and Israeli economies together. It accurately predicted that the "resulting network of interconnections between the two nations' economies…would strengthen the commitment the United States already has to Israel's survival and prosperity." Like the Iraq war, USIFTA brought few of the benefits to Americans that the Israel lobby had predicted.

Martin Indyk was a major contributor to USIFTA and the Iraq debacle, and his odyssey from native Australian to American Middle East policymaker is important to understand, as is the history of his key financial backer. When Indyk was researching AIPAC's lobbying material for USIFTA, he was not yet even a U.S. citizen; that he gained indirectly from his longtime benefactor, Israeli-American media entrepreneur and American Israel Public Affairs Committee (AIPAC) super donor Haim Saban.

Saban was famously quoted by the *New York Times* on Sept. 5, 2004 as saying he spent "hours at a time on the phone with Ariel Sharon" and declaring, "I'm a one-issue guy, and my issue is Israel." Saban played a decisive role in shaping President Bill Clinton's foreign policy by distributing largesse to the Democratic Party and subsidizing a stable of political appointees-in-waiting. Saban hosted a $3.5 million fundraiser for Democrats during Clinton's presidential campaign against George H.W. Bush, and was so anxious to maintain his lead donor influence with the Democratic Party that when he learned another donor had topped his contributions by a quarter-million dollars, he immediately sent the DNC a $1 bill clipped to a $250,000 check.

Saban served advising the White House on President Clinton's Export Council. In 1993 the Clinton administration adopted a copy of the Israeli strategy for "dual containment" first lobbied by Martin Indyk at the Washington Institute for Near East Policy. This strategy called for more direct U.S. presence against Iraq and Iran in the Middle East, rather than the less intensive strategy of "offshore balancing."[249] Saban lobbied to install Martin Indyk as U.S. ambassador to Israel in 1995. As an ineligible foreign national, Indyk first had to receive rush preferential naturalization. Then, while he was serving in Israel, Indyk had his State Department security clearances revoked for mishandling classified U.S. information.[250]

In 2001 Saban sold his interest in the cable television channel Fox Family Worldwide for $1.5 billion. Matthew G. Krane, who did tax planning for Saban, connected him with the Seattle-based Quellos Group in order to create a shelter to reduce Saban's taxes from $150 million to zero. This freed up the media-savvy Saban's resources, allowing him to pledge $13 million to fund the new Saban Center for Middle East Policy at the Brookings Institution in 2002. Martin Indyk became its director just in time to push for the U.S. invasion of Iraq.

In 2003, Brookings was the single most cited think tank in the American news media. The Saban Center played a vital public relations role by creating the appearance of full-spectrum left-right political support for the U.S. invasion of Iraq. Brookings' exhortations for war, immortalized in Martin Indyk's essay "Lock and Load," assured Americans that Saddam Hussein probably possessed weapons of mass destruction, but that Iraq could be neutralized by U.S. military force – if it moved quickly enough.[251]

In 2006, Saban's fortunes turned. He was forced to tell Senate investigators about Krane and the Quellos tax shelter. The shelter was invalidated and Saban was forced to pay $250 million in back taxes and penalties. But he soon bounced back. In the 2008 Obama-versus-Clinton race for the Democratic presidential nomination, Haim Saban offered two superdelegates at the Young Democrats of America a $1 million contribution to their nonprofit organization in return for voting for Hillary Clinton at the convention.[252] Four independent witnesses claimed this alleged bribe occurred right before the North Carolina and Indiana primaries, though Saban denied it and no criminal charges were ever filed.

Matthew G. Krane, who received $36 million from Quellos, soon came to the attention of investigators looking into his offshore banking arrangements and a passport application under the assumed name of "Christopher Sullivan." On July 21, 2009, Krane filed a civil suit against Saban in Los Angeles Superior Court. The suit threatened to expose "perpetual fraudulent and deceptive conduct" in business and tax strategies, as well as secret foreign policy dealings and demands for special treatment in return for political donations. Krane's suit details his contention that his criminal prosecution came in lieu of Saban's own and that it was evidence of corruption and influence peddling.[253]

A circumstantial case can be made that operating from behind the scenes, Saban attempted to rig an election (Young Democrats), mishandled classified U.S. national defense information (the Indyk security breach in Israel), and pushed a disastrous and costly war that was not in the American interest (Iraq). Saban is only the latest incarnation of an almost stereotypical archetype—the immune financial backer of illicit activity—that emerges repeatedly in the history of Israeli smuggling, espionage, and other wrongdoing against the U.S. A recently concluded incident illustrates how this archetype eludes both law enforcement and personal culpability.

In May of 1985, former Air Force and NATO advisor Richard Kelley Smyth was charged by a federal grand jury with smuggling over 800 krytons to Israel. The kryton, invented in 1934 for use in high-speed photography, was considered dual-use technology. Civilian uses of the small glass bulbs included laser photocopying machines and strobe lights, but because krytons were also used to trigger nuclear weapons, federal law forbade their sale overseas without a permit. The State Department specifically listed krytons as munitions requiring approval and a license for export.

At the time of his arrest, Smyth was president of an export and engineering business in Huntington Beach, California called Milco International Incorporated. Milco provided aviation consulting through U.S. military contracts as well as sales and export facilitation. Milco had close ties to Aaron Milchan, a partner in the Israeli-based Heli Trading Company, which imported the krytons. Milchan worked closely with Smyth to transfer the krytons to Israel for resale to the Israeli government. Milchan later claimed that his company was really used as a "conduit" by the Israeli government for trading with the United States.[254] Milchan also shared in Milco's profits, along with Smyth family members and friends who were stockholders.[255] Documents obtained by NBC News from Milco indicated Smyth had exported other equipment to Israel, including chemicals used to make missile fuel. Smyth posted $100,000 bail, but then failed to appear for his trial; soon afterward, he was seen in Israel, but the Israeli government refused to cooperate with the thwarted U.S. criminal prosecution.[256]

At the beginning of the incident, in the early 1980s, billionaire Aaron Milchan did not seem a likely candidate for nuclear technology smuggling. A dual citizen of Israel and Monaco and a personal friend of Shimon Peres, Milchan was most widely known in the U.S. as a Hollywood film mogul, cavorting with Robert De Niro, Jerry Lewis, and Martin Scorsese at the Cannes film festival in 1983.[liv] Milchan publicly denied that he had done anything illegal in collaboration with Smyth during interviews with NBC News in 1992 and 1993.[257]

But then, in July of 2001, Smyth was arrested in Costa del Sol in Malaga, Spain shortly after filling out a bank account application. At the age of 72, Smyth was extradited back to the United States and held without bail for trial in California's Central District Court. Although Smyth's defense lawyer James Riddet had already admitted to the news media that Smyth shipped the krytons after his client skipped bail, Smyth entered a not guilty plea.[258]

Before Smyth's arrest, during interviews with both *60 Minutes* and *Los Angeles Magazine*, Milchan alluded to both personal involvement and immunity. To *Los Angeles Magazine*, he brashly stated, "Let's assume that there's nothing that Israel and the United States do separately....I'll say it in my own words. I love Israel, and any way I can help Israel, I will. I'll do it again and again...If you say I am an arms dealer, that's your problem. In Israel, there is practically no business that does not have something to do with defense." Milchan probably felt free to speak by that time, since the statute of limitations had run out on any potential smuggling charge. But after Smyth was captured, U.S. customs officials expressed their interest in prosecuting anyone who had helped Smyth flee the U.S. on obstruction of justice charges. When the news media attempted to contact Milchan about Smyth's arrest in Spain, Milchan was "traveling and could not be reached for comments."[259]

The court ultimately dismissed all but two of 30 counts against Smyth, who was found guilty of violating the Arms Export Control Act and False Statements to Government Agencies. Smyth was fined $20,000 and sentenced to 40 months in federal prison, but also made eligible for immediate parole. The presiding judge, Pamela Ann Rymer, denied Smyth's request to reconsider or reduce the sentence and provide immediate parole, stating, "All of the mitigating circumstances applicable to Smyth and his family were fully and carefully considered before imposing sentence. Age, health, record, and family circumstances among other things were factored into the balance....Nothing presently brought to my attention causes me to reduce or alter the sentence."[260]

[liv] Milchan was born in Tel Aviv, British Mandate of Palestine. His father owned a fertilizer company that Aaron turned into a successful chemical business. Milchan produced the motion pictures *Once Upon a Time in America* (1984), *Brazil* (1985), and *Pretty Woman* (1990), as well as Oliver Stone's film *JFK* (1991) and many others. He launched New Regency Productions in 1991.

While the court allowed Smyth to continue using his assumed name, "Jon Shiller," it required that any employment requiring licensing by local state or federal officials be first approved by the probation office.[261] According to the Bureau of Prisons, Smyth was finally released on November 28, 2003. But like Daniel Halpern, the internationally mobile Milchan was a dead end and untouchable to prosecutors.

Smyth told the court that he had decided to flee the U.S. because his attorney told him he would go to prison, for a sentence the news media estimated could be as high as 105 years. "That was a grave mistake and error on my part...I wish I had never done it. My wife, Emilie and I wish to spend the rest of our lives surrounded by our families and peers."[262] Like Ben Ami Kadish, Smyth took advantage of his advanced age to escape both the harsh penalties of a long sentence and a plea bargain and collaboration with prosecutors that might have led to further prosecutions of the true masterminds and financiers of the operation. Smyth never answered the most important question—who had subsidized his 16 years on the run after he jumped bail? In 2009, as the news media began reporting that Milchan was an undercover Israeli agent, he made arrangements to relocate permanently to Israel.[263]

In the 1940s, Rudolph Sonneborn and Henry Montor successfully avoided prosecutorial attention, which lightly fell on lower-level operatives like Schwimmer, Winters, and Greenspun. Robert Nathan and the Sonneborn/Jewish Agency delegation lobbied FBI director J. Edgar Hoover by saying that none of their illegal activities would have an adverse impact on the United States. It paid off: the financial masterminds of the smuggling network evaded criminal liability for their front company operations. Their cause, when known, was popularized in the United States by favorable press. Their contemporary incarnations, such as media moguls Haim Saban and Aaron Milchan, operate in an even more favorable environment, bolstered by years of intense public relations efforts for Israel in the United States, including decades of Hollywood movies portraying Israelis as heroic and Arabs as evil untrustworthy terrorists.[264] History seems to be repeating itself, as even the Sonneborn network's Latin America operations appear to be periodically rejuvenated, with new twists, actors, and locales.

Israel shadowed the 2009 U.S. relocation of its primary Andean region air bases from facilities leased in Ecuador to Colombia. Colombia purchased $150 million in upgrades for its obsolete Kfir jet fighters, justified on the basis of fighting guerrillas. By purchasing Israeli weapons, the Colombian government may have been triangulating AIPAC's support in an arena where the lobby has already proven quite capable—passing preferential free trade legislation. Colombia has tried to move its stalled bilateral free trade agreement forward in Congress.[265] The key stumbling block is Colombia's long record of violence against journalists and labor rights activists—particularly at the hands of paramilitaries. Ironically, Israeli arms dealers in the past have trained and sold advanced weaponry to Colombian paramilitary groups. But if the Colombian government is trying to activate AIPAC and gain favor in Congress by providing a large market for Israeli weapons, it could get much more than it bargained for.

Shortly after an aged Colombian Kfir crashed in June of 2009, news reports circulated of successful Colombian air strikes on FARC guerillas. The U.S. does not appear to be interested in precipitating a wider regional conflict from its new airbases in the Andean region, and there appear to be no Israeli counterinsurgency trainers included as part of the new Kfir deal (unlike Israel's Honduras Kfir proposal made during the Contra war). Nevertheless, Israel's foreign minister, Avigdor Lieberman, has made conflict (and lucrative future arms sales for Israel) much more likely by turning up the rhetorical heat. Lieberman loudly accused Venezuela's president of cooperating with Islamic extremists and anti-Semites during his July 2009 "friendship" tour through Latin America.[266] Israel's deadly drive for arms sales appears poised to return to Latin America, even as Israel's lobby pushes for U.S. military strikes on Iran.

The disastrous invasion of Iraq and USIFTA-inspired trade policies have both contributed to the slowing economy and rising unemployment in the U.S. America may soon cease to be the source of limitless support that the Sonneborn network once tapped. AIPAC's subversion of U.S. industries, sensible foreign policymaking, support for the Iraq war, and potentially devastating new military adventures with Iran could take a final and fatal toll on the future prosperity of America. The continued failures of the Justice Department in this dangerous new environment are perhaps most troubling of all.

The Economic Espionage Act has been toothless against Israel and its lobby for lack of prosecutorial will and necessary political cover. As of 2009, six cases have been quietly settled before trial since the Economic Espionage Act was passed.[267] Only one has ever been successfully prosecuted—involving a Boeing engineer trafficking secrets to China.[268] Although the perpetrator's defense mirrored the standard Sonneborn/Israel lobby claims of "no harm," alleging that illicit tech transfers would make China more like the U.S. than the U.S. like China, jurors found it unconvincing and delivered a conviction in 2009.[lv] For Israeli espionage, however, the "no harm" plea still deters prosecutions.

The Department of Justice and FBI have rarely received enough political cover to investigate and prosecute the Israel lobby violators who really matter— powerful top-level operatives ensconced among the nation's elite and providing strategy and money. They are not only protected by a phalanx of lawyers, but also capable of leaving the country on very short notice to await more favorable conditions.

Marc Rich was one such case. Indicted in the U.S. for tax evasion and illegal oil deals with Iran during the 1970s-1980s hostage crisis, Rich simply stayed outside

---

[lv] In pre-trial defense motions to convince the presiding judge to drop espionage charges against AIPAC's Rosen and Weissman, the same argument was made— that the U.S.'s and Israel's objectives were "the same," so no espionage could have actually occurred.

the U.S. until he arranged an unprecedented pardon from President Bill Clinton on January 20, 2001. Eric Holder, acting as deputy attorney general, gave Clinton a "neutral, leaning towards favorable" opinion to pardon the Switzerland-based fugitive financier after a quiet and intense campaign by the Israel lobby and Ehud Barak and Shimon Peres of the Israeli government.[269] In the 1980s, DOJ officials evaluating the prospects for a successful prosecution of AIPAC looked up through the chain of command and saw William French Smith. In 2009, the person in that position is Eric Holder. When efforts to enforce U.S. laws against the Israel lobby appeared to be finally headed toward trial in 2009, it triggered spurious but highly effective charges of anti-Semitism in addition to the vast accommodations by ruling judge T.S. Ellis that would have seemed absurd if operatives for any other country had been under indictment.

The FBI seemed to finally win a long-delayed victory against the Israel lobby in 2005, when Pentagon Colonel Lawrence Franklin pled guilty to passing national defense information to two AIPAC employees, Steven J. Rosen and Keith Weissman. The FBI recorded conversations of classified national defense information exchanges between Rosen, Weissman, and Naor Gilon, the political officer at the Israeli embassy. In 2004, the FBI found Franklin in possession of 83 classified government documents at his home. Confronted and intimidated, Franklin agreed to wear a wire to future meetings with AIPAC officials in an FBI sting operation.

Perhaps mindful of past challenges handling classified material, the AIPAC officials refused to receive the documents Franklin offered as bait, but did read and quickly pass information favorable to their lobbying initiatives to contacts at the Israeli embassy and *Washington Post*. The FBI then raided AIPAC's Washington, DC headquarters twice, seizing hard drives for evidence. Colonel Franklin's boss, Douglas J. Feith, immediately resigned in January of 2005 as law enforcement officials raced to find out how information had leaked to the Iranian government via Ahmed Chalabi that the U.S. had broken Iranian communications codes. According to court documents, the investigation of AIPAC had been ongoing since 1999. Rosen and Weissman were criminally indicted and Franklin was sentenced to receive a $10,000 fine, 150 months in prison, and three years of supervised release, all suspended pending the outcome of a criminal trial against AIPAC operatives in which he would be the star witness.

But even with wiretap evidence and a credible witness, the prosecution quickly bogged down between 2005 and 2009 over pre-trial defense team maneuvers and appeals. In 2006, defense team lawyers rolled out their most eloquent "no harm" appeal for presiding Judge T.S. Ellis to get the Espionage Act[lvi] charges dropped:

[lvi] The Act reads, "Whoever, lawfully or unlawfully having possession of, access to, control over, or being entrusted with any document, writing, code book, signal book, sketch, photograph, photographic negative, blue print, plan, map,

> There's a disjunctive, your Honor. The disjunctive says "injure the
> United States or assist or benefit the advantage of a foreign
> country." How can anybody apply that in a context in which good
> foreign policy for the United States, that clearly is intended to help
> make the United States' foreign policy better, may also have a
> derivative impact that makes it an advantage to an ally of the
> United States, whose interest are exactly the same?[270]

The establishment media and First Amendment lawyers waded in, claiming that the "two lobbyists, in receiving and disseminating classified information, are doing what journalists, academics, and experts at think tanks do every day."[271] In 2007, a corporate media consortium[lvii] even filed an "Emergency Motion for Leave to Intervene" that Judge Ellis not allow Classified Information Procedures Act (CIPA) processes to protect secret information from being exposed in open court. [272]

In 2008, Judge Ellis ordered that incredible concessions be made to the defense, effectively scuttling the governing legal statutes. Ellis allowed expert testimony from a classification expert (whom prosecutors had consulted about the case and insisted was banned from testifying) about whether the defendants could have been in a "state of mind" in which they believed their conduct was lawful. The 1917 Espionage Act under which they were charged was silent on such issues.[273] In 2008, the *Washington Post* and *Wall Street Journal* ran editorials urging Attorney General Michael Mukasey to quash the case. The Jewish Telegraphic Agency (formerly a wholly owned subsidiary of the Jewish Agency[274]) even published an article from the defense counsel Abe Lowell urging an outright "uprising" across America.

> "I would like the community to rise up and, having seen all the
> public information, as a community start saying to the world, the
> Jewish world and the non-Jewish world, and the media, to the

---

model, instrument, appliance, or note relating to the national defense, willfully communicates or transmits or attempts to communicate or transmit the same to any person not entitled to receive it, or willfully retains the same and fails to deliver it on demand to the officer or employee of the United States entitled to receive it....shall be punished by a fine of not more than $10,000, or by imprisonment for not more than two years, or both."

lvii Newspaper Guild, Communications Workers of America, the Radio-Television News Directors Association, Reuters America LLC, the Society of Professional Journalists, Time Inc., the Washington Post, the Hearst Corp., the Reporters Committee for Freedom of the Press, ABC, the American Society of Newspaper Editors, the Associated Press, Dow Jones & Company, and the Newspaper Association of America.

> Justice Department and the attorney general: 'Reconsider. This is
> wrong. You made a mistake," Lowell said.
>
> "AIPAC and other groups that got snookered, they should admit
> they got snookered, and they should both embrace these men."[275]

The prosecution appealed the court's pre-trial "state of mind" ruling, but lost in the spring of 2009. After the election of Barack Obama, calls in the press shifted from pleas to protect "freedom of speech" toward quashing the trial as a rebuke to the legacy of pervasive Bush administration secrecy. The government prosecutors dropped their case against Rosen and Weissman on May 1, 2009, citing the "unexpectedly higher evidentiary threshold in order to prevail at trial." The *New York Times* noted that Joseph Persichini Jr. — the top official at the FBI's Washington office—was "disappointed," while FBI agents were "infuriated."

The *New York Times* also hinted at politicization, reporting that the decision chain extended from career attorneys through political appointees all the way up to Attorney General Eric Holder, who approved dropping the case. Dana J. Boente, Obama's new acting U.S. attorney for the Eastern District of Virginia, was omnipresent at negotiations. Boente's formal statement seemed to exude remorse: "Given the…inevitable disclosure of classified information that would occur at any trial in this matter, we have asked the court to dismiss the indictment." But with Lawrence Franklin's conviction still standing, for the Israel lobby, the case wasn't yet over.

On May 19, 2009, a coalition of 125 rabbis signed a letter to Attorney General Eric Holder requesting a probe into whether "anti-Semitism and/or anti-Israel sentiments" played any role in the original investigation of AIPAC. Michelle Boorstein and the *Washington Post* rolled out the heavy guns, publishing an article titled "Was Case Against AIPAC Lobbyists Anti-Semitic?" It sternly noted that the case "wasn't a total loss for the government" because it did win Franklin's guilty plea. That plea was the only remaining evidence that wrongdoing occurred, but for the Israel lobby, that was totally unacceptable. On May 14, 2009, U.S. attorneys filed sealed motions to reduce Lawrence Franklin's sentence to a fine and time in a halfway house, which Judge Ellis accepted.

That AIPAC had once again obtained classified information was never in doubt during the entire run up to the aborted trial. According to a legal filing by Steven J. Rosen (also present at AIPAC during the 1984 classified document affair), handling classified information continued to be routine:

> To control the flow of such information, government agencies in
> the field of foreign policy have designated individuals with the
> authority to determine and differentiate which information
> disclosures would be harmful to the United States, and which
> disclosures would benefit the United States through the work of
> their agencies and would not be harmful to the United States. To
> maintain liaison with the authorized agency officials who at times
> are willing to provide such information, organizations like AIPAC

have designated officials of their own who have the requisite
expertise and relationships to deal with government foreign policy
agencies. At AIPAC, Steve Rosen was one of the principal officials
who, along with Executive Director Howard Kohr and a few other
individuals, were expected to maintain relationships with such
agencies, receive such information, and share it with AIPAC Board
of Directors and its Senior Staff for possible further distribution.
AIPAC, and those defendants who were AIPAC officials and/or
members of its Board of Directors, knew that Mr. Rosen and others
at AIPAC were receiving such information and expected that they
would share it with them.[276]

But Israel lobby pundits continued to hammer away on "anti-Semitism" as the
sole explanation for why the FBI investigated and set up a sting against AIPAC.
Former FBI counterintelligence agent and supervisor I.C. Smith testified that
anti-Semitism in pursuing Israeli spying was "not my experience" during a
lengthy career in the FBI. "There was a great deal of frustration within the FBI in
dealing with the Israelis....In my time in the Intelligence Division [later the
National Security Division], the Israelis displayed a very real arrogance and with
their constant contacts on Capitol Hill, they showed a confidence that they could
do just about anything they wanted to do, and they could."[277]

But even after the latest AIPAC espionage flap was successfully put to rest by
the Department of Justice, questions linger and tug at the idea of equal justice
before the law. Haim Saban's name surfaced in a National Security Agency
phone intercept conducted in the year 2005 or 2006 between California
Congresswoman Jane Harman and an Israeli agent who was the target of a U.S.
government investigation. Harman, the ranking minority member of the House
Intelligence Committee, allegedly agreed to "waddle in" to the U.S. prosecution
of two AIPAC lobbyists. In return for Harman's help, the Israeli agent said he
would have one of House Minority Leader Nancy Pelosi's major campaign
donors—Haim Saban—withhold contributions to Pelosi until Harman was
appointed chair of the intelligence panel.[278]

The wiretap story was broken by Jeff Stein of *Congressional Quarterly* on April
19, 2009, shortly before the Obama administration folded the criminal
prosecution of Rosen and Weissman. Was it an effort by disgruntled law
enforcement officials angered by the DOJ's imminent capitulation to AIPAC? Or
was the information purposely leaked to Stein for his exposé (and independent
confirmation by the *New York Times*) as a warning to Obama that pursuing the
AIPAC prosecution would present a systemic risk to his party and
administration? In retrospect, the outcome was the same as that of the Jewish
Agency's warning to J. Edgar Hoover that "important individuals and
organizations could be harmed" if it challenged the Sonneborn Institute in the
1940s, or the AZC backing down on the DOJ's request for FARA registration in
the midst of assassination and upheaval in the 1960s.

Douglas Bloomfield, who never suffered any liability from his handling of classified information during the 1984 USIFTA affair, was by 2009 publicly upbraiding AIPAC for even firing Rosen and Weissman after they were criminally indicted. Bloomfield even threatened to reveal AIPAC as a de facto foreign agent if it did not provide Rosen and Weissman with adequate financial compensation.

> In cutting loose the pair, AIPAC insisted it had no idea what they were doing. Not so, say insiders, former colleagues, sources close to the defense, and others familiar with the organization.
>
> One of the topics AIPAC won't want discussed, say these sources, is how closely it coordinated with Benjamin Netanyahu in the 1990s, when he led the Israeli Likud opposition and later when he was prime minister, to impede the Oslo peace process being pressed by President Bill Clinton and Israeli Prime Ministers Yitzhak Rabin and Shimon Peres.
>
> That could not only validate AIPAC's critics, who accuse it of being a branch of the Likud, but also lead to an investigation of violations of the Foreign Agents Registration Act.
>
> "What they don't want out is that even though they publicly sounded like they were supporting the Oslo process, they were working all the time to undermine it," said a well-informed source."[279]

Large numbers of Israel's supporters, both in the U.S. and abroad, continue to operate on the presumption that almost no crime against U.S. or international law will ever be punished if it is done in the name of Israel. Like Bloomfield, Thomas Dine, who was head of AIPAC during the economic espionage incident, never suffered any consequences. In 2009, Dine was even contracted to consult and lobby for the U.S.-taxpayer-funded al-Hurra satellite television network to help improve its competitive stance in the Middle East against Al-Jazeera and win over Arab viewers. Al-Hurra has received more than $600 million from Congress since it began broadcasting in 2004.[280]

Only increasing public awareness of the rising stakes of such endemic criminal behavior and "two-track justice" may ultimately change the American public's tolerance. But Americans have little hope for help from establishment media. During and after the AZC DOJ registration battle in the 1960s, the *New York Times* was suspiciously quiet about the implications of foreign agent registration. It may have had a reason for such silence. In 2008 it was revealed that a high-profile *New York Times* reporter was receiving foreign-funded payments via the AZC, along with hundreds of others.[281] In 2005 criminal indictments, the *Washington Post* was revealed receiving purloined information from AIPAC lobbyists.

Credible allegations made by former FBI contract translator Sibel Edmonds that the Israel lobby, in collusion with members of Congress and political appointees spread across U.S. agencies, was deeply involved in money laundering and nuclear technology smuggling[282] appear to present another systemic threat, not only to government, but also to the establishment media. The DOJ refuses to publicly investigate Edmonds's allegations, and no major American media outlet has followed up on them. But the public calls for warranted law enforcement that have gone unanswered for so long may soon create such a monumental crisis in governance and rule of law that even the most manipulated Congress or politicized Department of Justice will be unwise to ignore it.

Sonneborn, NUMEC, the Jewish Agency/AZC, Iran-Contra, the USIFTA classified document incident, the Franklin Rosen and Weissman espionage scandal, and the Sibel Edmonds allegations all lie along a Möbius[lviii] strip of Israel lobby operations twisting America toward expensive policies that repeatedly corrupt U.S. national interests. The most recent have not yet been fully exposed, but they could cause low confidence in government to plummet still further.

Colonel Lawrence Franklin, the sole conspirator convicted in the 2005 AIPAC espionage affair, worked under Paul Wolfowitz and Douglas Feith in the Pentagon Office of Special Plans (OSP). Their activities may have been targets of the FBI investigation. The tactics of neoconservative ideologues who twisted the 9/11 attacks into the disastrous, but long awaited (for neoconservatives) U.S. invasion of Iraq are only gradually coming to light.

Franklin and another OSP colleague met with Iran-Contra arms dealer Manuchar Ghorbanifar as well as Iranian government officials, dissidents, and exiles. At the secret meetings, they pushed for "regime change" in Iraq and Iran and exchanged intelligence, even as the long-term neoconservative drive for a U.S. overthrow of Saddam Hussein's regime in Iraq to "secure the realm"[283] for Israel was reaching its zenith.[284] Unlike the USIFTA or Pollard situations, this one involved a document that was insinuated *into* the U.S. government, starting a chain reaction that cost the U.S. more than a trillion dollars and a severe crisis of confidence.

In the December 2001 meeting, Franklin, Harold Rhode, and Michael Ledeen[lix] met with Ghorbanifar and a former senior Iranian Revolutionary Guard member who claimed to possess information about ranks of dissidents in the military. Italy's head of military intelligence (SISMI) Nicolo Pollari and the Italian minister

---

[lviii] A Möbius strip can be created by taking a paper strip and giving it a half-twist, then joining the ends of the strip together to form a twisted loop. An insect crawling the length of the strip would return to its starting point having traversed both sides of the strip, without ever crossing a sharp edge.

[lix] Former consultant to MacFarlane under Reagan, then consulted for Douglas Feith during the George W. Bush administration.

of defense also attended.[285] By October 18, Elisabetta Burba, an Italian journalist working for the magazine *Panorama*, had delivered forged Iraqi purchase orders for uranium ore from Niger to the CIA's Rome office.[286] Ledeen later confirmed that he had worked for *Panorama* as a paid columnist since the mid-1990s.[287]

A second Italian job occurred in February 2002 as Harold Rhode, an Egyptian, an Iraqi, and another high-level U.S. government official reviewed events in Iraq and the rest of the Middle East. In July of 2002, Ledeen outlined plans to continue "his work" with the Iranians, and by June of 2003, a Paris round involving Rhode and Ghorbanifar was underway.[288] On September 9, 2002, Nicolo Pollari personally lobbied the White House with the Niger forgeries in a secret meeting with Deputy National Security Advisor Stephen Hadley. In January 2003, President George W. Bush used "uranium from Africa" as a prime justification for the U.S. invasion of Iraq in his State of the Union address. Though the International Atomic Energy Agency took only hours to determine that the Niger uranium documents were crude forgeries, by March of 2003 it was already much too late.[289] By mid-2004, Ahmed Chalabi, long supported by neoconservatives as a potential new leader for Iraq, was cut off from U.S. financial support for disclosing to Iran's Ministry of Intelligence and Security that the U.S. had broken the Iranian intelligence services' secret communications code.[290]

According to Colonel Lawrence Franklin, George W. Bush's National Security Council felt no trepidation in working with Ghorbanifar, despite the aftermath of the Iran-Contra affair and the wariness of other intelligence agencies. "There was a no-contact order by the CIA on Ghorbanifar because of the agency's past unsatisfactory relationship with him. However, our mission was approved by the NSC. Moreover, we worked for the secretary of defense and were not subject to CIA authority. The CIA viewed us as [being] 'in their lane.' I invited the Defense Intelligence Agency to join us, as well as military intelligence representatives in Europe. They declined, fearful of the CIA's no-contact order."[291]

As with the USIFTA classified document incident, the origins of the Niger forgeries have never been revealed and those responsible for producing them have never been held accountable. Seymour Hersh reported that the forgery was a CIA operation.[292] Former counterterrorism officer Philip Giraldi also implicated the CIA.[293] Former Director of Intelligence Programs for the National Security Council Vincent Cannistraro suggests the Niger documents were forged in the United States in conjunction with Iraqi exile groups.[294] Others point to an unredacted investigatory report from the Italian parliament implicating Michael Ledeen as the obvious conduit for a report produced by former CIA officers (and Iran-Contra intriguer) Duane Clarridge and Alan Wolf.[295]

This sordid history of unprosecuted crimes unfolding along the Israel lobby Möbius strip has had two attributes: high costs distributed across Americans with no say in matters of vast economic consequence, and zero accountability for the true perpetrators. It was first commemorated in a painting Rudolph Sonneborn commissioned for David Ben-Gurion after he assumed leadership of the newly independent state of Israel. It shows the room in Sonneborn's penthouse apartment where the fateful 1945 meeting of powerful Americans determined to finance and arm a state of Israel took place. The room is depicted in precise detail; the chairs are set up in a semicircle. The accountability of the elite members of the Israel lobby who defy the rule of law is revealed in the finest detail of all: the room in the painting is completely empty.[296]

During the four-year run-up to the abandoned 2009 AIPAC espionage trial, Colonel Lawrence Franklin, the government's key witness, was approached by a man offering to help him "disappear" by faking his own suicide in order to circumvent the trial. Colonel Franklin simply and precisely identified how an Israel lobby operative in the United States[297] could still propose such an audacious corruption of the rule of law: "He's beyond good and evil. They're not subject to the laws the rest of us are."[298]

Conclusion

The elite financiers and leadership of the Israel lobby remain as immune from criminal prosecution today as they were during the reign of the Sonneborn network. Multiple citizenship, international mobility, massive amounts of political patronage, and most importantly, credible threats of systemic risk to the U.S. government have turned law enforcement away from their harmful activities and toward initiatives that advance Israel's sovereign objectives.

The subversion of prosecutorial will in the Department of Justice and judiciary has been rigorously enforced by constant pressure from the lobby, its allies in establishment media, key donors, political appointees, and friends in Congress. As in the time of Kennedy, changes in presidential administrations provide ample opportunity for derailing major Justice Department enforcement actions. This means that even "open and shut" criminal cases such as the AIPAC espionage incident simply cannot be successfully prosecuted in the United States, under the doctrine that the Israel lobby is "too connected to regulate" and that "important individuals and organizations" will be harmed. This immunity has opened the door for new Israel lobby maneuvers offshore that both echo the past and pose ever greater dangers to the rule of law and the U.S. economy.

The Israel lobby has an enduring value system that is both alien and harmful to America, handed down from the Sonneborn Institute and Haganah through the Jewish Agency's American Section and American Zionist Council to AIPAC: that no crime is punishable if it advances the cause of Israel. Only when the broader American public becomes fully aware of how the Israel lobby's value system is slowly corrupting and bankrupting the nation will the call for long-overdue law enforcement finally be heeded.

Afterword

The Israel lobby has become a major determinant of both U.S. Middle East and broader economic policies. Those who believe such policies are too flawed and costly to continue must challenge the system—and by necessity challenge the Israel lobby. But how do concerned Americans influence policy in an environment where dominant groups achieve and wield power by flouting the law decade after decade with impunity? What is our future as a nation if we allow such corruption of the rule of law to continue? Does the success of Israel's lobby imply that the only way to exercise relevant power in the United States is by taking actions that subvert the Constitution and our entire system of advice and consent governance? Does the Israel lobby now provide the behavioral model others must adopt in order to have a relevant influence on the future? And if that's true, are we as a nation now truly bordering on suicide, as Michael F. Scheuer suggests?

These important questions go utterly unexplored in the establishment media. They are not debated in Congress. Much of the grist for public debate is classified—often grudgingly—by frontline government employees on orders from higher up. But the unpunished wrongdoing that has been the object of consternation within counterespionage and law enforcement agencies is beginning to slowly wash into the public sphere.

Declassified documents and unintended revelations reveal that the lobby itself, in private, has repeatedly suggested the single most important deterrent to its illegal activities. Simon Rifkind told the Justice Department in 1963 that a smaller but well-resourced Jewish organization[lx] would "so publicize" its money laundering that an American Zionist Council FARA registration would "kill the movement." AIPAC's Steven J. Rosen sent a memo to fellow employees in 1982 stating, "A lobby is like a night flower. It thrives in the dark and withers in the light."[299]

New watchdogs are advancing the public exposure of Israel lobby wrongdoing through books, essays, public events, alternative media, paid news releases, and, most importantly, interactive discussions conducted over the Internet. As Americans begin to stand up and take notice of the growing breach between vastly harmful illegal activities and warranted law enforcement, a new era must finally dawn. Otherwise, as Lincoln predicted, through continued forbearance, we will author our own dark fate as a nation.

[lx] The American Council for Judaism

Appendix

AIPAC Executive Committee Organizations

Ameinu
American Friends of Likud
American Gathering/Federation of Jewish Holocaust Survivors
America-Israel Friendship League
American Jewish Committee
American Jewish Congress
American Jewish Joint Distribution Committee
American Sephardi Federation
American Zionist Movement
Americans for Peace Now
Americans for Israel and Torah
Anti-Defamation League
Association of Reform Zionists of America
B'nai B'rith International
Bnai Zion*
Central Conference of American Rabbis
Committee for Accuracy in Middle East Reporting in America
Development Corporation for Israel / State of Israel Bonds
Emunah of America
Friends of Israel Defense Forces
Hadassah, Women's Zionist Organization of America*
Hebrew Immigrant Aid Society
Hillel: The Foundation for Jewish Campus Life
Jewish Community Centers Association
Jewish Council for Public Affairs
Jewish Institute for National Security Affairs
Jewish Labor Committee
Jewish National Fund
Jewish Reconstructionist Federation
Jewish War Veterans of the USA
Jewish Women International
MERCAZ USA, Zionist Organization of the Conservative Movement
NA'AMAT USA
NCSJ: Advocates on Behalf of Jews in Russia, Ukraine, the Baltic States & Eurasia
National Council of Jewish Women
National Council of Young Israel
Organization for Rehabilitation through Training-America
Rabbinical Assembly
Rabbinical Council of America
Religious Zionists of America*
Union for Reform Judaism
Union of Orthodox Jewish Congregations of America
United Jewish Communities
United Synagogue of Conservative Judaism
Women's International Zionist Organization
Women's League for Conservative Judaism
Women of Reform Judaism
Workmen's Circle
World Organization for Rehabilitation through Training
World Zionist Executive, U.S.
Zionist Organization of America*

*Formerly a constituent organization of the American Zionist Council

Organizations Lobbying USIFTA in 1984

76 against, 4 unclear, 23 for

Opposed
Abex Corporation
AFL-CIO
AG West, Inc.
American Butter Institute
American Dehydrated Onion and Garlic Association
American Farm Bureau
American Fiber Textile Apparel Coalition
American Hoechst Corporation
American Mushroom Institute
American Protective Services
Applewood Orchards
Apricot Producers of California
Arkansas Industrial Development
Axette Farms, Inc.
Belger Cartage Service
Bob Miller Ranch
Byrd Foods, Inc.
California Avocado Commission
California Dried Fig Advisory
California League Food Processors
California Tomato Growers Association
California Tomato Research
California-Arizona Citrus
Casa Lupe, Inc.
Davis Canning Company
Dow Chemical, U.S.A.
Ethyl Corporation
Florida Citrus Mutual
Furman Canning Company
Gangi Bros Packing Co.
Garden Valley Foods
George B. Lagorio Farms
Great Lakes Chemical Corporation
Greater Chicago Food Brokers
Harter Packing Co.
Hastings Island Land Company
Heidrick Farms, Inc.
Hunt-Wesson Foods
King Bearings, Inc.
Langon Associates
Leather Products Coalition
Letica Corporation
California Farm Bureau Federation
Liquid Sugar
Mallet and Sons Trucking Company
McGladdery & Gilton
Monsanto
Monticello Canning Company, Inc.
National Cheese Institute
National Milk Producers Federation
New Jersey Food Processors
Ohio Farm Bureau Federation
Otto Brothers Farms
Pacific Coast Producers
Perrys Olive Warehouse

Radial Warehouse Company
Rominger & Sons, Inc.
Roses, Inc.
Rubber Manufacturers Association Footwear Division
San Jose Chamber of Commerce
South Georgia Plant Growers
Sporting Arms and Ammunition Manufacturers Institute, Inc.
Stephen Investments, Inc.
Sun Garden Packing Company
Sunkist Growers, Inc.
Transport Associates, Inc.
Tri/Valley Growers
U.S. Bromine Alliance
United Midwest Manufacturing Company
University of California
Victor A. Morris Farms
Warren Hicks & Sons, Inc.
Western Growers Association
Westpoint Pepperell, Inc.
Woolf Farming Co.
Zonner, Inc.

Indeterminate
Elscint, Inc.
Manufacturing Jewelers & Silversmiths of America, Inc.
Solcoor
W. Braun Co.

In favor
A.P. Esteve Sales, Inc.
AARJOY, Inc.
Amalgamated Bank.
American Israel Chamber of Commerce and Industry, Inc.
American Israel Public Affairs Committee
Bake-N-Joy Foods
California Olive Growers Association
CMC Finance
Crisafulli Pump Company, Inc.
Dead Sea Bromine Group, Ameribrom
Deitsch Plastic Export Company
First Family of Travel
Gordon Brothers Corp.
H.S. Schnell & Co.
Heritage International Bank
Jewish War Veterans of the United States
Kings Super Markets, Inc.
Mast Industries, Inc.
Midbar Imports
Olive Growers Council
Printing Plus Enterprises
The Paul Rogers Company
Wembley Industries, Inc.

04/30/1984 AIPAC Legislative Update

AMERICAN ISRAEL PUBLIC AFFAIRS COMMITTEE
444 NORTH CAPITOL STREET, N.W. • SUITE 412 • WASHINGTON, D.C. 20001 • (202) 638-2256

MEMORANDUM   April 30, 1984

A U.S.-ISRAEL FREE TRADE AREA

On November 29, 1983, President Reagan and Prime Minister Shamir agreed to initiate formal negotiations on a Free Trade Area (FTA) between the United States and Israel. An FTA is defined as an agreement between two or more trading partners whereby tariffs are eliminated on substantially all of the two-way trade between them. In the case of a U.S.-Israel FTA, non-tariff barriers to trade would be addressed as well.

Such a reciprocal, two-way arrangement would benefit the American economy by expanding trade and maintaining the position of U.S. exporters in the Israeli market vis-a-vis their European competitors. An FTA would also strengthen the Israeli economy by increasing its export potential and by stabilizing commercial relations with the United States, its largest trading partner.

The commitment to an FTA by the two heads of state has given important impetus to the bilateral negotiations. Representatives from both governments have been meeting regularly to discuss the general parameters of such an agreement, and how it would be implemented. But Congressional action is required to provide the authorizing and implementing legislation necessary to conclude the agreement. The U.S. International Trade Commission (ITC) must also complete a product-by-product investigation. However, it is important to remember that in order to comply with the General Agreement on Tariffs and Trade (GATT), which specifically sanctions such arrangements, an FTA must cover "substantially all the trade" between the two territories.

TRADE EXPANSION

The permanent, stable trading framework that an FTA would provide should lead to a substantial expansion of trade between the U.S. and Israel. Already, the U.S. is Israel's largest trading partner. Twenty-three percent of Israel's exports go to the U.S. Israel is also one of the three largest markets for American products in the Middle East. About 20% of Israel's imports are from the U.S., although this share has been gradually declining, largely as a result of the Free Trade Agreement Israel has signed with the European Community.

Exports are vital to Israel's continued growth and self-reliance. By strengthening the economy of America's only reliable and democratic ally in the volatile Middle East, an FTA between the U.S. and Israel would provide important national security--as well as economic--benefits for the U.S.

BENEFITS TO THE U.S.

*Prevent loss of U.S. market share in Israel. Israel currently imports about $8 billion worth of goods, and $6 billion worth of services, excluding defense imports. The European Community, which is increasingly benefiting from duty-free access as the final stages of the EC-Israel FTA are being implemented, is enjoying a competitive advantage over U.S. exports in the

Israeli market. That competitive advantage will improve even further as tariffs are completely eliminated on EC products by 1989. Currently, about 40-45% of U.S. exports to Israel are affected by duties averaging approximately 10.3%.

*Expand U.S. exports. The U.S. has always had a favorable balance of trade with Israel. In 1983, the U.S. posted a surplus of over $400 million in its merchandise trade with Israel. An FTA with Israel would enlarge the potential for the U.S. to increase its already substantial exports to Israel of products such as computers and data processing equipment; paper products; automobiles, aircraft and other transportation equipment; specialized industrial machinery; electronic equipment; telecommunications systems; power generating machinery and equipment; chemicals; textiles; tobacco; and various consumer items such as home appliances. The U.S. also has a six-to-one surplus in agriculture products and textiles in its trade with Israel.

*Strengthen reciprocity. There is a mounting concern in Congress that the U.S. is at a disadvantage in international trade and that U.S. exports do not receive the same treatment that the U.S. provides to exports of other countries. A U.S.-Israel FTA would work against that trend by providing the U.S. with an open market in Israel and reciprocal duty-free trade relations. In fact, U.S. exporters would immediately benefit more than Israel's under an FTA since over 90% of Israeli exports to the U.S. already enter duty-free, while only 55-60% of U.S. exports now enter Israel without tariffs.

*Cause few problems to domestic industries. Israel already receives duty-free benefits on 90% of its imports to the United States; despite that, Israeli exports account for only one-half of 1% of total American imports. In areas such as textiles and apparel, for example, Israel's share of total U.S. imports is less than 0.2% and about 0.02% of total U.S. consumption in 1981. In addition, unlike other developing countries that receive duty-free benefits such as the GSP, Israel is not an enclave of inexpensive labor. It would not be able to flood U.S. markets with cheap, labor-intensive products. In agriculture, Israel's ability to increase exports is restricted by its limited amounts of land and water and the expensive costs of shipping perishable products long distances.

BENEFITS TO ISRAEL

*Provide a stable and dependable market for Israel's exports, particularly high-tech products, free from the uncertainties of the present GSP. Israel's fragile economy and lack of neighboring trading partners make it particularly vulnerable to changes in the import duties and policies of its principal markets.

*Make Israel more self-reliant and strengthen its economy through increased trade. The alternative to increasing exports through an FTA would be increased borrowing and foreign aid to finance the balance of payments gap, adding to Israel's growing debt which is already the highest per-capita in the world.

*Strengthen bilateral ties between the U.S. and Israel. As the only such arrangement the U.S. would have with any country in the world, an FTA with Israel would strengthen and reinforce the special political as well as economic bonds shared by the two democracies.

Top Global Arms Exporters[300]

	USA	Russia	Germany	France	UK	Spain	Netherlands	Italy	China	Israel
1984	11076		2883	2822	2415	262	315	1488	2147	296
1985	10278		1320	3677	2006	76	167	1037	1411	194
1986	11337		1421	2784	1906	137	357	435	2101	397
1987	12169		1103	1618	3301	137	445	727	3458	111
1988	11470		1575	1729	2278	151	757	489	2101	74
1989	10826		1245	1998	3305	227	581	381	1029	220
1990	10409		1776	1606	1861	114	405	359	931	101
1991	12660		2493	955	1459	100	441	534	1156	118
1992	14417	2719	1357	1009	1145	78	357	454	729	117
1993	14539	3477	1576	782	1412	101	443	455	1417	145
1994	11722	1555	2644	719	1522	204	580	312	1099	87
1995	11202	3528	1447	825	1525	82	414	369	1040	125
1996	10851	3842	1871	1783	1662	114	477	436	761	230
1997	14260	2989	878	3069	2452	638	607	441	443	236
1998	15348	2074	1760	3349	1426	164	596	414	357	204
1999	11448	4027	1728	1787	1313	30	320	509	289	134
2000	7526	4302	1603	1052	1474	46	258	176	268	354
2001	5808	5824	823	1261	1249	7	190	214	496	360
2002	4936	5602	893	1306	916	120	243	402	555	414
2003	5510	5249	1696	1287	621	158	342	312	623	358
2004	6648	6353	1048	2224	1169	56	208	200	253	593
2005	6786	5485	1899	1617	919	133	580	806	248	313
2006	7394	6186	2406	1541	871	757	1221	621	583	278
2007	7914	4559	3260	2639	1098	554	1241	649	396	414
2008	6159	5953	2837	1585	1075	623	554	484	428	410

Note about Declassified FBI Documents

Some of the document image scans of files released by the Federal Bureau of Investigation under the Freedom of Information Act have been altered.

FBI FOIA reviewers made deletions of data. The rectangular boxes were made by the FBI under the Freedom of Information/Privacy Acts (FOIPA). FOIPA section references appear in the margin. Such exemptions, when legitimately applied, are intended to prevent "unwarranted invasions" of privacy.

The author has restored the identity of individuals and organizations where possible by cross-referencing other FBI FOIA documents and consulting related primary and secondary sources.

No editing of information appearing outside rectangular FOIPA exclusion boxes has been made. The accuracy of restorations of FOIPA-excluded data is the sole responsibility of the author.

06/20/1984 FBI WFO: ITC Report

HD-36 (Rev. 8-26-82)

FBI

TRANSMIT VIA:
☒ Teletype
☐ Facsimile
☐ _____

PRECEDENCE:
☐ Immediate
☒ Priority
☐ Routine

CLASSIFICATION:
☐ TOP SECRET
☒ ~~SECRET~~
☐ CONFIDENTIAL
☐ UNCLAS E F T O
☐ UNCLAS
Date 6-20-84

FM   WASHINGTON FIELD (~~650-13183~~) (P) (C-2)

TO   DIRECTOR, FBI   PRIORITY

BT   DECLASSIFIED BY 60324 uc baw/dk/sbs
                                            ON 04-17-2009

~~C O N F I D E N T I A L~~

UNSUBS; THEFT OF CLASSIFIED DOCUMENTS FROM THE OFFICE OF

THE UNITED STATES TRADE REPRESENTATIVES; ESPIONAGE-ISRAEL;

OO:WASHINGTON FIELD

~~ALL MARKINGS, NOTATIONS AND ITEMS OF INFORMATION~~

~~CONTAINED IN THIS COMMUNICATION ARE CLASSIFIED "SECRET"~~

~~UNLESS OTHERWISE NOTED.~~

         ON JUNE 19, 1984, [   ] ASSOCIATE GENERAL

COUNSEL, OFFICE OF THE UNITED STATES TRADE REPRESENTATIVE,

600 17TH STREET, NORTHWEST, WASHINGTON, D.C. (WDC), ADVISED

THAT THE UNITED STATES TRADE REPRESENTATIVE FUNCTIONS TO

ASSIST THE PRESIDENT OF THE UNITED STATES IN NEGOTIATING

TRADE AGREEMENTS WITH FOREIGN COUNTRIES. AMBASSADOR

WILLIAM BROCK HEADS THIS AGENCY AND HOLDS CABINET LEVEL

RANK.

         [   ] EXPLAINED THAT BEFORE THE PRESIDENT CAN ENTER INTO

①-WFO
LBS:sgt
(4)

Approved: _____   Transmitted _____
                                          (Number)   (Time)

FD-36 (Rev. 8-28-82)

FBI

TRANSMIT VIA:
☐ Teletype
☐ Facsimile
☐ _____

PRECEDENCE:
☐ Immediate
☐ Priority
☐ Routine

CLASSIFICATION:
☐ TOP SECRET
☐ SECRET
☐ CONFIDENTIAL
☐ UNCLAS E F T O
☐ UNCLAS
Date _____

PAGE TWO DE WF #0017 CONFIDENTIAL

A TRADE NEGOTIATION HE OFTEN ASKES THE UNITED STATES
INTERNATIONAL TRADE COMMISSION (USITC) FOR ADVICE ON THE
PROBABLE ECONOMIC AFFECT OF ANY AGREEMENT HE MIGHT NEGOTIATE.
IN THIS CASE, ADVICE WAS REQUESTED IN FEBRUARY OF 1984,
CONCERNING AN AGREEMENT WITH THE STATE OF ISRAEL. THIS
INFORMATION WAS RECEIVED FROM THE USITC DURING THE LAST
WEEK OF MAY. THIS INFORMATION WAS CLASSIFIED CONFIDENTIAL.

     TWO DAYS PRIOR TO RECEIVING THE DOCUMENTS FROM THE
INTERNATIONAL TRADE COMMISSION, [   ] ADVISED THAT HE HEARD
A RUMOR THAT THE AMERICAN ISRAELI PUBLIC AFFAIRS COMMISSION
(AIPAC) ALREADY HAD RECEIVED COPIES OF THIS DOCUMENTS.
[   ] STATES THAT APPROXIMATELY TWO WEEKS PASSED AND WHILE
THEY WERE DECIDING WHERE AND WHO THIS INFORMATION WOULD BE
DIVULGED TO, A CONGRESSIONAL STAFFER ADVISED THEM THAT
THE ISRAELIS WERE OFFERING COPIES OF THIS DOCUMENT TO
MEMBERS OF CONGRESS BECAUSE THE UNITED STATES TRADE REPRE-
SENTATIVE WAS SLOW IN DELIVERING THEM.

     LAST FRIDAY, ON JUNE 15, 1984, GENERAL COUNSEL FOR THE
UNITED STATES TRADE REPRESENTATIVE, [CLAUD GINGRICH]

b6
b7C

b6
b7C

Approved: _____   Transmitted _____   Per _____
                    (Number)   (Time)

FD-36 (Rev. 8-26-82)

FBI

TRANSMIT VIA:
☐ Teletype
☐ Facsimile
☐ _____

PRECEDENCE:
☐ Immediate
☐ Priority
☐ Routine

CLASSIFICATION:
☐ TOP SECRET
☐ SECRET
☐ CONFIDENTIAL
☐ UNCLAS E F T O
☐ UNCLAS
Date _____

PAGE THREE DE WF #0017 ~~CONFIDENTIAL~~

CONTACTED ESTER KURZ OF THE AMERICAN ISRAELI PUBLIC AFFAIRS

COMMISSION AND ASKED HER IF AIPAC HAD A COPY OF THIS REPORT.

KURZ REPLIED YES AND GINGRICH SAID THE MATERIAL WAS

CLASSIFIED AND ASKED FOR IT TO BE RETURNED.

LATER ON, THE DIRECTOR OF AIPAC TELEPHONED

AND ADVISED THAT HE HAD NO KNOWLEDGE THAT AIPAC HAD OBTAINED

A CLASSIFIED DOCUMENT AND HE STATED THAT THE MATERIAL WOULD

BE RETURNED AND THAT THEY WOULD COOPERATE IN EVERY WAY IN

ANY INVESTIGATION TO DETERMINE HOW THEY RECEIVED A COPY OF

A CLASSIFIED DOCUMENT.

LATER ON THAT DAY, AN UNBOUND XEROX COPY OF THIS

DOCUMENT WAS DELIVERED BY AN AIPAC MESSENGER TO THE UNITED

STATES TRADE REPRESENTATIVE OFFICE.

ADVISED THAT ALL INFORMATION CONTAINED IN THIS

DOCUMENT WAS CLASSIFIED CONFIDENTIAL OR BUSINESS CONFIDEN-

TIAL. THE HIGHEST LEVEL OF CLASSIFICATION IN THIS REPORT IS

CONFIDENTIAL. ESTIMATES THAT BY OBTAINING THIS DOCU-

MENT, THE PRESIDENT'S NEGOTIATING ~~PHYSICIAN~~ POSITION CONCERNING A

TRADE AGREEMENT BETWEEN THE UNITED STATES AND THE STATE OF

ISRAEL IS COMPROMISED BECAUSE THIS REPORT DIVULGES THOSE

Approved: _____ Transmitted _____ Per _____
                                  (Number)   (Time)

FD-36 (Rev. 8-29-82)

FBI

TRANSMIT VIA:
☐ Teletype
☐ Facsimile
☐ _____

PRECEDENCE:
☐ Immediate
☐ Priority
☐ Routine

CLASSIFICATION:
☐ TOP SECRET
☐ SECRET
☐ CONFIDENTIAL
☐ UNCLAS E F T O
☐ UNCLAS
Date _____

PAGE FOUR DE WF #0017 ~~CONFIDENTIAL~~

PRODUCTS AND INDUSTRIES THAT HAVE BEEN IDENTIFIED BY THE
INTERNATIONAL TRADE COMMISSION AS BEING THE MOST SENSITIVE
TO IMPORTS FROM ISRAEL. ALSO, THE REPORT BASICALLY STATES
THAT THE UNITED STATES CAN LOWER DUTIES ON ALL GOODS BEING
IMPORTED FROM ISRAEL AND IT WILL ONLY ~~NOT~~ HURT ~~ANY UNITED STATES~~
~~INDUSTRIES EXCEPT~~ SEVEN INDUSTRIES. THESE INDUSTRIES ARE
LISTED IN THIS REPORT.

[   ] ADVISED THAT THIS DOCUMENT WAS STOLEN OR GIVEN
TO THE AIPAC BY EITHER A MEMBER OF THE UNITED STATES TRADE
REPRESENTATIVE STAFF OF THE INTERNATIONAL TRADE COMMISSION.

[   ] ADVISED THAT HE BELIEVES THE COPY CAME FROM THE
INTERNATIONAL TRADE COMMISSION BECAUSE ALL INTERNAL COPIES
KEPT AT THE UNITED STATES TRADE REPRESENTATIVE ASSOCIATION
WOULD HAVE AN INTERNAL DOCUMENT CONTROL NUMBER IN THE UPPER
RIGHT HAND CORNER OF THE COVER PAGE. THE DOCUMENT IDENTIFIED
AS HAVING BEEN RETURNED FROM AIPAC HAD NO SUCH NUMBER.

INVESTIGATION CONTINUING, FBIHQ WILL BE ADVISED OF
PERTINENT DETAILS.

~~C BY 5054. DECL: OADR.~~

BT

b6
b7C

#0017

Approved: _____ Transmitted _____ Per _____
                         (Number)   (Time)

08/13/1984 FBI WFO: Status Update

Airtel

Date: 8/13/84

TO: DIRECTOR, FBI

FROM: SAC, WASHINGTON FIELD OFFICE (65C-13191)(P)(CI-7)

UNSUBS:
THEFT OF CLASSIFIED DOCUMENTS FROM
THE UNITED STATES TRADE REPRESENTATIVES;
ESPIONAGE-ISRAEL
OO:WFO

SECRET

~~All markings, notations, and items of information
contained in this communication are classified "SECRET" unless
otherwise noted.~~

Re WFO tel to Director dated 6/20/84.

Enclosed for the Bureau are the original and four
copies of an LHM dated and captioned as above.

Preliminary investigation by WFO indicates that the
confidential report on trade with Israel was likely taken while
being prepared at the International Trade Commission (ITC). A
cursory review of security procedures at ITC disclosed no
security procedures are in place that would prevent outright
theft or the printing of an "extra" copy of the report.

This confidential report contains no national defense
information and was orignally classified to protect the U.S.
bargaining position during negotiations with Israel. The
"Business Confidential" information identifies seven U.S.
industries that would be harmed by lowering import tariffs on
Israel products.

SECRET

Classified by: 55B
Declassify on: OADR

2-Bureau (Enc. 5)
1-Washington Field

MFR:ldj
(3)

WFO 55C-13191   SECRET

Personnel at USTR and ITC were most angered by the fact that the American-Israeli Public Affairs Commission (AIPAC) had apparently attempted to influence members of Congress with the use of a purloined copy of the ITC report and had unsurped their authority.

-       WFO files disclose that AIPAC is a powerful pro-Israel lobbying group staffed by U.S. citizens. WFO files contain an unsubstantiated allegation that a member of the Israeli Intelligence Service was a staff member of AIPAC.

REQUEST OF THE BUREAU

The Bureau is requested to coordinate this matter with the appropriate officials at the DEPARTMENT OF JUSTICE for a prosecutive opinion.

- 2 -   SECRET

U.S. DEPARTMENT OF JUSTICE
FEDERAL BUREAU OF INVESTIGATION
WASHINGTON FIELD OFFICE
WASHINGTON, D.C. 20535
August 6, 1984

UNKNOWN SUBJECTS:
THEFT OF CLASSIFIED DOCUMENTS FROM
THE OFFICES OF
THE UNITED STATES TRADE REPRESENTATIVES:
ESPIONAGE-ISRAEL
PRELIMINARY INQUIRY
(INITIATED JUNE 19, 1984)

~~All markings, notations, and items of information
contained in this communication are classified "SECRET" unless
otherwise noted.~~

OFFICE OF ORIGIN: WASHINGTON FIELD OFFICE

DATE INVESTIGATIVE SUMMARY PREPARED: August 13, 1984

BASIS FOR INVESTIGATION:

Investigation is based upon a complaint received from
[   ] Associate General Counsel, Office of the
United States Trade Representative (USTR), 600 17th Street, NW,
Washington, D.C. (WDC). This complaint alledges that person(s)
unknown had made available to the government of Israel, a
confidential report published by the International Trade
Commission outlining The Probable Effect of Providing Duty-Free
Treatment of Imports from Israel (332-180).

INVESTIGATION TO DATE:

On January 25, 1984, the U.S. International Trade
Commission (ITC), WDC, was requested by the USTR to prepare a
report for the President relating to the establishment of a free
trade area with Israel. This report was to be available within
four month. The first "prehearing report" was published April 4,
1984, by ITC. Twenty copies were distributed within ITC to key

This document contains neither recommendations nor
conclusions of the FBI. It is the property of the FBI
and is loaned to your agency; it and its contents are
not to be distributed outside your agency.

SECRET

Classified by: 558
Declassify on: OADR

UNKNOWN SUBJECTS   SECRET

personnel. On May 3, 1984, five more copies were distributed
within ITC for senior staff/editorial review and for review by
the six ITC Commissioners. On May 18, 1984, 13 more copies
called "Action Jacket" copies were distributed within ITC as a
device for recording the clearances and comments of the
commissioners. On May 31, 1984, 40 copies of the final report
were distributed with one copy to the President, 28 copies to
USTR, and 11 copies within ITC. One copy of the statistical
appendix to the subject report was made available to USTR on May
9, 1984, to assist in the preparation of testimony before
Congress. No other copies were available to any other
individuals or agencies until May 30, 1984.

On May 21, 1984, a DEPARTMENT OF COMMERCE (DOC)
employee was in Jerusalem following the formal U.S.-Israeli
negotiations which had been held the week before. This employee
met with a [   ] of the Israeli delegation and
an Israeli Embassy official from WDC. [   ] stated he had
received a cable from the Israeli Embassy in WDC and then
proceeded to read from this cable what appeared to be a full
summary of the report including the conclusions regarding
sensitive products.

On or about May 30, 1984, prior to the USTR
distribution of the "final report," a member of the Trade
Subcommittee of the Senate Finance Committee notified USTR that
after a conversation with an employee of the AIPAC, WDC, this
member was left with the impression that AIPAC had a copy of the
subject report although they did not offer a copy to this
employee. This AIPAC member was familiar with the report's
contents and conclusions.

On June 7, 1984, the Israeli trade minister and [   ]
lunched with Ambassador WILLIAM BROCK [   ] USTR.
[   ] recalled that [   ] was aware of the contents of the
report.

On June 12 and 13, 1984, information passed to USTR
indicated that certain members of Congress could acquire copies
of the ITC report through AIPAC.

On June 15, 1984, the USTR general counsel telephoned
AIPAC employee ESTER KURZ and inquired if AIPAC had a copy of
the USTR report. KURZ advised they did. KURZ was asked to
return this confidential report and all copies. Subsequently,
THOMAS DINE of AIPAC, contacted USTR, to claim no
knowledge of the report himself and to disassociate himself from
such activities. A copy of the USTR report was subsequently

- 2 -   SECRET

delivered to USTR. Also delivered was a substantial portion of a
second copy of the report in an unsorted condition. The full
report copy was a copy of the "final report" and had no.
identifying mark on the outside cover which was clearly stamped
confidential. This indicates that this copy was probably made
prior to the May 30 delivery to USTR. USTR officials advised the
significance of the unauthorized disclosure of the contents of
the ITC report is that the bargaining position of the United
States was compromised and "Business Confidential" information
used in the report was made available to the public. This
disclosure also impacts on the effectiveness of the ITC to
solicit data from the U.S. business community. No national
defense information was utilized in the preparation of the ITC
report.

OBJECTIVE:

         To identify individual(s) responsible for the
unauthorized disclosure of the contents of the ITC report to the
government of Israel and employees of AIPAC through interviews of
ITC personnel and congressional staff aides.

11/01/1985 AAG to FBI: Case Reopened

Memorandum

SECRET

Subject	Date
Unknown Subjects, Theft and Unauthorized Disclosure of Documents From the United States International Trade Commission	NOV 1 1985 SST:GEMcD:GAC:mtf

To
The Director
Federal Bureau of Investigation

From
Stephen S. Trott
Assistant Attorney General
Criminal Division

The Criminal Division has determined that additional investigation should be conducted to ascertain responsibility for the
unauthorized disclosure of the report of the United States
International Trade Commission (No. 332-180). This matter was
the subject of a previous FBI inquiry which may be identified by
reference to file no. 52B-18153.

The known information indicates that it is likely that
offenses under 18 U.S.C. §641 (theft of government property) and
18 U.S.C. §1905 (disclosure of confidential business information)
have occurred; therefore, please conduct an appropriate investigation, designed to identify the offender or offenders and to
determine the details regarding the disclosure(s).

Reports of your investigation should be made to the Public
Integrity Section to the attention of
Any questions regarding the investigation should
be addressed to him.

b6
b7C

ALL FBI INFORMATION CONTAINED
HEREIN IS UNCLASSIFIED
DATE 04-17-2009 BY 60324 uc baw/dk/sbs

52B - 18153 - 4
SEARCHED
SERIALIZED
INDEXED
FILED
12-2-85

SECRET

12/19/1985 FBI Interviews Ester Kurz

FD-302 (REV. 3-10-82)

FEDERAL BUREAU OF INVESTIGATION

ALL INFORMATION CONTAINED
HEREIN IS UNCLASSIFIED
DATE 04-20-2009 BY 60524 uc baw/dR/pbs   Date of transcription ___1/6/86___

1

MRS ESTER KURZ, DEPUTY LEGISLATIVE DIRECTOR
American Israel Public Affairs Committee (AIPAC), 500 North
Capitol Street, N.W., Suite 300, Washington, D.C. (WDC),
telephone #638-2256 was interviewed by FEDERAL BUREAU OF
INVESTIGATION Special Agents (SAs)[   ] and
[   ] regarding a trade report published by
the United States Trade Representatives (USTR) which alledegly
was in the possession of AIPAC in 1984.

KURZ was interviewed in the presence of her
Attorney, [   ] representing the law firm of
DICKSTEIN, SHAPIRO, AND MORIN, 2101 L Street, N.W., WDC,
telephone #628-2236. KURZ provided the following information:

KURZ advised that she has been employed with
AIPAC from January 1982 until present. She advised that in
April of 1984, she received a document from an Israeli Embassy
Official, DAN HALPERN KURZ advised that HALPERN
is the ECONOMIC MINISTER at the Israeli Embassy. ESTER
KURZ described this document as being an International Trade
Commission (ITC) report studying free trade between Israel
and America and the implications resulting from possible
agreements. She stated that the document was 50-80 pages in length and
that she was not aware of the title of this report. She further
advised that this document was marked "confidential".

Regarding the receipt of this document, KURZ
stated that HALPERN came to the AIPAC office for a meeting
and prior to the meeting he handed her an envelop which was
unmarked. At that time, she said she was unaware of the contents
of the envelop. She further stated that this meeting was a
conference on the free trade issue between America and Israel
but she advised she cannot recall who else was attending this
meeting.

Investigation on __12/19/85__ at Washington, D.C.   File # __52B-18153-7__

SAs [   ]
by   JAH:rlw   12/23/85
                                    Date dictated

This document contains neither recommendations nor conclusions of the FBI. It is the property of the FBI and is loaned to your agency;
it and its contents are not to be distributed outside your agency.

FD-302a (Rev. 11-15-83)

Continuation of FD-302 of **ESTER KURZ** , On 12/19/85 , Page 2*

KURZ stated that **HALPERN** never discussed the document with her and that he never explained to her how he received it. She stated that after she received the document, she placed the document in her desk and subsequently gave it a cursory examination a short time later before passing it on to **MARGARET BLAIR** for AIPAC. She advised that she provided **BLAIR** with this document approximately one week after she had received it from **HALPERN** **KURZ** advised that when she gave this document to **BLAIR** she does not recall any specific instructions she gave to **BLAIR**

KURZ advised that she paid no attention to this document until she received a phone call from the U.S. Trade Representative (USTR) General Counsel **CLAUD GINGRICH** several weeks later. **GINGRICH** called to ascertain if AIPAC had this trade report in their possession. She further advised that prior to that call she was given a duplicate copy of the report by AIPAC official **DOUGLAS BLOOMFIELD** She advised she had no information as to who duplicated this report but that after AIPAC received a call from **GINGRICH** she then received a call from **BLOOMFIELD** telling her to destroy the duplicate copy of the report. **KURZ** advised that she destroyed this duplicate copy by throwing it down the garbage shute at her residence. She stated that the original report was then returned to the U.S. Trade Representatives but that she does not know the identity of the person who returned the report.

Regarding the availability of the report, **KURZ** advised that the document was known to be "floating around town" and that the contents of the report were common knowledge to those interested in these matters.

KURZ advised that she could provide no opinion or comments regarding what other officials at AIPAC may have seen the report or in what manner **HALPERN** obtained the report. It was then requested by her Attorney, , that if the FBI had any further request of **KURZ** that the FBI should contact and he would submit any questions to **KURZ** **KURZ** otherwise did not wish to furnish any additional information regarding this matter.

12/19/1985 FBI Interviews Margaret Blair

FD-302 (REV. 3-10-82)

FEDERAL BUREAU OF INVESTIGATION

ALL INFORMATION CONTAINED
HEREIN IS UNCLASSIFIED
DATE 04-20-2009 BY 60324 uc baw/dk/sbs

Date of transcription _____ 1/6/86

1

MARGARET BLAIR
Maryland, home telephone _____ was interviewed by FEDERAL
BUREAU OF INVESTIGATION (FBI) Special Agents (SAs) _____ regarding a classfied report
received by the American Israel Public Affairs Committee (AIPAC)
in June 1984.

BLAIR was interviewed in the presence of her
Attorney _____ representing the law firm of FRIED,
FRANK, HARRIS, SHRIVER AND JACOBSON, 600 New Hampshire Avenue,
N.W., Washington, D.C. (WDC), telephone #342-3622. BLAIR
provided the following information:

BLAIR advised that while she was employed by
AIPAC, she was TRADE ANALYST She advised that she had been
employed by AIPAC from the period of _____. She stated that the address
for AIPAC is 500 North Capitol Street, N.W., Suite 300, WDC,
telephone #638-2256. She furthered advised that she does not
plan on returning to AIPAC

BLAIR advised that she first became aware of the
U.S. International Trade Commission Report on American Israeli
Free Trade when she received the report in June of 1984. She
stated that she received the report from ESTER KURZ who
as employed as DIRECTOR with AIPAC. BLAIR advised
that when she was given the report by KURZ she was told to
"keep it in a safe place" but was otherwise given no specific
instructions regarding the report or regarding who initially
received the report for AIPAC.

BLAIR advised that as TRADE ANALYST it was
her responsibility to study any reports or documents pertaining
to American Israeli trade and considered the receipt of this
report a very ordinary event. She did not know if it was common
knowledge at AIPAC whether or not AIPAC had possession of this
report. She stated she received the report in June of 1984 and

Investigation on 12/19/85 at Wheaton, Maryland File # 52B-18153-8

SAs _____

by _____ JAH:rlw Date dictated 12/23/85

This document contains neither recommendations nor conclusions of the FBI. It is the property of the FBI and is loaned to your agency;
it and its contents are not to be distributed outside your agency.

FD-302a (Rev. 11-15-83)

Continuation of FD-302 of _____   , On _____ 12/19/85 , Page _____ 2*

held on to it for a few weeks. She stated that sometime in
July of 1984, the General Counsel for the U.S. Trade Representatives (USTR) CLAUD GINGRICH asked her if she had seen a copy of
this report. She advised GINGRICH that she had seen a copy
and for her to check with AIPAC General Counsel
if he had any further questions regarding this document.

BLAIR advised that subsequent to her conversation
with_____ she turned the report over to someone at
AIPAC but she does not remember specifically who it was. She
further advised that she had no information regarding who
provided this report to KURZ and that KURZ did not
indicate to her how she received it.

BLAIR described the report as being approximately
100 pages in length but stated she did not see a title to this
report. She further described this report as being a study by
the International Trade Commission (ITC) examining the different
product sectors in America and the possible impact these
sectors if duty free imports from Israel were allowed. She
advised that she did not utilize any of the information gleaned
from this report. She could not recall whether the report was
classified or not.

BLAIR does not specifically recall to whom she
returned the report at AIPAC but thinks it could have been
_____ She further advised that there was
general discussion of the report at AIPAC but that this was not
considered an especially significant matter. BLAIR advised
that her_____ became aware of the report
at the time of the newspaper articles regarding this matter.

BLAIR could otherwise provide no other
information relating to how the report was received by AIPAC
or who initially received the report. BLAIR advised
that she has no pertinent information regarding this
matter and requested that any future contact of her by the FBI
be coordinated through her Attorney,_____

02/13/1985 FBI Interviews Doug Bloomfield

ALL INFORMATION CONTAINED
HEREIN IS UNCLASSIFIED
DATE 04-20-2009 BY 60724 uc baw/dk/sbs

FD-302 (REV 3-10-82)

FEDERAL BUREAU OF INVESTIGATION

Date of transcription 3/21/86

DOUGLAS BLOOMFIELD
American Israel Public Affairs Committee (AIPAC), 500 North
Capitol Street, N.W., Suite 300, Washington, D.C., telephone
(202) 638-2256 was interviewed by Federal Bureau of Investigation
(FBI) Special Agents (SAs)
regarding a classified report received by AIPAC in June
of 1984.

BLOOMFIELD was interviewed in the presence of his
Attorney, representing the law firm of
WILLIAMS & CONNOLLY, the HILL Building, Washington, D.C.,
telephone (202) 331-5000. BLOOMFIELD provided the following
information:

BLOOMFIELD advised that he is employed at AIPAC in
the capacity of LEGISLATIVE DIRECTOR with responsibilities
pertaining to Congressional Relations and for Lobbying on Capitol
Hill. BLOOMFIELD advised that he first became aware of the
International Trade Commission (ITC) report being at AIPAC on a
Friday afternoon in the spring of 1984. He stated that on this
occasion ESTER KURZ DEP LEGIS. DIR. with AIPAC advised that
she received a call from the U.S. Trade Representative (USTR)
General Counsel CLAUD GINGRICH asking her whether she or anyone
at AIPAC had this document. BLOOMFIELD advised that KURZ
stated to GINGRICH that she had the document and at that point
GINGRICH asked that she return it to the USTR. BLOOMFIELD
asked KURZ if it was true that she had this report and she
advised that she did have it. subsequently examined
the document to determine if it had any secret classification or
pertained to any United States National Defense matters.
BLOOMFIELD advised that he and KURZ went to the office of
THOMAS DINE EXEC DIRECTOR of AIPAC and informed him of the
incident. DINE inquired as to whether KURZ actually
had the report and if AIPAC had done anything illegal in having
it. BLOOMFIELD advised that he stated to DINE that it

Investigation on 2/10/86 at Washington, D.C. File# 52B-18153-73
SAs
By   DDR:erw Date dictated 2/14/86
This document contains neither recommendations nor conclusions of
the FBI. It is the property of the FBI and is loaned to your
agency; it and its contents are not to be distributed outside
your agency.

FD-302a (Rev 11-13-83)

Continuation of FD-302 of [_____] On 2/13/86 Page2*   b6
                                                                     b7C

contained no National Defense information and that AIPAC did not
solicit the report. Both [_____] were
satisfied that AIPAC had not acted improperly in possessing the
report.

    [DINE] immediately called [GINGRICH] at the USTR to
make arrangements to return the document. The report was
subsequently returned to the USTR by a member of the AIPAC office
staff. Prior to returning this document, [BLOOMFIELD] asked to
have a duplicate copy of the document made so that the staff of
the AIPAC could further examine the report. [BLOOMFIELD]   b6
advised that he saw no "secret classifications" on the report and   b7C
there were no indications that this was a report pertaining to
United States National Security. He further believed that AIPAC
had not acted improperly or illegally in having this report in
its possession and thereafter, asked [_____] for
AIPAC to examine the document regarding the free trade issue
between the U.S. and Israel. He stated that [KURZ] retained
the duplicate copy of the report and that the original report was
returned to the USTR. [BLOOMFIELD] advised that he did not
consider this report to be especially important and thought that
any controversy regarding the report had ended.

    In November of 1985, [BLOOMFIELD] asked [KURZ]   b6
about the report and she stated to him that it was generally   b7C
useless and that she had eventually thrown it away.

    Regarding the identity of the individual who provided
the report to AIPAC, [BLOOMFIELD] advised that he has no first
hand knowledge pertaining to this matter. He did advise that he   b6
was told that Israeli Embassy official [DAN HALPERN] had   b7C
initially provided the report to a representative of AIPAC. [____]
[BLOOMFIELD] further advised that he had no information pertaining
to who may have provided the report to [DAN HALPERN]

    [BLOOMFIELD] stated that it was his understanding
that several other industries had copies of this report as well
as several people on Capitol Hill and that AIPAC did not consider
possessing this report an especially significant matter. [____]   b6
[BLOOMFIELD] could otherwise provide no additional information   b7C
relating to who may have provided the report to [DAN HALPERN] He
further requested that any future contact of him by the FBI be
coordinated through his Attorney, [_____]

03/07/1986 FBI Interviews Dan Halpern

FD-302 (REV. 3-10-82)

FEDERAL BUREAU OF INVESTIGATION

ALL INFORMATION CONTAINED
HEREIN IS UNCLASSIFIED
DATE 04-20-2009 BY 60324 uc kaw/dk/sbs

Date of transcription _____3/13/86_____

1

DAN HALPERN, ECONOMIC MINISTER

Embassy of Israel, 3514 International Drive, N.W., Washington,
D.C. telephone (202) 364-5692 was interviewed by Federal
Bureau of Investigation Special Agents[   ]
and [   ] regarding the receipt of a U.S.
Internationl Trade Commission (USITC) report pertaining
to free trade between the U.S. and Israel.

During this interview, HALPERN was accompanied
by[   ]
[   ] for the Embassy of Israel, Washington, D.C.

HALPERN advised that at some unrecalled
time in 1984 he received this USITC report pertaining to
free trade between America and Israel. HALPERN advised
that he received this document from someone that he
would not identify. He indicated that he received this
information in his official capacity as a diplomat and that it
would be against the principles of diplomatic work to divulge
any information pertaining to the identity of the individual
who provided him the report. He further advised that it
is impossible within the professional ethics of a diplomat
to identify individuals who provide certain information
to a diplomat.

HALPERN did state that the individual who
provided him with the report was not a U.S. Government Official
nor was he an employee of the U.S. Government. HALPERN
indicated that there were numerous negotiators regarding
this free trade issue representing several U.S. Government agencies
including the U.S. Trade Representatives, the U.S. Treasury,
the U.S. Commerce Commission, the U.S. Department of State,
and the U.S. Department of Agriculture. He advised that
there were usually one or two principales representing each
of these agencies which would attend most negotiations.
He further advised that he thinks certain U.S. negotiators
wanted the person who provided HALPERN the report to know
about certain aspects pertaining to the United States

Investigation on __3/7/86__ at __Washington, D.C.__ File # __52B-18153-12__

by __SAs[   ]__   JAH:cjc Date dictated __3/13/86__

This document contains neither recommendations nor conclusions of the FBI. It is the property of the FBI and is loaned to your agency;
it and its contents are not to be distributed outside your agency.

FD-302a (Rev. 11-15-83)

Continuation of FD-302 of ___52B-18153;___ [ ]_____ , On _3/7/86_____ , Page __2__

and Israel.

      Regarding the availability of this report, HALPERN advised that the report had been widely circulated among the staff and members of Capitol Hill, as well as among various consultants representing the interest of each agency affected by the free trade issue. He advised that the Government of Israel did not ask to receive the report and stated that when the individual provided him with the report, the transaction was not conducted in a discreet or secretive manner.

      HALPERN advised that he furnished the report to an employee at the American Israel Public Affairs Committee (AIPAC) during the Spring or Summer of 1984. He believes he gave the report to either ESTER KURZ or to [ ] HALPERN indicated that this report was only part of a package that he provided to AIPAC with other routine information.

      [ ] advised that he could not recall the specific period of time when he was given the report but stated that the contents of the report were well known by the time he had received it. HALPERN advised that he did not try to conceal the fact that representatives of Israel had this report in their possession. He further stated that he believes that the controversy regarding this report is extremely exaggerated and that in his opinion, the fact that representatives of Israel viewed this report, caused no economic damage to any U.S. business or interest.

08/25/1986 USAT Closes Investigation

Memorandum

SECRET

Subject Unknown Subjects, Theft and Unauthorized Disclosure of Documents from the United States International Trade Commission	Date **AUG 25 1986** SST:GEMcD:GAC:mtf

To
The Director
Federal Bureau of Investigation

From
Stephen S. Trott
Assistant Attorney General
Criminal Division

The investigative reports of the Federal Bureau of
Investigation concerning the theft and unauthorized disclosure of
a copy or copies of the report of the United States International
Trade Commission (No. 332-180) have been examined in the Public
Integrity Section of the Criminal Division. We have decided that
it is improbable that additional investigation would be productive; therefore, no further investigation is necessary. Thank
you for your assistance.

ALL FBI INFORMATION CONTAINED
HEREIN IS UNCLASSIFIED
DATE 04-20-2009 BY 00324 uc baw/dk/sbs

52-18153-15

SECRET

Derived from FBI 558
Declassify on: OADR

SEARCHED_____ INDEXED_____
SERIALIZED_____ FILED_____

JAN 1 6 1987

FBI — WASH. FIELD OFFICE

AIPAC USIFTA Report Cover Page

A U.S.-ISRAEL FREE TRADE AREA

How Both Sides Gain

Peggy Blair

AIPAC Papers on U.S.-Israel Relations

Editors: Steven J. Rosen
Martin Indyk
Business Manager: Peggy Shay

1996 U.S. Defense Investigation Service Memo

COUNTRY: ISRAEL

KEY JUDGMENTS:

* Israeli espionage intentions and capabilities are determined by their traditional desire for self reliance.

*Israel aggressively collects military and industrial technology. The United States is a high priority collection target.

* Israel possesses the resources and technical capability to successfully achieve its collection objectives.

BACKGROUND:

Non-traditional Adversary

Israel is a political and military ally of the United States. However, the nature of espionage relations between the two governments is competitive. The Israelis are motivated by strong survival instincts which dictate every facet of their political and economic policies. This results in a highly independent approach determining those policies which they consider to be in their best interests. Consequently, the Israelis have established an intelligence service capable of targeting military and economic targets with equal facility. The strong ethnic ties to Israel present in the United States coupled with aggressive and extremely competent intelligence personnel has resulted in a very productive collection effort. Published reports have identified the collection of scientific intelligence in the United States and other developed countries as a the third highest priority of Israeli Intelligence after information on its Arab neighbors and information on secret U.S. policies or decisions relating to Israel.

The primary Israeli collection agencies are the Mossad, equivalent to the CIA, Aman, the Israeli Military Intelligence branch, and a little known agency identified as the LAKAM, which translates to the Science and Liaison Bureau. It has been reported that the LAKAM was disbanded after it was identified as the agency responsible for recruiting and running Jonathan Pollard. However, there is no doubt that the Israeli intelligence community has adjusted its collection efforts and continues to closely target the scientific and industrial community within the United States.

John Davitt, formerly the head of the Justice Department's Internal Security Section, was quoted as stating the Israeli intelligence services were "more active than anyone but the KGB....They were targeted on the United States about half the time and on Arab countries about half the time."

METHOD OF OPERATION/TECHNIQUES:

The Israeli Intelligence Service employs traditional collection tools. It has a trained agent cadre well versed in espionage tradecraft. Collection requirements are identified by the national leadership based on factors relating to defense and the national economy. The most compelling requirement deals with immediate threats to the existence of Israel posed by its geographic neighbors. Therefore, collection information relating to the existence of nuclear, chemical and biological weapons is the first order of priority. Israeli personnel are always seeking to recruit knowledgeable human sources with access to this information. Recruitment techniques include ethnic targeting, financial aggrandizement, and identification and exploitation of individual frailties. Selective employment opportunities (placing Israeli nationals in key industries) is a technique utilized with great success.

DOCUMENTED INCIDENTS:

a) The most highly publicized incident involving Israeli espionage directed against the United States is the 1985 arrest of Navy Intelligence analyst Jonathan Pollard. Pollard conveyed vast quantities of classified information to Israel for ideological reasons and personal financial gain.

b) In 1986, Israeli agents stole proprietary information from Chicago-based Recon Optical, Inc., an Illinois optics firm. Significant financial damages were incurred by Recon an in 1993, the Israelis agreed to pay three million dollars in damages.

c) In the mid-eighties, a large DoD contractor hosting Israeli visitors experienced the loss of test equipment during field testing relating to the manufacture of a radar system. Two years later, a request was received from Israel to repair the piece of missing equipment.

d) In 1994, a small firm utilizing a proprietary PC-based product to upgrade Israeli radar systems sent an engineer to Israel with its product. Upon arrival, the PC-based equipment was malfunctioning. Examination by the engineer traveling to Israel revealed the proprietary chip had been tampered with.

e) Israel is suspected of furnishing the People's Republic of China with U.S. export-controlled technology desired by the Chinese to upgrade their indigenous capability to develop a fighter aircraft.

f) Author Peter Schweizer maintains Israeli Air Force personnel have repeatedly gained access to top secret military research projects by paying off Pentagon employees.

INFORMATION DESIRED:

The Israelis have a voracious appetite for information on intentions and capabilities relating to proliferation topics, i.e. nuclear, chemical and biological weapons. Specific types of technology desired includes avionics equipment, spy satellite data, theater missile defense information. Israel had developed an arms industry which produces weapons platforms for each branch of its military service, information relating to the technologies relating to these platforms is actively sought. Israeli industry manufactures the Merkava Mark III battle tank, the Sa'ar class corvette missile boat and the Kfir jet fighter. United States firms engaged in research, development, and manufacturing associated with these technologies together with radar and missile defense technologies are high priority collection targets.

2009 Draft Order: AIPAC FEC Regulation after 20 Years[lxi]

UNITED STATES DISTRICT COURT
FOR THE DISTRICT OF COLUMBIA

JAMES E. AKINS, *et al.*,	)	
	)	
Plaintiffs,	)	
	)	
v.	)	Civ. A. No. 92-1864 (RJL)
	)	Civ. A. No. 00-1478 (RJL)
FEDERAL ELECTION COMMISSION,	)	Civ. A. No. 03-2431 (RJL)
	)	
Defendant.	)	
	)	

ORDER

On consideration of plaintiffs' motion for summary judgment, it is this _____ day

of _____, 20___,

ORDERED that plaintiffs' motion is granted. It also is

ADJUDGED and ORDERED as follows.

1. Defendant Federal Election Commission's dismissals of plaintiffs'

administrative complaints in MUR 2804 and MUR 5272 are unlawful and are set aside;

the dismissals are "arbitrary, capricious, an abuse of discretion, . . . otherwise not in

accordance with law," and "without observance of procedure required by law." 5 U.S.C.

§ 706(2).

2. The case is remanded to the Commission.

3. The Commission is ordered, on remand,

(a) to explain its interpretation of "organized primarily" as that phrase is

used in 2 U.S.C. § 431(9)(B)(iii);

[lxi] This order is proposed by the plaintiffs. It is not a court order at the time of publication.

(b) to investigate and find whether lobbying by the American Israel Public Affairs Committee (AIPAC) is based "primarily" on AIPAC's influencing of federal elections;

(c) if the Commission finds that AIPAC's lobbying is based primarily on influencing elections, to find that AIPAC is "organized primarily for the purpose of influencing" them, within the meaning of § 431(9)(B)(iii);

(d) if the Commission finds that AIPAC is not organized primarily for the purpose of influencing elections, to decide whether AIPAC's membership communication is disentitled to the § 431(9)(B)(iii) exemption because it solicits campaign contributions and is coordinated with candidates and therefore is not "by" AIPAC, within the meaning of the statute;

(e) if the Commission finds that AIPAC is organized primarily for the purpose of influencing federal elections or that its membership communication is disentitled to the § 431(9)(B)(iii) exemption, to investigate and find whether AIPAC is a "political committee," within the meaning of § 431(4), due to its election communication to its members;

(f) if the Commission finds that AIPAC is not a political committee due to its election communication to its members, to investigate and find whether AIPAC is a political committee due to other expenditures;

(g) if the Commission finds that AIPAC is a political committee, to require AIPAC to comply with the applicable disclosure requirements;

(h) if the Commission finds that AIPAC is not a political committee and not organized primarily for the purpose of influencing federal elections, to

2

investigate and find whether AIPAC's membership communication includes

"communication expressly advocating the election or defeat of . . . clearly

identified candidate[s]," within the meaning of § 431(9)(B)(iii), irrespective of

whether communication that expressly advocates election or defeat is separate

from communication that identifies candidates and their political views; and

(i) if the Commission finds that AIPAC is not a political committee and

not organized primarily for the purpose of influencing federal elections, but that

AIPAC's membership communication includes communication expressly

advocating the election or defeat of a clearly identified candidate, to investigate

and find whether the cost of the communication requires AIPAC to report it under

§ 431(9)(B)(iii), and, if so, to require AIPAC to comply with the applicable

reporting requirements.

_____

Richard J. Leon
United States District Judge

Copies to:

Greg J. Mueller
Federal Election Commission
999 E Street, N.W.
Washington, D.C. 20463

Daniel M. Schember
Gaffney & Schember, P.C.
1666 Connecticut Avenue, N.W., Ste. 225
Washington, D.C. 20009

3

2009 USTR FOIA Rejection

EXECUTIVE OFFICE OF THE PRESIDENT
OFFICE OF THE UNITED STATES TRADE REPRESENTATIVE
WASHINGTON, D.C. 20508

March 9, 2009

Mr. Grant Smith
Institute for Research
Middle Eastern Policy
Calvert Station
P.O. Box 32041
Washington, D.C. 20007

Dear Mr. Smith:

This letter is USTR's final response to your request for **"the complete report prepared by the International Trade Commission to U.S. Trade Representative William E. Brock in preparation for the U.S.-Israel Free Trade Agreement in 1984"**, under the Freedom of Information Act.

Please be advised that, after a thorough review, it has been determined that the report should not be declassified. The report is classified in its entirety, leaving no segregable portions available for public viewing.

The report is being withheld in full pursuant to 5 U.S.C. §552(b)(1), which pertains to information that is properly classified in the interest of national security pursuant to Executive Order 12958.

Inasmuch as this constitutes a complete grant of your request, I am closing your file in this office.

In the event that you are dissatisfied with USTR's determination, you may appeal such a denial, within thirty (30) days, in writing to:

FOIA Appeals Committee
Office of the United States Trade Representative
1724 F Street, N.W.
Washington, DC 20508

Both the letter and the envelope should be clearly marked: "Freedom of Information Act Appeal". In the event you are dissatisfied with the results of any such appeal, judicial review will thereafter be available to you in the United States District Court for the judicial district in which you reside or have your principal place of business, or in the District of Columbia, where we searched for the records you seek. Should you have any questions, please feel free to contact me or my assistant Jacqueline Caldwell at (202) 395-3419.

Sincerely,

Jacqueline B. Caldwell

Jacqueline B. Caldwell
FOIA Specialist

Case File #08122049

Index

Sources

[1] Smith, Grant F., *America's Defense Line: The Justice Department's Battle to Register the Israel Lobby as Agents of a Foreign Government*, Institute for Research: Middle Eastern Policy, 2008

[2] Slater, Leonard, *The Pledge*, New York: Simon and Schuster, 1970, p. 76

[3] Evans, John, "Help for Jews Fleeing Europe is Asked of U.S.," *Chicago Daily Tribune*, April 25, 1938. The United Jewish Appeal was on a major fundraising push under Montor as Nazi Germany increased repression in 1938, increasing its Palestine settlement fundraising to $25 million.

[4] "Rudolf Sonneborn, American Zionism Leader, 87," *Boston Globe*, June 5, 1986

[5] Kollek, Teddy and Amos, *For Jerusalem, a Life*, New York: Random House, p. 10

[6] Slater, Leonard, *The Pledge*, New York: Simon and Schuster, pp. 137-140

[7] Calhoun, Ricky-Dale, "Arming David: The Haganah's Illegal Arms Procurement Network in the United States, 1945-1949," *Journal of Palestine Studies*, Vol. 36, No. 4 (Summer 2007)

[8] Calhoun, Ricky-Dale, "Arming David: The Haganah's Illegal Arms Procurement Network in the United States, 1945-1949," *Journal of Palestine Studies*, Vol. 36, No. 4 (Summer 2007)

[9] Brackman, Harold, "Hawaii Residents Aided Underdog Israel's Struggle," *Honolulu Star Bulletin*, October 15, 2006

[10] Calhoun, Ricky-Dale, "Arming David: The Haganah's Illegal Arms Procurement Network in the United States, 1945-1949," *Journal of Palestine Studies*, Vol. 36, No. 4 (Summer 2007)

[11] Central Intelligence Agency, "Clandestine Air Transport Operations: Memorandum for the Secretary of Defense," May 28, 1948; declassified and released on September 27, 2001, CIA Freedom of Information Act electronic reading room

[12] Clark, Alfred E., "Henry Montor is Dead at 76; U.J.A. and Israel Bond Leader," *New York Times*, April 16, 1982

[13] Slater, Leonard, *The Pledge*, New York: Simon and Schuster, p. 301

[14] Schiesel, Seth, "Robert R. Nathan, 92, Dies; Set Factory Goals in War," *New York Times*, September 10, 2001

[15] Slater, Leonard, *The Pledge*, New York: Simon and Schuster, p. 76

[16] Brackman, Harold, "Hawaii Residents Aided Underdog Israel's Struggle," *Honolulu Star Bulletin*, October 15, 2006

[17] Burston, Bradley, "Al Schwimmer," *The Jewish Daily Forward*, March 2, 2001

[18] Shahak, Israel, *Jewish History, Jewish Religion: The Weight of Three Thousand Years*, Pluto Press, 1997, Foreword

[19] Kenen, Isaiah L., *Israel's Defense Line: Her Friends and Foes in Washington*, New York: Prometheus Books, p. 106

[20] Senate Foreign Relations Committee Investigation into the Activities of Agents of Foreign Principals in the United States, 88th Congress, 1st session, Washington, US Government Printing Office, August 1, 1963, p. 1735

[21] Senate Foreign Relations Committee Investigation into the Activities of Agents of Foreign Principals in the United States, 88th Congress, 1st session, Washington, US Government Printing Office, August 1, 1963, p. 1719

[22] Hoover, J. Edgar, FBI Memo, "American Zionist Council – Registration Act—Israel," August 14, 1963; declassified and released under Freedom of Information Act on June 10, 2008, http://www.irmep.org/ILA/AZCDOJ/p6100050/default.asp

[23] Hall, Thomas K., Executive Assistant, Internal Security Division, Department of Justice, Memo to Nathan Lenvin, FARA section chief, August 15, 1963, p. 1

[24] Memo from J. Walter Yeagley, Assistant Attorney General, Internal Security Division to Files, pp. 1-3, October 17, 1963; released under Freedom of Information Act on June 10, 2008

[25] Yeagley, J. Walter, DOJ Memo, "American Zionist Council," March 31, 1965; released under Freedom of Information Act on June 10, 2008, http://www.irmep.org/ILA/AZCDOJ/p6100012-13/default.asp

[26] Lenvin, Nathan B., Memo, "Isaiah L. Kenen," to US Department of Justice Internal Security Section central files, January 27, 1951. The memo records a visit from AIPAC founder Isaiah Kenen as he considers leaving the employment of the Israeli Ministry of Foreign Affairs to lobby. The memo partially reads, "Mr. Kenen stated that his first client would probably be the Government of Israel and consequently I told him that he should file a new registration statement..." Kenen never refiled with the FARA section. http://irmep.org/ILA/Kenen/FARA/01kenenlenvin.htm

[27] "Federal Agent Dies," *Chicago Tribune*, October 26, 1968

[28] Smith, Grant F., *America's Defense Line: The Justice Department's Battle to Register the Israel Lobby as Agents of a Foreign Government*, Institute for Research: Middle Eastern Policy, 2008

[29] Smith, Grant F., *America's Defense Line: The Justice Department's Battle to Register the Israel Lobby as Agents of a Foreign Government*, Institute for Research: Middle Eastern Policy, 2008, p. 185

[30] Smith, Grant F., *America's Defense Line: The Justice Department's Battle to Register the Israel Lobby as Agents of a Foreign Government*, Institute for Research: Middle Eastern Policy, 2008, pp. 188-191

[31] American Israel Public Affairs Committee, "Bylaws," January 28, 2003, pp. 1, 10. The bylaws specifically state that "the chief lay officer of each organization that is a member of the Conference of Presidents of Major Jewish Organizations shall be invited to serve as a member of the Executive Committee." The Conference of Presidents has 52 members, including the AZC's original constituent organizations, Hadassah and the Zionist Organization of America, and the American Section of the World Zionist Organization.

[32] Curtiss, Richard H., *Stealth PACs: Lobbying Congress for Control of US Middle East Policy*, Washington, DC: American Educational Trust, 1996, p. 27

[33] Curtiss, Richard H., *Stealth PACs: Lobbying Congress for Control of US Middle East Policy*, Washington, DC: American Educational Trust, 1996,

[34] Pear, Robert and Berke, Richard L., "Pro-Israel Group Exerts Quiet Might as it Rallies Supporters in Congress," *New York Times*, July 7, 1987

[35] Pear, Robert and Berke, Richard L., "Pro-Israel Group Exerts Quiet Might as it Rallies Supporters in Congress," *New York Times*, July 7, 1987

[36] Babcock, Charles R., "Papers Link Pro-Israel Lobby to Political Funding Efforts," *Washington Post*, November 14, 1988

[37] Babcock, Charles R., "Papers Link Pro-Israel Lobby to Political Funding Efforts," *Washington Post*, November 14, 1988

[38] Kaplan, Fred, "Report Raised Question of PAC Fund Collusion," *Boston Globe*, November 2, 1988

[39] Associated Press, January 12, 1989

[40] *Washington Report on Middle East Affairs*, January/February 1997

[41] Barnes, Lucille, *Washington Report on Near East Affairs*, February 1991

[42] Curtiss, Richard, *Washington Report on Near East Affairs*, January/February 1997

[43] Curtiss, Richard, *Washington Report on Near East Affairs*, January/February 1997

[44] Gitell, Seth, *The Forward*, June 5, 1998

[46] American Israel Public Affairs Committee, "Bylaws," January 28, 2003, pp. 1, 10. The bylaws specifically state that "the chief lay officer of each organization that is a member of the Conference of Presidents of Major Jewish Organizations shall be invited to serve as a member of the Executive Committee." The Conference of Presidents has 52 members, including the AZC's original constituent organizations, Hadassah and the Zionist Organization of America, and the American Section of the World Zionist Organization.

[47] American Israel Public Affairs Committee, "Bylaws," January 28, 2003, p. 1

[48] Blair, Peggy, "A U.S.-Israel Free Trade Area: How Both Sides Gain," AIPAC Papers on US-Israel Relations #9, 1984, p. 4

[49] Cockburn, Andrew and Leslie, *Dangerous Liaisons: The Inside Story of the U.S. Israeli Covert Relationship*, New York: Harper Perennial, 1992, p. 216

[50] O'Brien, Thomas F., *Making the Americas: The United States and Latin America from the Age of Revolutions to the Era of Globalization*, UNM Press, 2007

[51] Needler, Martin C., *Political Systems of Latin America*, Van Nostrand Reinhold Co, 1970, p. 127

[52] Cockburn, Andrew and Leslie, *Dangerous Liaisons: The Inside Story of the U.S. Israeli Covert Relationship*, New York: Harper Perennial, 1992, p. 216

[53] Kinzer, Stephen, *All the Shah's Men: An American Coup and the Roots of Middle East Terror*, New York: John Wiley & Sons, 2004

[54] Bill, James A., *The Eagle and the Lion: The Tragedy of American-Iranian Relations*, New Haven: Yale University Press, p. 403.

[55] Davar, 11/29/1985.

[56] "Israel, Economic Growth and Structural Change," http://countrystudies.us/israel/66.htm

[57] CIA intelligence report on Israeli Intelligence, derived from volumes seized from the US embassy in Tehran in 1979 by Iranian students and published; document #11 of Documents from the US Espionage Den titled "America: Supporter of Usurpers of the Qods" (Tehran: 1981), p. 28

[58] Beit-Hallahmi, Benjamin, *The Israeli Connection: Who Israel Arms and Why*, London: I.B. Tauris & Co., 1988, pp. 11-12

[59] Cockburn, Andrew and Leslie, *Dangerous Liaisons: The Inside Story of the U.S. Israeli Covert Relationship*, New York: Harper Perennial, 1992, p. 242

[60] Beit-Hallahmi, Benjamin, *The Israeli Connection: Who Israel Arms and Why*, London: I.B. Tauris & Co., 1988, p. 12

[61] Wilentz, Sean, *The Age of Reagan: A History, 1974-2008*, New York: Harper, 2008, p. 211

[62] Central Intelligence Agency, "Clandestine Air Transport Operations: Memorandum for the Secretary of Defense," May 28, 1948; declassified and released on September 27, 2001, CIA Freedom of Information Act electronic reading room

[63] Cockburn, Andrew and Leslie, *Dangerous Liaisons: The Inside Story of the U.S. Israeli Covert Relationship*, New York: Harper Perennial, 1992, p. 107

[64] Bradley, Burston, "Adolph 'Al' Schwimmer," *The Forward*, January 3, 2001

[65] Beit-Hallahmi, Benjamin, *The Israeli Connection: Who Israel Arms and Why*, London: I.B. Tauris & Co., 1988, p. 13

[66] Bradley, Burston, "Adolph 'Al' Schwimmer," *The Forward,* January 3, 2001

[67] Beit-Hallahmi, Benjamin, *The Israeli Connection: Who Israel Arms and Why,* London: I.B. Tauris & Co., 1988, p.13

[68] Beit-Hallahmi, Benjamin, *The Israeli Connection: Who Israel Arms and Why,* London: I.B. Tauris & Co., 1988, p.14

[69] Independent Counsel, Court Record, "U.S. Government Stipulation on Quid Pro Quos with Other Governments as Part of Contra Operation," April 6, 1989, http://www.gwu.edu/~nsarchiv/NSAEBB/NSAEBB210/11-Stipulation%20(IC%2004305).pdf

[70] Turnipseed, Max, "US Bromine Alliance Letter to Dr. Paula Stern, ITC," ITC Public File, November 1, 1984, http://irmep.org/ILA/FTA/11011984US_Bromine/default.asp

[71] Independent Counsel, Court Record, "U.S. Government Stipulation on Quid Pro Quos with Other Governments as Part of Contra Operation," April 6, 1989, http://www.gwu.edu/~nsarchiv/NSAEBB/NSAEBB210/11-Stipulation%20(IC%2004305).pdf

[72] Wingerter, Rex B., "Israel's Search for Strategic Interdependence and the 1983 U.S.-Israeli Strategic Cooperation Agreement," *American-Arab Affairs,* 14, September 30, 1985, p. 81

[73] Carus, Seth W., "U.S. Procurement of Israeli Defense Goods and Services," AIPAC Papers on US-Israel Relations #8, p. 19

[74] Cockburn, Andrew and Leslie, *Dangerous Liaisons: The Inside Story of the U.S. Israeli Covert Relationship,* New York: Harper Perennial, 1992, p. 161

[75] "What Is Bird," The Bird Foundation Website, http://www.birdf.com/Index.asp?CategoryID=22&ArticleID=79, accessed Summer 2009

[76] According to its website, "BIRD supports approximately 20 projects annually with a total investment of around $11 million per year. To date, BIRD has invested over $245 million in 740 projects, which have produced sales of over $8 billion. Since the establishment of the Foundation 30 years ago, the accumulated repayments have totaled $82 million." http://www.birdf.com/Index.asp?CategoryID=22&ArticleID=79

[77] National Archives and Records Administration, "What Is Fast Track?" http://clinton2.nara.gov/Initiatives/FastTrack/what.html

[78] Bard, Mitchell Geoffrey, *The Water's Edge and Beyond: Defining the Limits to Domestic Influence on U.S. Middle East Policy,* New Jersey: Transaction Publishers, 1991, p. 36

[79] National Archives and Records Administration, "What Is Fast Track?" http://clinton2.nara.gov/Initiatives/FastTrack/what.html

[80] Editorial, "The Trade Deal With Israel," *New York Times,* October 22, 1984

[81] Brock, William E., "USTR Letter to Alfred Eckes, Chairman of the ITC," January 31, 1984.

[82] Federal Register Vol. 49, No. 32/ Notices February 15, 1984

[83] It further stated, "All submissions requesting confidential treatment must conform with the requirements of 201.6 of the Commission's Rules of Practice and Procedure (19 CFR 201.6). All written submission, except for confidential business information, will be made available for inspection by interested persons. All submissions should be addressed to the Secretary at the Commission's office in Washington, D.C." Federal Register Vol. 49, No. 32/ Notices February 15, 1984

[84] Independent Counsel, Court Record, "U.S. Government Stipulation on Quid Pro Quos with Other Governments as Part of Contra Operation," April 6, 1989, http://www.gwu.edu/~nsarchiv/NSAEBB/NSAEBB210/11-Stipulation%20(IC%2004305).pdf

[85] Dine, Thomas A., Written Testimony of AIPAC, before the ITC, 4/10/1984, http://irmep.org/ILA/FTA/AIPAC_Testimony/default.asp

[86] Dine, Thomas A., Written Testimony of AIPAC, before the ITC, 4/10/1984, http://irmep.org/ILA/FTA/AIPAC_Testimony/default.asp

[87] Cockburn, Andrew and Leslie, *Dangerous Liaisons: The Inside Story of the U.S. Israeli Covert Relationship*, New York: Harper Perennial, 1992, p. 193

[88] "A U.S.-Israel Free Trade Area," Memorandum, American Israel Public Affairs Committee, April 30, 1984, http://irmep.org/ILA/FTA/04301984/default.asp

[89] Gossage, Thomas L., "Monsanto Letter to Kenneth Mason, ITC," ITC Public File, May 2, 1984, http://irmep.org/ILA/FTA/Monsanto/default.asp

[90] Gossage, Thomas L., "Monsanto Letter to Kenneth Mason, ITC," ITC Public File, May 2, 1984, http://irmep.org/ILA/FTA/Monsanto/default.asp

[91] Electronic docket report generated May 9, 1994, "Probable Economic Effect of Providing Duty Free Treatment for Imports from Israel," International Trade Commission, Public File, p. 46

[92] FBI Report, "Theft and Unauthorized Disclosure of Documents from the United States International Trade Commission, Theft of Government Property," January 14, 1986; declassified on April 20, 2009, released July 31, 2009

[93] Hudgins, Edward L., "The Case for a U.S.-Israel Free Trade Area," Executive Memorandum #53, The Heritage Foundation, May 22, 1984, http://www.heritage.org/research/tradeandeconomicfreedom/em53.cfm

[94] FBI Report, "Theft and Unauthorized Disclosure of Documents from the United States International Trade Commission, Theft of Government Property," January 14, 1986; declassified on April 20, 2009, released July 31, 2009

[95] Eckes, Alfred, "Letter to President Ronald Reagan from the ITC," ITC Public File, May 30, 1984, http://www.irmep.org/ila/FTA/05301984_ITC_POTUS/default.asp

[96] Hudgins, Edward L., "The Case for a U.S.-Israel Free Trade Area," Executive Memorandum #53, The Heritage Foundation, May 22, 1984, http://www.heritage.org/research/tradeandeconomicfreedom/em53.cfm

[97] Priority Teletype, FBI Washington Field Office to Director, "Theft of Classified Documents from the Office of the United States Trade Representatives; Espionage-Israel," June 20, 1984

[98] Priority Teletype, FBI Washington Field Office to Director, "Theft of Classified Documents from the Office of the United States Trade Representatives; Espionage-Israel," June 20, 1984

[99] Priority Teletype, FBI Washington Field Office to Director, "Theft of Classified Documents from the Office of the United States Trade Representatives; Espionage-Israel," June 20, 1984

[100] FBI Report, "Theft and Unauthorized Disclosure of Documents from the United States International Trade Commission, Theft of Government Property," January 14, 1986; declassified on April 20, 2009, released July 31, 2009

[101] Priority Teletype, FBI Washington Field Office to Director, "Theft of Classified Documents from the Office of the United States Trade Representatives; Espionage-Israel," June 20, 1984

[102] FBI Report, "Theft and Unauthorized Disclosure of Documents from the United States International Trade Commission, Theft of Government Property," January 14, 1986; declassified on April 20, 2009, released July 31, 2009

[103] White House, "Presidential Finding on Covert Operations in Nicaragua (with attached Scope Note)," SECRET, September 19, 1983,

http://www.gwu.edu/~nsarchiv/NSAEBB/NSAEBB210/2-NSPG%20minutes%206-25-84%20(IC%2000463).pdf

[104] Auerbach, Stuart, "FBI Investigates Leak on Trade to Israel Lobby," *Washington Post*, August 3, 1984

[105] FBI Report, "Theft and Unauthorized Disclosure of Documents from the United States International Trade Commission, Theft of Government Property," January 14, 1986; declassified on April 20, 2009, released July 31, 2009

[106] Auerbach, Stuart, "FBI Investigates Leak on Trade to Israel Lobby," *Washington Post*, August 3, 1984

[107] Priority Teletype, FBI Washington Field Office to Director, "Theft of Classified Documents from the Office of the United States Trade Representatives; Espionage-Israel," June 20, 1984, Document H

[108] FBI Report, "Theft and Unauthorized Disclosure of Documents from the United States International Trade Commission, Theft of Government Property," January 14, 1986; declassified on April 20, 2009, released July 31, 2009

[109] Priority Teletype, FBI Washington Field Office to Director, "Theft of Classified Documents from the Office of the United States Trade Representatives; Espionage-Israel," June 20, 1984; declassified on April 20, 2009, released July 31, 2009

[110] FBI Report, "Theft and Unauthorized Disclosure of Documents from the United States International Trade Commission, Theft of Government Property," January 14, 1986; declassified on April 20, 2009, released July 31, 2009

[111] Turnipseed, Max, "US Bromine Alliance Letter to Dr. Paula Stern, ITC," ITC Public File, November 1, 1984, http://irmep.org/ILA/FTA/11011984US_Bromine/default.asp

[112] Cockburn, Andrew and Leslie, *Dangerous Liaisons: The Inside Story of the U.S. Israeli Covert Relationship*, New York: Harper Perennial, 1992, p. 159

[113] Seib, Gerald F., "Israel Is Promised U.S. Economic Support But Reagan Didn't Give a Specific Pledge," *Wall Street Journal*, October 10, 1984

[114] McCartney, James, "U.S. Said to Pledge More Aid to Israel," *Philadelphia Inquirer*, October 10, 1984

[115] Stern, Dr. Paula, "ITC Letter to Max Turnipseed, US Bromine Alliance," ITC Public File, November 29, 1984, http://irmep.org/ILA/FTA/11291984USITC/default.asp

[116] Stern, Dr. Paula, "ITC Letter to Max Turnipseed, US Bromine Alliance," ITC Public File, November 29, 1984, http://irmep.org/ILA/FTA/11291984USITC/default.asp

[117] FBI Washington Field Office Report on Theft and Unauthorized Disclosure of Documents from the US International Trade Commission, March 31, 1986; declassified on April 20, 2009, released July 31, 2009

[118] FD-302 Federal Bureau of Investigation interview transcript, Douglas Bloomfield, AIPAC deputy legislative director, February 13, 1986; dictated February 14, 1985, transcribed March 21, 1986; declassified April 20, 2009 and released July 31, 2009

[119] Melman, Yossi, "Accused Israel Spy Hints at FBI Anti-Semitism in AIPAC Probe," *Haaretz*, July 27, 2009, http://www.haaretz.com/hasen/spages/1102358.html

[120] Beit-Hallahmi, Benjamin, *The Israeli Connection: Who Israel Arms and Why*, London: I.B. Tauris & Co., 1988, pp. 1-14

[121] Walsh, Lawrence, *Firewall, the Iran-Contra Conspiracy and Cover-up*, New York: W. W. Norton and Co, 1997, pp. 36-37

[122] Mason, Kenneth R., ITC Notice, ITC Public File, January 7, 1985

[123] Farnsworth, Clyde H., "U.S. and Israel Set Pact to End Tariffs by 1995," *New York Times*, March 5, 1985

124 "Israeli/U.S. Trade Benefits," *Providence Journal*, March 10, 1985.

125 Johnston, Oswald, "U.S., Israel to Mutually End Trade Barriers," *Los Angeles Times*, April 23, 1985

126 "Israeli Cabinet OKs U.S. Free-Trade Pact,"_*Chicago Tribune*, August 19, 1985

127 "House Passes Bill to Lift U.S.-Israel Trade Barriers," *San Francisco Chronicle*, May 8, 1985.

128 "Reagan OK'd Our Role in Deals: Israelis," *Montreal Gazette*, December 11, 1986

129 Patience, Martin, "Spy Case Still Makes Waves in Israel," BBC News, January 15, 2008, http://news.bbc.co.uk/2/hi/middle_east/7181277.stm

130 Werner, Leslie Maitland, "U.S. Jurors Indict an Israeli Officer on Spying Counts," *New York Times*, March 4, 1987, http://www.nytimes.com/1987/03/04/us/us-jurors-indict-an-israeli-officer-on-spying-counts.html?pagewanted=2

131 Wright, Claudia, "Did US Government Funds Pay Costs of Pollard Espionage?" *Washington Report on Middle East Affairs*, August 1987, http://www.wrmea.com/backissues/0887/8708001.html

132 Cockburn, Andrew and Leslie, *Dangerous Liaisons: The Inside Story of the U.S. Israeli Covert Relationship*, New York: Harper Perennial, 1992, p. 206

133 Memo to FBI Director from Washington Field Office, "Theft and Unauthorized Disclosure of Documents from the United States International Trade Commission, Theft of Government Property – Espionage-Israel," August 13, 1984

134 FBI Report, "Theft and Unauthorized Disclosure of Documents from the United States International Trade Commission, Theft of Government Property," January 14, 1986; declassified on April 20, 2009, released July 31, 2009

135 Hosinki, John, "FBI Washington Field Office Memo to Special Agent in Charge on Theft and Unauthorized Disclosure of Documents from the US International Trade Commission," December 17, 1985; declassified on April 20, 2009, released July 31, 2009

136 FD-302 Federal Bureau of Investigation interview transcript, Ester Kurz, AIPAC deputy legislative director, December 19, 1985; dictated December 23, 1985, transcribed January 6, 1986; declassified April 20, 2009 and released July 31, 2009

137 FD-302 Federal Bureau of Investigation interview transcript, Margaret Blair, AIPAC deputy legislative director, December 19, 1985; dictated December 23, 1985, transcribed January 6, 1986; declassified April 20, 2009 and released July 31, 2009

138 FD-302 Federal Bureau of Investigation interview transcript, Douglas Bloomfield, AIPAC deputy legislative director, February 13, 1986; dictated February 14, 1985, transcribed March 21, 1986; declassified April 20, 2009 and released July 31, 2009

139 FD-302 Federal Bureau of Investigation interview transcript, Douglas Bloomfield, AIPAC deputy legislative director, February 13, 1986; dictated February 14, 1985, transcribed March 21, 1986; declassified April 20, 2009 and released July 31, 2009

140 FBI Washington Field Office Report to FBI Director on Theft and Unauthorized Disclosure of Documents from the US International Trade Commission, March 7, 1986, Interview with Embassy of Israel Official, Washington, DC; declassified on April 20, 2009, released July 31, 2009

141 FBI Washington Field Office original handwritten notes, Theft and Unauthorized Disclosure of Documents from the US International Trade Commission, March 7, 1986, Interview with Embassy of Israel Official, Washington, DC; declassified on April 20, 2009, released July 31, 2009

142 FBI Washington Field Office Report to FBI Director on Theft and Unauthorized Disclosure of Documents from the US International Trade Commission, March 7, 1986,

Interview with Embassy of Israel Official, Washington, DC; declassified on April 20, 2009, released July 31, 2009

[143] Beit-Hallahmi, Benjamin, *The Israeli Connection: Who Israel Arms and Why*, London: I.B. Tauris & Co., 1988, p 14

[144] Limbert, John W., *Negotiating with Iran: Wrestling with Ghosts of History*, US Institute of Peace, September 2009; quote from discussion of his on point #4, "Talk with the Right People," from his book on National Public Radio's *Weekend Edition*, September 20, 2009

[145] "Noriega Wins a Round/Defense to Get Key Papers, Source Says," Houston Chronicle, August 8, 1991

[146] Department of Defense FOIA 09-F-1077, dated May 30, 2009

[147] Memo to Washington DC Field Office, "Theft and Unauthorized Disclosure of Documents from the United States Trade Commission; Theft of Government Property," January 14, 1987; declassified on April 20, 2009, released July 31, 2009

[148] FBI Washington Field Office Report on Theft and Unauthorized Disclosure of Documents from the US International Trade Commission, March 31, 1986; declassified on April 20, 2009, released July 31, 2009

[149] Abbot, Marilyn, "ITC Letter to the Institute for Research: Middle Eastern Policy denying FOIA Request for Probable Economic Effect of Providing Duty Free Treatment for U.S. Imports from Israel, Investigation No. 332-180 (redesignated TA-131(b)-10)" from ITC, December 29, 2009; Caldwell, Jacqueline B., "Letter from United States Trade Representative Denying FOIA," March 9, 2009

[150] Gibson, Robert, "Aid Makes Israel Ward of U.S.; $4-Billion-a-Year Dependency Provokes Unease in Both Nations," *Montreal Gazette*, July 25, 1987

[151] Thomas, Gordon, *Gideon's Spies: The Secret History of the Mossad*, New York: St. Martin's Griffin, 2000, p. 286

[152] Source: Stockholm International Peace Research Institute

[153] Sciolino, Elaine, "Israeli Arms Office Is Given Immunity," *New York Times*, October 7, 1988, http://www.nytimes.com/1988/10/07/world/israeli-arms-office-is-given-immunity.html

[154] "Study Sees Need for More Aid to Israel," *New York Times*, June 26, 1983

[155] Twing, Shawn L., "Retired Israeli General Investigated for Embezzling $10 Million in U.S. Aid Funds," *The Washington Report on Middle East Affairs*, February 28, 1997

[156] Cockburn, Andrew and Leslie, *Dangerous Liaisons: The Inside Story of the U.S. Israeli Covert Relationship*, New York: Harper Perennial, 1992, p. 205

[157] *Near Armageddon: The Spread of Nuclear Weapons in the Middle East*, ABC Television program, 1981

[158] Rice, Bruce D., NUMEC security manager, "Letter to Harry R. Walsh, Director of AEC Security and Property Management, Seeking AEC Approval for the Visit," September 12, 1968

[159] Cockburn, Andrew and Leslie, *Dangerous Liaisons: The Inside Story of the U.S. Israeli Covert Relationship*, New York: Harper Perennial, 1992

[160] Thomas, Mary Ann and Santanam, Ramesh, "Despite Doubts, Shapiro Maintains Innocence," *Valley News Dispatch*, August 26, 2002, http://www.pittsburghlive.com/x/pittsburghtrib/news/specialreports/buriedlegacy/s_879 59.html

[161] Thomas, Gordon, *Gideon's Spies: The Secret History of the Mossad*, New York: St. Martin's Griffin, 2000, p. 98

162 Jin, Liyun, "89-Year-Old Oakland Inventor Receives 15th Patent," *Pittsburgh Post-Gazette*, June 26, 2009

163 Aubele, Michael, "Nuclear Waste Dump Cleanup Could Start This Year," *McClatchy Tribune Business News*, April 29, 2009.

164 Cockburn, Andrew and Leslie, *Dangerous Liaisons: The Inside Story of the U.S. Israeli Covert Relationship*, New York: Harper Perennial, 1992, pp. 78-81

165 Ben-David, Amir, "Israel Wants Nuclear Power Plant: Officials in Jerusalem Seek American Assistance in Building Civilian Reactor in South," *Ynet News*, July 31, 2009, http://www.ynetnews.com/articles/0,7340,L-3755000,00.html

166 Complaint, United States of America v Ben-Ami Kadish, Southern District of New York, April 21, 2008, http://www.irmep.org/ila/kadish.pdf

167 "US Man Fined in Israeli Spy Case," BBC News, May 30, 2009, http://news.bbc.co.uk/2/hi/americas/8075029.stm

168 Smith, Jeffrey R., "Defense Memo Warned of Israeli Spying Ethnic Ties," *Washington Post*, January 30, 1996

169 *Washington Times*, June 27, 2006

170 Nelson, Jack, "Spies Took $300-Billion Toll on U.S. Firms in '97," *Los Angeles Times*, January 12, 1998, http://articles.latimes.com/1998/jan/12/news/mn-7575

171 "FBI Suspects Israel of Industrial Espionage," *Jerusalem Post*, January 31, 1998, http://www.amnotes.net/doc_jpost_industrial.html

172 Richardson, Lee and Luchsinger, Vince, "Strategic Marketing Implications in Competitive Intelligence and the Economic Espionage Act of 1996," *Journal of Global Business Issues*, 1(2), Summer 2007, pp. 41-45

173 Richardson, Lee and Luchsinger, Vince, "Strategic Marketing Implications in Competitive Intelligence and the Economic Espionage Act of 1996," *Journal of Global Business Issues*, 1(2), Summer 2007, pp. 41-45

174 Golan, Matti, *The Road to Peace: A Biography of Shimon Peres*, New York: Warner Books, 1989, p. 11

175 Clarke, Duncan "Israel's Unauthorized Arms Transfers," Foreign Policy Magazine, Summer 1995

176 Carr, Chris and Gorman, Larry, "The Revitalization of Companies by the Stock Market Who Report Trade Secret Theft under the Economic Espionage Act," *The Business Lawyer*, 57(1), November 2001, pp. 25-53

177 Green, Stephen, "Serving Two Flags: Neocons, Israel and the Bush Administration," *Counterpunch*, February 28, 2004, http://www.counterpunch.org/green02282004.html

178 Krieger, Hilary Leila, "Congress Votes $37.5m for Arrow-3 Program," *Jerusalem Post*, June 28, 2009

179 "Israeli Officials Reported Mulling Effects of Possible US Military Aid Freeze," BBC Monitoring Middle East, July 23, 2009

180 National Security Archive, "Israel Crosses the Threshold," April 28, 2006, http://www.gwu.edu/~nsarchiv/NSAEBB/NSAEBB189/index.htm

181 The White House, " Memorandum for the Heads of Executive Departments and Agencies, Subject: Freedom of Information Act," January 21, 2009

182 National Security Archive, "2009 Rosemary Award for Worst FOIA Response," George Washington University, March 13, 2009, http://www.gwu.edu/~nsarchiv/news/20090313/index.htm

[183] Meiners, Regina, Acting Deputy Director, "Letter about Fee Waivers to Author," Office of the Secretary of Defense, September 16, 2009. Information about denial rates provided by Mike Bell, Department of Defense Fee Waiver Appeals area.

[184] "Israel and U.S. Facing Hurdles on Trade Pact," *New York Times*, January 10, 1985

[185] Maltz, Judy, "U.S. Fines Israeli Firm Heavily for Dumping," *Jerusalem Post*, February 2, 1989

[186] Maltz, Judy, "U.S. Fines Israeli Firm Heavily for Dumping," *Jerusalem Post*, February 2, 1989

[187] Brown, Bill, "Good but Not Good Enough," *Jerusalem Post*, July Special Edition, "Americanization of Israel," 1989

[188] "Notice of Request for Public Comments on the Review and Renegotiation of the United States-Israel Agreement on Trade in Agricultural Products," *Federal Register*, 65(232), December 1, 2000, http://www.fas.usda.gov/info/fr/2000/120100.html

[189] "Letter Pursuant to Renegotiation of the US-Israel Agreement on Trade in Agricultural Products," California Pistachio Commission, December 29, 2000, USTR Public File

[190] "Letter Pursuant to Renegotiation of the US-Israel Agreement on Trade in Agricultural Products," National Sunflower Association, December 21, 2000, USTR Public File

[191] "Letter Pursuant to Renegotiation of the US-Israel Agreement on Trade in Agricultural Products," Manatt, Phelps & Phillips, LLP, December 28, 2000, USTR Public File

[192] "Letter Pursuant to Renegotiation of the US-Israel Agreement on Trade in Agricultural Products," JBC International, January 3, 2001, USTR Public File

[193] "Letter Pursuant to Renegotiation of the US-Israel Agreement on Trade in Agricultural Products," Grocery Manufacturers of America, December 27, 2000, USTR Public File

[194] "Letter Pursuant to Renegotiation of the US-Israel Agreement on Trade in Agricultural Products," Philip Morris, December 29, 2000, USTR Public File

[195] "Letter Pursuant to Renegotiation of the US-Israel Agreement on Trade in Agricultural Products," Chocolate Manufacturers Association – National Confectioners Association, January 3, 2001, USTR Public File

[196] "Letter Pursuant to Renegotiation of the US-Israel Agreement on Trade in Agricultural Products," Corn Refiners Association, November 14, 2007, USTR Public File

[197] "Letter Pursuant to Renegotiation of the US-Israel Agreement on Trade in Agricultural Products," Blue Diamond Growers November 5, 2007, USTR Public File

[198] "Letter Pursuant to Renegotiation of the US-Israel Agreement on Trade in Agricultural Products," California Dried Plum Board, 2007, USTR Public File

[199] "Letter Pursuant to Renegotiation of the US-Israel Agreement on Trade in Agricultural Products," Paramount Farms, November 14, 2007, USTR Public File

[200] "Letter Pursuant to Renegotiation of the US-Israel Agreement on Trade in Agricultural Products," Distilled Spirits Council of the United States, November 14, 2007, USTR Public File

[201] "Letter Pursuant to Renegotiation of the US-Israel Agreement on Trade in Agricultural Products," Western Growers Association, November 9, 2007, USTR Public File

[202] "Letter Pursuant to Renegotiation of the US-Israel Agreement on Trade in Agricultural Products," US Grain Council, November 13, 2007, USTR Public File

[203] Baseline derived from "Exports from Manufacturing Establishments," US Census Bureau, 2006

[204] "Using Data in Commercial Diplomacy," International Commercial Diplomacy, Inc.

[205] Farnsworth, Clyde H., "Washington Watch; U.S.-Israeli Trade Issue," *New York Times*, September 10, 1984

[206] "Israel," *CIA World Factbook*, https://www.cia.gov/library/publications/the-world-factbook/geos/IS.html

[207] "U.S. Trade in Goods - Balance of Payments (BOP) Basis vs. Census Basis Value in Millions of Dollars 1960 Thru 2008," US Census Bureau, June 10, 2009, http://www.census.gov/foreign-trade/statistics/historical/goods.txt

[208] US Trade Representative, US-Israel Free Trade Agreement. The Preamble Agreement on the Establishment of a Free Trade Area between the Government of Israel and the Government of the United States of America states, "Determined to strengthen and develop the economic relations between them for their mutual benefit; The Government of the United States of America and the Government of Israel, Desiring to promote mutual relations and further the historic friendship between them; Determined to strengthen and develop the economic relations between them for their mutual benefit; Recognizing that Israel's economy is still in a process of development, wishing to contribute to the harmonious development and expansion of world trade; Wishing to establish bilateral free trade between the two nations through the removal of trade barriers; Wishing to promote cooperation in areas which are of mutual interest; Have decided to conclude this Agreement."

[209] Bard, Mitchell, "Israel's Ties that Bind," *Los Angeles Times*, January 10, 2008

[210] Francis, David R., "Economic Scene: Sanctions on Iran and Israel Could Defuse Middle East," *Christian Science Monitor*, August 5, 2009, http://features.csmonitor.com/economyrebuild/2009/08/05/economic-scene-sanctions-on-iran-and-israel-could-defuse-middle-east/

[211] Weintraub, Sidney, "A U.S.-Israel Free-Trade Area," Challenge, Armonk, 28(3), July/August 1985, p. 47

[212] Editorial, "The Trade Deal with Israel," *New York Times*, October 22, 1984

[213] Sawyer, Jon, "Gephardt Urges Expansion of U.S.-Israeli Trade Zone," *St. Louis Post-Dispatch*, July 26, 1994

[214] "U.S. Firm Hires Speaker's Wife to Aid Trade," *Los Angeles Times*, February 7, 1995.

[215] "Egypt/Israel Regulations: QIZ Agreement Revised," *Economist Intelligence Unit ViewsWire*, October 29, 2007

[216] Mahdi, Mazen, "Few Takers for Engaging Israel," *The National*, July 22, 2009, http://www.thenational.ae/apps/pbcs.dll/article?AID=/20090723/FOREIGN/707229809/1135

[217] Institute for Research: Middle Eastern Policy, "Special Report: Dividends of Fear: America's $94 Billion Arab Market Export Loss," *Washington Report on Middle East Affairs*, July/August 2003, http://www.wrmea.com/archives/july_aug2003/irmep.pdf

[218] "U.S. Trade in Goods—Balance of Payments (BOP) Basis vs. Census Basis Value in Millions of Dollars 1960 Thru 2008," US Census Bureau, June 10, 2009, http://www.census.gov/foreign-trade/statistics/historical/goods.txt

[219] Faux, Jeff, "Globalization That Works for Working Americans," Economic Policy Institute, Briefing Paper #179, January 11, 2007

[220] Faux, Jeff, "Globalization That Works for Working Americans," Economic Policy Institute, Briefing Paper #179, January 11, 2007

[221] Blair, Peggy, "A U.S.-Israel Free Trade Area: How Both Sides Gain," AIPAC Papers on US-Israel Relations #9, 1984, p. 41

[222] PhRMA "Special 301" Submission, 2005, pp. 140-141

[223] PhRMA "Special 301" USTR Submission, 2005, p. 141

224 Lappin, Yaakov, "Local Drug Companies Cry Foul Play. Pharmaceutical Firms Claim Foreign Rivals Want to Push Them Out," *Jerusalem Post*, February 7, 2008

225 World Trade Organization – Statistics Database, Time Series, http://stat.wto.org/StatisticalProgram/WSDBStatProgramHome.aspx?Language=E

226"Israel's Intellectual Property Law," Israel Ministry of Foreign Relations, March 16, 2008, http://www.mfa.gov.il/MFA/Government/Law/Legal+Issues+and+Rulings/Israel%20intellectual%20property%20law%2016-Mar-2008

227 Factor, Michael, "Israel Remains on US Priority Watch List," *The IP Factor*, http://blog.ipfactor.co.il/2008/05/04/israel-remains-on-us-priority-watch-list/

228 Krieger, Hilary Leila, "Congress Tries to Get Israel off of US Intellectual Property Blacklist," *Jerusalem Post*, May 31, 2008, http://www.jpost.com/servlet/Satellite?pagename=JPost%2FJPArticle%2FShowFull&cid=1212041440082

229 Lappin, Yaakov, "Local Drug Companies Cry Foul Play. Pharmaceutical Firms Claim Foreign Rivals Want to Push Them Out," *Jerusalem Post*, February 7, 2008

230 Abboud, Leila, "Clone Wars: An Israeli Giant in Generic Drugs Faces New Rivals; Arab Boycott Gave Teva Edge; Now It's No. 1 in Industry, but U.S. Market Toughens; An Army Colonel and CEO," *Wall Street Journal*, October 28, 2004

231 Habib-Valdhorn, Shiri, "Teva's Patent Marathon Runner: Dr. Yehudah Livneh, General Patent Counsel at Teva, Talks to "Globes" About the Company's Patent Policy and Gives a Behind-the-Scenes View of the Global Battle for the Generics Market," *McClatchy Tribune Business News*, April 24, 2008

232 Breitstein, Joanna, "I Pray for the Welfare of Your Company...," *Pharmaceutical Executive*, 26(10), October 2006

233 Breitstein, Joanna, "I Pray for the Welfare of Your Company...," *Pharmaceutical Executive*, 26(10), October 2006

234 Habib-Valdhorn, Shiri, "Teva's Patent Marathon Runner: Dr. Yehudah Livneh, General Patent Counsel at Teva, Talks to "Globes" About the Company's Patent Policy and Gives a Behind-the-Scenes View of the Global Battle for the Generics Market," *McClatchy Tribune Business News*, April 24, 2008

235 Lappin, Yaakov, "Local Drug Companies Cry Foul Play. Pharmaceutical Firms Claim Foreign Rivals Want to Push Them Out," *Jerusalem Post*, February 7, 2008

236 Linder-Ganz, Ronny, "Israel Ranks High in Counterfeit Pharmaceutical Trade," *Haaretz*, July 16, 2009, http://www.haaretz.com/hasen/spages/1100607.html

237 Guttman, Nathan, "The Agony of Ecstasy," *Haaretz*, July 7, 2007, http://www.haaretz.com/hasen/pages/ShArt.jhtml?itemNo=477978&contrassID=2&subContrassID=1&sbSubContrassID=0&listSrc=Y

238 "Israel Releases List of Top Diamond Exporters," *Diamond World News Service*, January 22, 2009, http://www.diamondworld.net/contentview.aspx?item=3472

239Letter to Lev Leviev, Office of the Executive Director, United Nations Children's Fund, June 19, 2008

240 "No One Knows Full Cost of Israel's Settlement Ambitions," *USA Today*, August 14, 2005

241 "No One Knows Full Cost of Israel's Settlement Ambitions," *USA Today*, August 14, 2005

242 Peck, Sarah E., "The Campaign for an American Response to the Nazi Holocaust, 1943-1945," *Journal of Contemporary History*, 15(2), April 1980, pp. 367-400

243 Senate Foreign Relations Committee Investigation into the Activities of Agents of Foreign Principals in the United States, May 23, 1963, p. 1235

[244] National Journal, "US Senator Richard C. Shelby (R-AL) Holds Hearing on Terror Finance Program," *Political/Congressional Transcript Wire*, August 29, 2004

[245] Indyk, Martin, Interview on the *Diane Rehm Show*, WAMU Radio, August 18, 2009

[246] American Israel Public Affairs Committee, "Fifty Years of Friendship between the U.S. Congress and Israel," 1998, p. 8

[247] Mearsheimer, John J. and Walt, Stephen M., *The Israel Lobby and US Foreign Policy*, New York: Farrar, Straus and Giroux, 2007, p. 230

[248]"The Israel Lobby: Does It Have Too Much Influence on Foreign Policy?" Debate sponsored by the Cooper Union, New York City, September 28, 2006, http://www.scribemedia.org/2006/10/11/israel-lobby/

[249] Mearsheimer, John J. and Walt, Stephen M., *The Israel Lobby and US Foreign Policy*, New York: Farrar, Straus and Giroux, 2007, p. 286-287

[250] "State Dept. Suspends Security Clearance of 5," *Seattle Times*, September 26, 2000, http://community.seattletimes.nwsource.com/archive/?date=20000926&slug=TT681MDQR

[251] Indyk, Martin and Pollack, Kenneth M., "Lock and Load," *Los Angeles Times*, December 19, 2002, http://www.brookings.edu/opinions/2002/1219iraq_indyk.aspx

[252] "Superdelegates Turned Down $1 Million Offer From Clinton Donor," *Huffington Post*, May 29, 2008, http://www.huffingtonpost.com/2008/05/19/superdelegates-turned-dow_n_102450.html

[253] *Matthew Gale Krane and Goldfleugel Partnershaft, LLC v. Haim Saban*, Superior Court for the State of California for the County of Los Angeles, July 21, 2009

[254] "US Nuclear Parts Trafficker Sentenced," BBC, April 30, 2002

[255] S'ad, Najwa, "The Great Kryton Caper," *Washington Report on Middle East Affairs*, July 15, 1985, http://www.wrmea.com/backissues/071585/850715006.html

[256] "Israelis Illegally Got U.S. Devices Used in Making Nuclear Weapons," *New York Times*, May 16, 1985; "Computer Expert Used Firm to Feed Israel Technology," *Washington Post*, October 31, 1986; "US Asks Israel to Account for Nuclear Timers," *Washington Post*, May 15, 1985; "Israel Arms Deals Strain US Ties," Raviv, Dan and Melman, Yossi, *Friends in Deed: Inside the US Israel Military Alliance*, New York: Hyperion Books, 1995, p. 299

[257] Windrem, Robert, "Israel Hollywood Nuclear Connection," MSNBC, July 2001, http://www.msnbc.msn.com/id/3340725

[258]"Engineer Pleads Not Guilty to Bomb Component Exports," *New York Times*, November 27, 2001

[259] Windrem, Robert, "Israel Hollywood Nuclear Connection," MSNBC, July 2001, http://www.msnbc.msn.com/id/3340725

[260] *United States of America v. Richard Kelly Smith*, Case Number CR 85-483, Order from Pamela Ann Rymer, United State Circuit Judge, August 27, 2002

[261] *United States of America v. Richard Kelly Smith*, Case Number CR 85-483, Case Docket

[262] "US Nuclear Parts Trafficker Sentenced," BBC ,April 30, 2002

[263] Gedalyahu, Tzvi Ben, "US Billionaire Hollywood Producer to Make Aliyah," *Israel National News*, October 12, 2009

[264] Shaheen, Jack, "Reel Bad Arabs," Media Education Foundation, 2009

[265] http://www.bilaterals.org/article.php3?id_article=15552

[266] "FB Lieberman: Chavez Supports Islamic Extremists," Arutz Sheva, http://www.israelnationalnews.com/News/Flash.aspx/168800

[267] Flaccus, Gillian, "Economic Espionage Trial Winds Down," Associated Press, *Deseret News*, June 25, 2009

268 Abdollah, Tami, "Orange County Man Convicted in First-Ever Economic Espionage Trial," *Los Angeles Times*, July 16, 2009, http://latimesblogs.latimes.com/lanow/2009/07/oc-man-convicted-in-firstever-economic-espionage-trial.html

269 Conason, Joe, "The Real Reason Bill Clinton Pardoned Marc Rich," *Salon*, January 16, 2009, http://www.salon.com/opinion/conason/2009/01/16/holder/index.html

270 *United States of America v. Steven J. Rosen and Keith Weissman*, Reporter's Transcript, Motions Hearing, March 24, 2006, http://www.fas.org/sgp/jud/rosen032406.html

271 Pincus, Walter, "Lobbyists' Prosecutors Pointing to Spy Case," *Washington Post*, April 11, 2006, http://www.washingtonpost.com/wp-dyn/content/article/2006/04/10/AR2006041001423_pf.html

272 *United States of America v. Steven J. Rosen and Keith Weissman*, Emergency Motion to Intervene, March 13, 2007, http://www.irmep.org/PDF/emergencymotion.pdf

273 *United States of America v. Steven J. Rosen and Keith Weissman*, Memorandum Opinion, February 17, 2009, http://www.fas.org/sgp/jud/aipac/rosen021709.pdf

274 Smith, Grant F., *Foreign Agents: The American Israel Public Affairs Committee from the 1963 Fulbright Hearings to the 2005 Espionage Scandal*, Institute for Research: Middle Eastern Policy, 2007, p. 57

275 "Rosen Lawyer Wants Jews to 'Rise Up,'" Jewish Telegraphic Agency, May 14, 2008, http://www.irmep.org/05142008jta.htm

276 *Steven J. Rosen v. The American Israel Public Affairs Committee, et. al.*, Civil Action Number 0001256-09, March 2, 2009, http://www.irmep.org/ila/rosen/default.asp#9

277 Gertz, Bill, "Pro-Israel Lobby Probe Linked to Anti-Semitism: Ex-Informant Points to FBI," *Washington Times*, July 30, 2009, http://www.washingtontimes.com/news/2009/jul/30/pro-israel-lobby-probe-linked-to-anti-semitism/?page=3

278 Rutten, Tim, "The Real Story Behind the Faux Jane Harman Scandal," *Los Angeles Times*, April 22, 2009; Stein, Jeff, "Wiretap Recorded Rep. Harman Discussing Aid for AIPAC Defendants," *Congressional Quarterly*, April 29, 2009

279 Bloomfield, Douglas M., "The AIPAC Two Aren't the Only Ones on Trial," *New Jersey Jewish News*, March 5, 2009, http://www.njjewishnews.com/njjn.com/030509/opedAIPACtwo.html

280 Linzer, Dafna, "Alhurra Targeted for Review by State Department Inspector General," September 2009, http://www.alternet.org/rss/breaking_news/90852/alhurra_targeted_for_review_by_state_dept._inspector_general/; Fingerhut, Eric, "Tidbits," Jewish Telegraphic Agency, September 21, 2009, http://blogs.jta.org/politics/article/2009/09/21/1008027/tidbits-glenn-beck-and-yom-kippur

281 Smith, Grant F., *America's Defense Line: The Justice Department's Battle to Register the Israel Lobby as Agents of a Foreign Government*, Institute for Research: Middle Eastern Policy, 2008, p. 179

282 Giraldi, Philip, "Who's Afraid of Sibel Edmonds? The Gagged Whistleblower Goes On the Record," *The American Conservative*, November 1, 2009

283 "Clean Break or Dirty War: Israel's Foreign Policy Directive to the United States," Institute for Research: Middle Eastern Policy, March 2003, http://www.irmep.org/Policy_Briefs/3_27_2003_Clean_Break_or_Dirty_War.html

[284] Micah, Joshua Marshall and Rozen, Laura, "Iran-Contra II? Fresh Scrutiny on a Rogue Pentagon Operation," *The Washington Monthly*, September 2004, http://www.washingtonmonthly.com/features/2004/0410.marshallrozen.html

[285] Micah, Joshua Marshall and Rozen, Laura, "Iran-Contra II? Fresh Scrutiny on a Rogue Pentagon Operation," *The Washington Monthly*, September 2004, http://www.washingtonmonthly.com/features/2004/0410.marshallrozen.html

[286] Drum, Kevin, "Forged Documents Update," Political Animal, *Washington Monthly*, July 20, 2003, http://www.washingtonmonthly.com/archives/individual/2003_07/001693.php

[287] Alexandrovna, Larisa, "Conversations with Machiavelli's Ghost: Denials Mark Neoconservative's Account of Past and Present Scandal," *The Raw Story*, March 7, 2006, http://www.rawstory.com/news/2006/Conversations_with_Machiavellis_ghost_Denials_mark_0307.html

[288] Micah, Joshua Marshall and Rozen, Laura, "Iran-Contra II? Fresh Scrutiny on a Rogue Pentagon Operation," *The Washington Monthly*, September 2004, http://www.washingtonmonthly.com/features/2004/0410.marshallrozen.html

[289] Transcript of IAEA Director General Mohamed ElBaradei's Presentation to the U.N. Security Council, March 7, 2003, CNN.com

[290] Risen, James and Johnston, David, "The Reach of War: The Offense: Chalabi Reportedly Told Iran That U.S. Had Code," *New York Times*, June 2, 2004, http://www.nytimes.com/2004/06/02/world/the-reach-of-war-the-offense-chalabi-reportedly-told-iran-that-us-had-code.html

[291] Melman, Yossi, "Accused Israeli Spy Hints at FBI Anti-Semitism in AIPAC Probe," *Haaretz*, July 27, 2009, http://www.haaretz.com/hasen/spages/1102358.html

[292] Hersh, Seymour, "The Stovepipe: How Conflicts Between the Bush Administration and the Intelligence Community Marred Reporting on Iraq's Weapons," *The New Yorker*, October 27, 2003, http://www.newyorker.com/archive/2003/10/27/031027fa_fact?printable=true

[293] Raimondo, Justin, "Niger Uranium Forgery Mystery Solved?" *Antiwar.com*, October 20, 2005, http://original.antiwar.com/justin/2005/10/19/niger-uranium-forgery-mystery-solved/

[294] Masters, Ian, "Who Forged the Niger Documents?" Alternet, April 7, 2005, http://www.alternet.org/world/21704/?page=1

[295] Raimondo, Justin, "Niger Uranium Forgery Mystery Solved?" *Antiwar.com*, October 20, 2005, http://original.antiwar.com/justin/2005/10/19/niger-uranium-forgery-mystery-solved/

[296] Slater, Leonard, *The Pledge*, New York: Simon and Schuster, pp. 321-322

[297] Melman, Yossi, "Accused Israeli Spy Hints at FBI Anti-Semitism in AIPAC Probe," *Haaretz*, July 27, 2009, http://www.haaretz.com/hasen/spages/1102358.html

[298] Roth, Zachery, "AIPAC Spy Figure: 'Zionist' Wanted Me Dead," TPMMuckraker, July 2, 2009, http://tpmmuckraker.talkingpointsmemo.com/2009/07/aipac_spy_figure_zionist_wanted_me_dead.php

[299] Rosenberg, M.J. "Steve Rosen, Former Indictee on Espionage, Lectures Obama" Huffington Post, September 18, 2009. http://www.huffingtonpost.com/mj-rosenberg/steve-rosen-former-indict_b_291223.html

[300] Source: Stockholm International Peace Research Institute

LaVergne, TN USA
02 November 2009
162686LV00003B/2/P

9 780976 443711